The Genesis of South Asian Nuclear Deterrence

Pakistan's Perspective

The Genesis of South Asian Nuclear Deterrence

Pakistan's Perspective

NAEEM SALIK

OXFORD
UNIVERSITY PRESS

OXFORD
UNIVERSITY PRESS

Great Clarendon Street, Oxford OX2 6DP

Oxford University Press is a department of the University of Oxford.
It furthers the University's objective of excellence in research, scholarship,
and education by publishing worldwide in

Oxford   New York

Auckland   Cape Town   Dar es Salaam   Hong Kong   Karachi
Kuala Lumpur   Madrid   Melbourne   Mexico City   Nairobi
New Delhi   Shanghai   Taipei   Toronto

with offices in

Argentina   Austria   Brazil   Chile   Czech Republic   France   Greece
Guatemala   Hungary   Italy   Japan   Poland   Portugal   Singapore
South Korea   Switzerland   Turkey   Ukraine   Vietnam

© Oxford University Press 2009

The moral rights of the author have been asserted

First published 2009

ISBN   978-0-19-547716-0

Typeset in Adobe Garamond Pro
Printed in Pakistan by
Pixel Graphics, Karachi.
Published by
Ameena Saiyid, Oxford University Press
No. 38, Sector 15, Korangi Industrial Area, PO Box 8214
Karachi-74900, Pakistan.

Contents

Abbreviations

ABM	Anti-Ballistic Missile
ACDA	Arms Control and Disarmament Agency
AEC	Atomic Energy Commission
ASEAN	Association of South East Asian Nations
ASFC	Army Strategic Force Command
ATBM	Anti Tactical Ballistic Missile
BARC	Bhabha Atomic Research Centre
BJP	Bhartiya Janata Party
BWC	Biological Weapons Convention
CANDU	Canadian Deuterium Uranium (a reactor which runs on natural uranium and is moderated by heavy water)
CBMs	Confidence Building Measures
CD	Conference on Disarmament
CENTO	Central Treaty Organization
CHASHNUPP	Chashma Nuclear Power Plant
CHICOM	Chinese Communists
CIA	Central Intelligence Agency
CIRUS	Canadian Indian US Reactor
CIR	Canadian Indian Reactor (short for CIRUS)
CPPNM	Convention on Physical Protection of Nuclear Materials
CSI	Container Security Initiative
CTBT	Comprehensive Test Ban Treaty
CWC	Chemical Weapons Convention
DAE	Department of Atomic Energy
DBT	Design Based Threat
DCC	Defence Committee of the Cabinet
DGMOs	Directors General Military Operations
DNSRP	Directorate of Nuclear Safety and Radiation Protection

DPRK	Democratic People's Republic of Korea
DRDO	Defence Research and Development Organization
EIF	Entry into Force
EMP	Electromagnetic Pulse
ENDC	Eighteen Nation Disarmament Committee (precursor of Conference on Disarmament)
ERL	Engineering Research Laboratories
EU	European Union
FBR	Fast Breeder Reactor
FBTR	Fast Breeder Test Reactor
FCNA	Force Command Northern Areas
FMCT	Fissile Materials Cut Off Treaty
FPAG	Foreign Policy Advisory Group
GCC	Gulf Cooperation Council
GHQ	General Headquarters
GOI	Government of India
GSLV	Geosynchronous Space Launch Vehicle
GWH	Gegawatt Hours
HEU	Highly Enriched Uranium
IAEA	International Atomic Energy Agency
ICBM	Inter Continental Ballistic Missile
ISRO	Indian Space Research Organization
IDSA	Institute of Defence Studies and Analysis
IGMDP	Integrated Guided Missiles Development Programme
IISS	International Institute for Strategic Studies
IRBM	Intermediate Range Ballistic Missile
KANUPP	Karachi Nuclear Power Plant
KRL	Kahuta Research Laboratories (also known as Khan Research Laboratory)
LIS	Laser Isotope Separation
LSG	London Supplier's Group (precursor to NSG established in the wake of 1974 Indian nuclear test)
MFN	Most Favoured Nation

MOU	Memorandum of Understanding
MOX	Mixed Oxide (Fuel)
MP	Member of Parliament
MPC&A	Material Protection Control & Accounting
MRBM	Medium Range Ballistic Missile
MTCR	Missile Technology Control Regime
MW	Megawatts
MWe	Megawatt Electrical
NASA	National Space Agency
NATO	North Atlantic Treaty Organisation
NCA	Nuclear Command Authority (India)
NCA	National Command Authority
NDC	National Development Complex
NIE	National Intelligence Estimate
NNWS	Non Nuclear Weapons States
NPPA	Nuclear Proliferation Prevention Act of 1994, also known as the Glenn Amendment
NPT	Non-proliferation Treaty
NSAB	National Security Advisory Board
NSC	National Security Council
NSG	Nuclear Supplier's Group
NWFZ	Nuclear Weapons Free Zone
NWS	Nuclear Weapons States
OIC	Organisation of Islamic Conference
OPEC	Organisation of Petroleum Exporting Countries
PAEC	Pakistan Atomic Energy Commission
PALs	Permissive Action Links
PDCC	Power Development Coordination Committee
PINSTECH	Pakistan Institute of Science and Technology
PNE	Peaceful Nuclear Explosion
PNRA	Pakistan Nuclear Regulatory Authority
PRP	Personnel Reliability Programme
PSI	Proliferation Security Initiative
PTBT	Partial Test Ban Treaty
R&D	Research and Development

SAARC	South Asian Association for Regional Cooperation
SAM	Surface to Air Missile
SEATO	South East Asian Treaty Organisation
SECDIV	Strategic Export Controls Division
SLBM	Submarine Launched Ballistic Missile
SLCM	Submarine Launched Cruise Missile
SLV	Space Launch Vehicle
SNIE	Special National Intelligence Estimate
SPD	Strategic Plans Division (secretariat of Pakistan's NCA)
SROs	Statutory Regulatory Orders
SUPARCO	Space and Upper Atmosphere Research Commission
UNGA	United Nations General Assembly
UNMOVIC	United Nations Monitoring Verification and Inspection Commission
UNSC	United Nations Security Council
UNSCOM	United Nations Special Commission
URENCO	European Energy Consortium
W	Watts
WMDs	Weapons of Mass Destruction

Prologue

The nuclearization of South Asia in May 1998 challenged the basis of the non-proliferation regime and policies of the existing nuclear weapons powers that had been intended to discourage others from acquiring nuclear capability. It also raised the spectre of a catastrophic nuclear war between India and Pakistan, that could result from miscalculations, misperceptions, misinterpretation of intelligence information, false warnings or accidents. Some observers of the South Asian scene also believe that a disastrous nuclear crisis could even be precipitated by non-state actors and groups outside the control of either government. Given the long history of mistrust and hostility, accentuated by the festering dispute over Kashmir, the prophets of doom can readily find all the ingredients for an impending disaster waiting to happen. Small wonder, then that South Asia has often been characterized as a nuclear flashpoint and the most likely venue for a nuclear exchange. As British journalist Owen Bennett-Jones remarked, 'South Asia's nuclearization has rendered it one of the most politically sensitive regions on earth and made the dispute over Kashmir one of the world's most potentially dangerous conflicts.'[1]

There are a multitude of concerns and doubts about the ability of the two new entrants into the nuclear club to ensure the security of their respective nuclear arsenals against theft, sabotage, accidents or unauthorized use, especially during a crisis situation, and to show the requisite degree of restraint and caution in contemplating their use or threat to use. These concerns are mainly due to the fact that the situation in South Asia does not neatly fit into any Cold War deterrence model and has its own distinctive features.

The situation therefore demands a dispassionate and objective analysis of these concerns, and the peculiar dynamics of the emerging nuclear deterrence equation in South Asia, that distinguish it from the traditional Cold War models. Much has been written about the South Asian nuclear environment by western analysts, but generally their analyses are coloured by ethnocentric biases and lack of first hand information of the ground realities. There are some seminal works on India's nuclear programme and policies by George Perkovich[2] and Ashley Tellis[3] respectively. Indian strategic analysts and academics have also been prolific in writing on the nuclear issues, but their writing naturally reflect an Indian perspective, betraying a degree of arrogance and a general tendency to be dismissive of Pakistan's indigenous strategic capabilities which have evolved over the years, and conveniently label it as imported Chinese and/or Korean technology. Unfortunately, no serious or substantive study on the subject has emerged from Pakistan, barring a lone book by Lt.-Gen. (retired) Kamal Matinuddin.[4] This work provides a broad overview of the subject but is rather weak on technical aspects. There have, however, been a few serious articles on Pakistan's nuclear programme and related policies, and some journalistic accounts of Pakistan's nuclear development mainly eulogizing personalities, mixing up facts with fiction, and showing a poor understanding of the technical and operational issues involved.[5] It may, however, be appropriate, before attempting to address the issue, to study its background and historical context in order to place it in the right perspective.

NOTES

1. Owen Bennett-Jones, *Pakistan: Eye of the Storm*, Yale University Press, New Haven & London, 2002, p. xii.
2. George Perkovich, *India's Nuclear Bomb: The Impact on Global Proliferation*, University of California Press, Berkeley, 1999.
3. Ashley J. Tellis, *India's Emerging Nuclear Posture: Between Recessed Deterrence and Ready Arsenal*, Rand Corporation, Santa Monica, 2001.
4. Kamal Matinuddin, *The Nuclearization of South Asia*, Oxford University Press, Pakistan, 2002.
5. Zahid Malik's book, *A.Q. Khan and the Islamic Bomb*, and Shahid-ur-Rehman's, *The Long Road to Chaghi* are typical of this category of books.

Acknowledgements

This project could not have been undertaken without the support and encouragement provided by Lieutenant General (retd) Khalid Ahmed Kidwai, DG, SPD. I would also like to express my gratitude to my wife Mrs Nighat Naeem Salik and my sons Ahsan and Ahmad who assumed the responsibility of looking after the family affairs, including the move to our new home, without making any demands on my time while I was working on my manuscript for two long years.

My work was greatly facilitated by the intellectually stimulating atmosphere provided by the Brookings Institution and the Nitze School of Advanced International Studies at Johns Hopkins University, with which I was affiliated as a visiting scholar. My gratitude is also owing to Professor Stephen Cohen, Dr Walter Andersen, Michael Krepon, Professor Scott Sagan, Dr Rodney Jones, and Dr Hasan-Askari Rizvi for sparing time to read parts of my manuscript and proffering very useful suggestions for improvement.

1

Historical Background

South Asia is a conglomeration of states ranging from India with a population of over a billion people and an area in excess of 3 million sq km, to the tiny island state of the Maldives with a population of around 0.3 million and a land area of merely 300 sq km.[1] Geographically, India occupies a pivotal position and shares common land borders with Pakistan, China, Bangladesh, Nepal, Bhutan and Myanmar, while a narrow strait separates it from Sri Lanka. As a geographical unit, South Asia is bounded in the north and north-west by the mighty Himalayan and Hindu Kush mountains, in the south by the Arabian Sea, in the east it shares its borders with the ASEAN Region, and in the west, it links up with West and Central Asia. The region as a whole is home to one-fifth of humanity. However, from the point of view of power potential and politico-diplomatic significance India and Pakistan are the two paramount states in the South Asian subcontinent and their mutual hostility and unresolved disputes have always cast a dark shadow on the overall regional environment with regard to peace, security and economic cooperation. Mainly for this reason the South Asian Association for Regional Cooperation (SAARC) has failed to realize its full potential and emulate other regional groupings such as ASEAN and the European Union. The overt nuclearization of India and Pakistan in May 1998 brought this region to the forefront of international attention, as is evident from former US President Clinton's characterization of the region as a 'nuclear flash point.'[2] For the purpose of this study, therefore, the focus will remain on India and Pakistan and the evolving deterrent equation between the two South Asian rivals.

Indo–Pakistani antagonism has its roots deeply embedded in history far beyond their post-independence relationship. The Muslims of India fearing domination by the Hindu majority after the departure of the British from their most valuable colonial possession, and after having failed to obtain constitutional guarantees to safeguard their legitimate rights, demanded a separate homeland based on the Muslim majority areas mainly in the north-west and south-east of the Indian subcontinent. This demand was based on the two-nation theory, revolving around the argument that Hindus and Muslims, despite co-existence for a thousand years, had maintained their distinctive identities, and despite mixing with each other had never fused into a single nation. Chaudhri Mohammad Ali, former prime minister of Pakistan, has very aptly described this phenomenon as follows:

> The encounter between Hindu and Muslim cultures which began over a thousand years ago has profoundly influenced both. They have met at a thousand points on battlefields and at festivals around market places and in homes on spiritual heights and in the lowlands of mundane affairs. They have learnt from each other, interacted with each other and penetrated each other; their tongues have mixed to produce new and rich languages; in music and poetry, painting and architecture in styles of dress and in ways of living they have left their mark on each other. And yet they have remained distinct with an emphasis on their separateness. They have mixed but never fused; they have coexisted but have never become one. Hindu and Muslim families, that have lived in the same neighbourhood for generations can be distinguished at a glance from one another. The clothes, the food, the household utensils, the layout of homes, the manner of speech, the words of salutation, the postures, the gestures, everything about them will be different and will immediately point to their origin. These outer differences are only the reflection of an inner divergence. For among the varied social groups of mankind, it is difficult to imagine a more striking contrast than between Hindu and Muslim social organization.[3]

The Muslim demand for a separate homeland was viewed by Gandhi and Nehru as the bifurcation of 'Mother India'. While some of the Muslim political parties representing mainly religious groups were opposed to the creation of Pakistan, some very prominent Hindu leaders came out in support of the idea.[4] Interestingly, though, the last chance to maintain the unity of post-independence India, which presented itself in the form of the Cabinet Mission proposals of 1946, was lost due to the refusal of Jawaharlal Nehru, while the Muslim League under the leadership of Mohammad Ali Jinnah had accepted the proposed plan.[5]

The partition of India did not result from a secessionist movement but came about through a politico-legal process mutually agreed between the three main players, i.e. the British, the Indian National Congress and the Muslim League. However, the mass migration and large scale communal violence triggered by the decision has left such deep scars on the psyche of the two nations, that they have not been able to overcome the traumatic experience even after the passage of more than half a century. The Congress leadership had accepted the creation of Pakistan grudgingly with the hope that it would be a short-lived experiment.[6] As such Pakistan's existence as an independent state was never accepted at heart, and it took 52 years for an Indian prime minister to acknowledge this reality by visiting the monument erected at the site where the Muslim aspirations for a separate homeland were codified in an historic resolution which has come to be known as the 'Pakistan Resolution'.[7] Similarly, General Musharraf became the first Pakistani leader to formally visit Mahatma Gandhi's final resting place to pay his respects during his July 2001 visit to India.[8]

GEO-STRATEGIC/SECURITY ENVIRONMENT

Following the departure of the British from the South Asian subcontinent, India viewed itself as the rightful successor to the British Indian empire. However, it was unable to fulfil its ambitions of replaying the 'Great Game' in Afghanistan and the north-western reaches of the subcontinent, and found its access to West and Central Asia impeded by what was then known as West Pakistan.

In the north the options were, in any case, restricted by the gigantic Himalayas, while the Arabian Sea in the south, in the absence of a sea-going tradition and a strong naval force, did not allow much freedom of action. Unable, therefore, to project its power beyond its geographical confines and forced to deploy its forces inside the newly created borders, India felt frustrated and irritated by Pakistan. A similar situation has been witnessed in the recent past when, despite all its eagerness and enthusiasm, India could not play a direct role in the ongoing war against terrorism in Afghanistan due to limitations imposed by geography. Pakistan was again viewed as an obstacle, leading to an acute sense of frustration and anger. This magnified the reaction to the 13 December 2001 attack on the Indian Parliament, resulting in the 2001–02 military standoff between India and Pakistan.

Pakistan on the other hand, despite its location at the crossroads of west, central and south-east Asia, and overlooking the entrance to the strategic Persian Gulf region, also suffers from some serious limitations of geography. Firstly, it is shadowed by two of the most populous and largest states, namely, China and India; and until the break-up of Soviet Union in the early 1990s it also cast its long shadow over Pakistan. A country with over 160 million people and a land area of over 0.8 million sq km would otherwise have been a major player in any region of the world. Secondly, the rectangular shape of the country, with its longest borders in the east being shared with a hostile and antagonistic India, and in the west with a turbulent Afghanistan, means that the country has minimal strategic depth and an enormous burden of defence. The emergence of the Kashmir problem soon after independence, which still remains unresolved, despite half a century of confrontation with a much larger neighbour, has meant that the preservation of national security and integrity has been its predominant concern throughout its history. This has turned Pakistan, like Israel, into a national security state. Until the creation of Bangladesh, out of the former East Pakistan in 1971, the two wings of the country were separated by 1000 miles of Indian territory. This has greatly compounded Pakistan's security problems. However, due to this peculiar geography Pakistan was at the same time part of south-west as well as south-east Asia, which facilitated its entry into military alliance systems spanning both the regions.[9]

A newly independent Pakistan, with its limited resources, especially the almost negligible industrial base and non-existent defence industry, attempted to counterbalance the Indian preponderance in conventional security by means of entering into alliances with powerful outside powers and by developing close security ties with the Muslim states in the Middle East and West Asia. This approach manifested itself in the form of Pakistan's participation in multilateral treaties such as SEATO and CENTO in 1954 and 1955 respectively, and a bilateral security arrangement with the US in 1959.[10] However, during the 1965 and 1971 wars with India, these alliances proved to be of little consequence in terms of their impact on the course and the ultimate outcome of the wars.

The Pakistani people have strongly felt that they have been betrayed by their American allies. This feeling was a natural consequence of the delusion, nurtured for years by the Pakistani leadership in the public mind, about the commitments accruing out of these military pacts. The United States clearly viewed these treaties as being directed solely against Communist aggression, while the Pakistanis, because of the self-created misconceptions, tended to believe that these would also serve as an insurance policy against any ingress by India. The frustrating experiences with the military pacts led to Pakistan's ultimate withdrawal from these treaties by the mid-1970s. The traumatic memories of the dismemberment of the eastern wing of the country through foreign military intervention, and the realization that no outside power would underwrite its security or come to its assistance in another crisis became critical factors in Pakistan's decision to develop its military nuclear capability. By the late 1970s serious differences started to emerge between the US and Pakistan over Pakistan's nascent nuclear enterprise, and led to the imposition of military and economic sanctions by the Carter administration in April 1979. However, the Soviet invasion of Afghanistan in December

1979 once again turned Pakistan into a frontline state, with its attendant benefits as well as dangers.[11] On the positive side, it restored the American military and economic assistance, which enabled Pakistan to embark on a long overdue programme of military modernization, replacement of some of its obsolescent military hardware and induction of frontline aircraft in its air force. The succour provided to Pakistan by the Afghanistan interlude was, however, to be short lived, and the umbilical chord was snapped in 1990 due to continued US concerns over the trajectory of Pakistan's nuclear programme.

India and Pakistan have both traditionally perceived the other as their prime enemy. Though the Indians project the Chinese as their main military threat, the deployment of the Indian army and air force does not correspond to that perceived threat. The bulk of India's forces remain arrayed along its borders with Pakistan, and the sizeable armoured and mechanized component of its military can only be used against Pakistan. The rugged Himalayan terrain astride the Sino–Indian border is obviously unsuited for the employment of mechanized forces. This mutual perception of hostile intent with long, contiguous and easily assailable borders, has set in motion an action–reaction syndrome in the South Asian subcontinent. As a result of this, both countries have devoted a significant proportion of their limited resources on building their respective military apparatus.

The two South Asian nations are prominent among the third world countries not merely as two quarrelsome neighbours. They have earned for themselves a respectable status amongst the developing nations due to significant achievements in the fields of industry, agriculture, science and technology. One aspect of their progress in the field of science and technology that has attracted the attention of the world is that made by both India and Pakistan in the field of nuclear technology. India had already displayed its nuclear prowess through its first nuclear explosion on 18 May 1974, though this test was characterized as a 'Peaceful Nuclear Explosion' (PNE) at that time, and was only acknowledged as a weapons test in 1996 by Dr Raja Ramanna, who had led the team that had conducted this test. India conducted multiple nuclear tests on 11 and 13 May 1998 and declared itself as a nuclear weapons power, while Pakistan also demonstrated its nuclear capability by conducting six nuclear tests on 28 and 30 May 1998 in response to the Indian tests. Both countries are non-signatories to the Non-Proliferation Treaty (NPT). India refused to sign it on the grounds of its inherent inequity and discrimination between the nuclear 'haves' and 'have nots', while Pakistan considered it a political suicide to sign it as long as India did not do so. With their newly acquired nuclear status it would be impossible for the two states to sign away their hard-earned capabilities by joining the NPT as non-nuclear weapon states under the existing framework of the NPT. Both countries are also pursuing broad-based and advanced missile development programmes.

For some time both India and Pakistan maintained that they did not intend to produce nuclear weapons and that their nuclear programmes were meant for the utilization of nuclear energy for peaceful purposes, such as the generation of electricity, medicine and agriculture. In the case of India, the desire to achieve a regional/global power status and to deter the perceived nuclear threat from China and Pakistan, or as the Indians stated on many occasions during the cold war days, to avoid nuclear blackmail by the superpowers, could be regarded as some of the motives. On the other hand, it would have been politically impossible for Pakistan, given the antagonistic relationship between the two countries, to allow India to have the nuclear monopoly in the South Asian subcontinent. From Pakistan's point of view its nuclear programme is mainly driven by its security concerns, and it does not hide the fact that its nuclear capability is India-centric. The action/reaction phenomenon, which has dominated the relationship between the two countries and has spurred competition in the military field for decades, may also have been a contributory factor in the Pakistani quest to achieve some sort of parity with India in the nuclear field as well. There have always been misgivings about the nature and the real objectives of the Indian and especially the Pakistani nuclear programmes in the western world.

There has, however, been a basic difference in the approach of the two countries in dealing with external criticism of their respective nuclear policies. The Indians have always been very critical of the efforts on the part of the nuclear weapon powers to maintain their monopoly in the nuclear field and prevent other states from developing this technology, even for peaceful purposes. The Indians have also been very assertive in advocating their legitimate right to develop and benefit from nuclear technology. The 1974 nuclear test explosion was a clear manifestation of this attitude. As a result of that explosion the world at large slowly and gradually became reconciled to a nuclear India, and the opposition to India's nuclear programme continued to wane, while efforts directed at Pakistan, to prevent it from following suit, were redoubled.

The technology control regimes such as the NSG (Nuclear Suppliers Group) and MTCR (Missile Technology Control Regime) were instituted in the aftermath of India's nuclear test in 1974. However, these affected Pakistan more seriously, since India had already gone past the 'road block'. The 18 July 2005 agreement between US and India, signed during Prime Minister Manmohan Singh's visit to Washington, is an unambiguous acknowledgement of India's de-facto status as a nuclear weapons power. The deal was sealed during President Bush's visit to New Delhi in early March 2006, wherein the US interlocutors agreed to the separation plan offered by India and, in their eagerness to clinch an agreement during the presidential visit, retreated from their earlier demands, to bring all civilian power plants and the breeder reactors under the safeguards regime. At the same time President Bush and Secretary of State Condoleezza Rice made it amply clear, during their visit to Pakistan, that this deferential treatment was only reserved for India and that Pakistan did not qualify, as yet, to be offered a similar favour. This statement was further reinforced when the Bush administration sent a bill to the US Congress, asking for passage of an India-specific amendment to the existing US laws which prohibit such a deal with a non-NPT member state that does not accept full scope safeguards for all its nuclear facilities.

By contrast with India, Pakistan's approach has been mainly defensive, to the extent of being apologetic in trying to justify the need for pursuing a comparatively modest nuclear programme. Pakistan, however, has had to face relentless political pressure to roll back its nuclear programme and has had to pay for the sins committed by others. Canada, for instance, unilaterally withdrew its technical assistance from the Karachi Nuclear Power Plant (KANUPP) in 1976, because of its changed policy. This was in view of the Indian nuclear explosion in May 1974 that had utilized the plutonium extracted from the Canadian supplied 'CIRUS' reactor. In 1976 France signed an agreement with Pakistan for the provision of a reprocessing plant, covered by stringent IAEA (International Atomic Energy Agency) safeguards. In 1978, under great political and diplomatic pressure from the USA, France was forced to renege on the agreement. This pressure on Pakistan's nuclear programme has continued unabated. Even at the height of the Afghanistan crisis in the 1980s there was no let up in US Congressional concerns about Pakistan's nuclear programme. Consequently, security and economic assistance for Pakistan could not proceed through the American Congress without a presidential certification as to the peaceful intent of Pakistan's nuclear programme. More recently, despite Pakistan's significant contribution in the US led war against terrorism, accusations and insinuations keep appearing in the western media with monotonous regularity. This campaign has of late exploited the involvement of a prominent Pakistani scientist, Dr Abdul Qadeer Khan (A.Q. Khan), and some of his close associates, in the proliferation of nuclear knowledge and technology to Libya, Iran and North Korea, to malign the Pakistani nuclear programme and the country itself, conveniently forgetting the role of European suppliers. Moreover, nobody seems to remember the network involving many western companies and dozens of individuals who had been supplying the Iraqi nuclear programme in the 1980s.

Due to the many controversies and relative opacity surrounding the Indian and Pakistani nuclear policies, and their serious implications for the future of the non-proliferation regime and the security of the South Asian region, an analysis of the nuclear programmes and policies of India and Pakistan, with a view to putting in perspective the dynamics of the evolving South Asian nuclear deterrence, is in timely. During the course of this study an effort will be made to address the following critical questions, which will hopefully clarify many of the myths and misconceptions and help in presenting a clearer and more realistic picture to the reader.

- How did the Indian and Pakistani nuclear programmes evolve in the historical context?
- How was the direction of the two programmes determined by politico-strategic and technological imperatives?
- What is the future of non-proliferation in South Asia?
- What are the Indian and Pakistani nuclear doctrines? Are there viable command and control system in place in India and Pakistan? What are the nuclear channels of command?
- How provocative are the Indian and Pakistani missile testing and development programmes, and how can their destabilizing effects be moderated?
- Have the 'Kargil Crisis' and the 2001–02 military standoff proved the viability of a regional nuclear deterrence or otherwise? Have the conventional doctrines of the two countries been tailored to take account of the evolving nuclear environment? How robust is the South Asian nuclear deterrence and what are the prospects of its stabilization in the near or long term? Was the A.Q. Khan proliferation episode a product of the peculiar circumstances prevalent during a particular phase of development of Pakistan's nuclear programme, and are there any possibilities of recurrence of such events in future?

NOTES

1. CIA World Fact Book, (http://www.odci.gov/cia/publications/factbook/index. html).

2. President Clinton quoted in Kaushik Kapisthalan, 'Pakistan leaves arms calling card', *South Asia*, 10 February 2005, Asia Times Online, www.atimes. com. Also see Edwin Chen and Dexter Filkins, 'US backs India, sees no role now in Kashmir', *Los Angeles Times*, 22 March 2000, and Arathi R Jerath, 'President's proactive speech leaves the government shocked', *Indian Express*, New Delhi, 23 March 2000 and Timothy D. Hoyt, 'Politics, Proximity and Paranoia: The Evolution of Kashmir as a Nuclear Flashpoint', in Sumit Ganguly (ed.), *The Kashmir Question, Retrospect and Prospect*, Routledge, London, 2003, p. 117.

3. Chaudhri Mohammad Ali, *The Emergence of Pakistan*, Columbia University Press, New York & London, 1967, p. 1.

4. Hafeez Malik, *Dilemmas of National Security and Cooperation*, Macmillan, London, 1993, pp. 10–15.

5. Ibid., p.11.

6. Ibid., p. 5.

7. Indian Prime Minister Vajpayee's visited the Minar-e-Pakistan at Lahore during his historic bus journey to Lahore in February 1999. See Owen Bennett-Jones, op. cit., p. xiv.

8. 'First Pak Head of State to Visit Rajghat', *The Tribune*, Chandigarh, India, 15 July 2001.

9. Bharat Karnad, 'India's Weak Geopolitics and What to Do About It', in Bharat Karnad (ed.), *Future Imperilled: India's Security in the 1990s and Beyond*, Viking, New Delhi, 1994, p. 24.

10. Kail C. Ellis, 'Pakistan's Foreign Policy: Alternating Approaches', in Hafeez Malik (ed.), *Dilemmas of National Security and Cooperation in India and Pakistan*, Macmillan, London, 1993, pp. 131–3.

11. Ibid., pp. 141–2.

2

Evolution of India's Nuclear Programme

India has made major strides in the development of its nuclear capability and build-up of a sprawling nuclear infrastructure over the past six decades. In the 1950s, the very early days of the nuclear age, it had already become the leading Asian nation in the nuclear field and had, by the late 1960s, acquired mastery over the complete nuclear fuel cycle. However, in the history of Indian nuclear endeavours, the years 1974 and 1998 constitute two major landmarks. Whereas, in 1974 India demonstrated its technical prowess in nuclear technology through what it preferred to call then a 'Peaceful Nuclear Explosion' (PNE), ironically code named as the 'Smiling Buddha', in 1998 when the Buddha smiled again, though the grin was much wider this time, India had no qualms about openly declaring itself a nuclear weapon state.[1]

The nuclear explosion in 1974 was a watershed event because, from the technical point of view, there is no basic difference between the initial stages of a programme to develop peaceful nuclear explosive devices and the ones intended to produce nuclear weapons.[2] What matters is the decision to cross the psychological and qualitative threshold in the face of possible international reprimand and sanctions, and India did cross the psychological barrier by detonating a so-called 'peaceful nuclear device' on 18 May 1974. However, it succeeded in mellowing down the international reactions by insisting on the peacefulness of the explosion. Nuclear explosive testing aimed at developing an operational military nuclear capability has to be followed up with the development of the requisite nuclear delivery systems, appropriate command, control and communications arrangements and of course the articulation of a suitable nuclear use doctrine.

After the 1974 test India slowly but surely started moving into the aforementioned fields, but the slow pace of development and a low-key posture helped maintain a high degree of ambiguity about its actual intentions. The 1998 tests, however, removed the veil of ambiguity from India's nuclear ambitions and brought about far reaching changes to the security landscape in the South Asian region and far beyond its geographical confines. A study of the Indian nuclear programme can, therefore, be logically divided into three segments: the first covering the period from its inception to 1974, the second covering the developments from 1974 to 1998, and the third encompassing developments post-1998.

THE INDIAN NUCLEAR PROGRAMME
FROM ITS ORIGIN TO 1974

The Indian nuclear programme was initiated on 2 March 1944, fifteen months before the 'Alamogordo explosion', almost a year and a half before the first public demonstration of the awesome power of nuclear weapons at Hiroshima and Nagasaki, and more than three years before the country actually achieved its independence.[3] This unique but relatively little known aspect of the Indian nuclear programme can be attributed to the personal efforts of an enthusiastic young physicist, Dr Homi J. Bhabha, who had just returned after completing his studies with Lord Rutherford, an internationally renowned British nuclear scientist, at Cambridge University. Dr Bhabha managed to establish the 'Institute for Fundamental Research', with the assistance of 'Sir Dorabji Tata Trust', for the expressed purpose of preparing a crop of Indian nuclear scientists and engineers. Bhabha was certainly much ahead of his time in visualizing the peaceful uses of nuclear energy, at a time when the Manhattan Project in the US and other similar secretive efforts in some other countries, notably the UK and Germany, were focused only on the military potential of the atom. This is evident from the letter Homi Bhabha wrote to the trust declaring that:

When nuclear energy has been successfully applied for power production in say a couple of decades from now India will not have to look abroad for its experts but will find them ready at hand.[4]

The five established nuclear weapons powers USA, USSR, UK, France and China began their nuclear programmes for the explicit purpose of producing nuclear weapons, and developed civilian applications of nuclear technology as a spin off at a much later stage. India, however, embarked on a civilian nuclear programme to begin with and achieved nuclear explosive capability as a by-product.[5] An Atomic Energy Commission was set up in India by an act of parliament in 1948, within eight months of independence, and naturally enough under the stewardship of Dr Homi Bhabha. The commission covered both technical as well as managerial aspects of the atomic research activities. Once again it was Dr Bhabha, in the early 1950s, who laid down the technological objectives of the country's nuclear programme, the phases in which these goals were to be achieved and the time frame within which various phases were to be completed. The main objectives to be achieved within the first 25-year period were as follows:[6]

- Long term technological autarky in aspects of nuclear research and development;
- Acquisition of technology in the interim period from all possible sources;
- Mastering the designing and manufacturing techniques along with the import of technology;
- Development of breeder reactor technology;
- Training of large numbers of technicians at home and abroad.

The importance assigned to the nuclear research and development can be gauged from the fact that right from the beginning the Indian Atomic Energy Commission was under the direct supervision of Prime Minister Jawaharlal Nehru, himself a Cambridge graduate in Natural Sciences as well as Law. Later on, when a more powerful 'Department of Atomic Energy' (DAE) was established in 1954, the prime minister remained personally in charge of the department.

The biggest advantage of this arrangement was that it freed Dr Bhabha from bureaucratic impediments in the pursuit of his objectives. It also gave him access to, and influence at, the highest executive level in the country. The allocation of resources, although limited in the beginning, started to expand after the establishment of the DAE in 1954. Within two years a team of well-trained Indian scientists led by Bhabha succeeded in carrying out the first sustained chain reaction in Asia. This test was conducted at the indigenously constructed 1 MW research reactor, code named 'APSARA', the only foreign component being the enriched uranium fuel purchased from Britain.

By 1958, Bhabha felt confident enough to publicly proclaim that India could produce a nuclear explosive device within eighteen months of the political decision to do so.[7] In retrospect, however, this certainly was an ambitious claim in view of the fact that, at that time, India had no source of fissile material, the most critical element, without which the production of a nuclear explosive device is unimaginable. Interestingly, the claim was made two years before the French conducted their first nuclear explosion and six years ahead of the Chinese nuclear test of 1964. Therefore, the widespread perception that India's decision to embark on a nuclear weapons programme was triggered by the Chinese nuclear test in October 1964 and India's embarrassing experience in the 1962 border war with China is at best questionable.

India's first source of fissile material, the Canadian supplied CIRUS reactor, came on line in 1960.[8] This reactor, which runs on natural uranium fuel, and is moderated by heavy water is ideally suited for plutonium production. CIRUS has a capacity of 40 MW and can produce up to 15 kg of plutonium working on 100 per cent capacity. However, nuclear reactors seldom run on 100 or close to 100 per cent capacity, and usually operate on 60–80 per cent capacity, which would mean that its annual output could be anywhere between 9–12 kg of plutonium. This reactor therefore, has been the major source of India's fissile material inventory. As shown in some recently declassified US government documents, right from the outset the Indians had been removing fuel from

CIRUS at 'low burn up', which meant that, once separated in a reprocessing plant, the plutonium obtained would be ideally suited for nuclear weapons.[9] The plutonium used for the Pokhran-I test in 1974 was produced in this plant, which was in contravention to the understanding with the US and Canada that this plant would only be used for peaceful purposes.[10] This agreement, however, was based only on trust and no stringent safeguards were built into it. In the event the parties to the agreement interpreted its terms in differing ways and while the Canadians and the Americans were inclined to insist that a nuclear explosion of any type did not constitute a peaceful use, the Indians persisted in their stance that PNEs fall into the category of peaceful applications. Indian Prime Minister Manmohan Singh has recently announced in the Indian Parliament that CIRUS would be shut down in 2010 after completing fifty years of operation.[11] India's third research reactor, Zerlina, with a power output of 100 W became operational in 1961.[12] This reactor, which was designed engineered and built entirely by Indian scientists and technicians, was decommissioned and dismantled in 1983. In 1962 India's first heavy water plant was commissioned at Mangal and in 1963 an agreement was signed with the US for assistance in the construction of a nuclear power station comprising two nuclear power plants at Tarapur.[13]

It is generally believed that from 1958 till the early 1970s, when the decision to conduct the 'peaceful nuclear explosion' is thought to have been taken, the Indian policy makers deliberately kept in check the demands of the scientific lobby, led by Bhabha, for the production of nuclear explosive devices. This belief in the peaceful intent of the Indian nuclear programme was a common strand in almost all the analyses of the Indian nuclear programme carried out by various US government agencies, including the intelligence agencies, from the late 1950s to the early 1970s. For instance, a 1958 Scientific Intelligence Report on 'Indian Nuclear Energy Programme' prepared by the Central Intelligence Agency stated:

> There are no indications of Indian interest to exploit the military applications of nuclear energy. The government is pledged to devote

its entire effort to the peaceful uses of nuclear energy and no divergence from this pledge is anticipated.

The report went on to emphasize the Indian traditions of 'passivity and mediation' to reinforce its earlier conclusion.[14]

There was obviously a major change in US outlook towards India because of the 1962 Sino–Indian border war, and this feeling of empathy and support for India was further reinforced after the Chinese nuclear test in October 1964. From then on all efforts were directed at assuring the Indians of the US support in the event of a Chinese nuclear threat to that country, as a means of alleviating India's security concerns and to prevent it, as far as possible, from developing nuclear weapons. At the same time there was an understanding of India's predicament in view of the perceived Chinese threat, and a benign view was taken of its motivation for going nuclear should it ultimately do so. Efforts were mainly directed at persuading the Indians that although it was well within their capability to develop or test a few nuclear devices, the costs for India to develop and maintain a credible operational nuclear arsenal and the requisite delivery systems would be prohibitive, and a drain on India's economy. To make the argument more persuasive, classified US data on the expenditure on developing and maintaining an operational nuclear capability was shared privately by the US diplomats with key Indian officials.[15]

In April 1964, when India's first Plutonium Separation Plant was inaugurated by Prime Minister Shastri, the American Consulate in Bombay's Airgram reporting the event stated that the purpose of the was to 'extract plutonium' which it described as a 'material and atomic fuel for future reactors, besides being valuable fissionable material. The emphasis of the report was clearly on the futuristic use of plutonium as part of the MOX (mixed oxide fuel), a technology which has not seen widespread use and applications, while the potential use of plutonium as a fissile material was assigned a lower priority. The fact that India had thus become the fifth country in the world after the USA, USSR, UK and France and the first in Asia to have that technology,[16] did not ring any alarm bells. This important development, therefore, went largely unnoticed and did not attract the kind of international opprobrium which such facilities with proliferation potential were to attract from the 1970s onwards to this day. While embarking on the construction of this plant in 1963, the Indian scientists must surely have been aware of the dual purposes for which the plutonium could be used. However, it may be relatively difficult at this stage to pass a judgment on the motives of the political leaders for sanctioning the establishment of this facility,[17] which was immediately put to use for the separation of plutonium from the spent fuel being generated by CIRUS.[18]

The tenor of rejoinders given by the American diplomats and officials to their Indian counterparts was in fact more in the way of friendly advice rather than any threats of sanctions or deprivation. The State Department, for instance, in a brief for Governor Harriman, who was embarking on a visit to India in February 1965, unequivocally asserted that:

> We are aware that India has decided against developing its own nuclear weapons programme, which we consider a commendable example worthy of emulation around the world.[19]

Great care was also taken to ensure that no American statement or action in support of India should in any way affect India's non-aligned status, or its pre-eminent political and technological position amongst the Afro–Asian nations.[20] However, one must remember that this was the pre-NPT era, during which there were no international norms, treaties or agreements against nuclear testing or development of nuclear weapons by any state. Therefore, there was greater tolerance for nuclear activities, especially on the part of countries which were not deemed to be hostile by the US. Technology control arrangements such as the NSG, MTCR and the Australia Group did not exist at the time. Interestingly, this is not very different from the current US policy, that nuclear weapons in the hands of 'good guys' are okay but they are bad in the hands of 'bad guys'.

An October 1964 CIA appraisal of 'Indian Government Policy on Nuclear Weapons' while stating that India has all the wherewithal necessary to produce a nuclear weapon and assemble a nuclear bomb in a short time, added that India did not plan to embark on the bomb project as yet because of the conviction of the Indian government that the Chinese would not have a meaningful operational nuclear capability for at least a further five years and should the situation change in the meantime, India would be relying on President Johnson's assurances to come to the aid of all nations threatened by China.[21]

A scientific intelligence report prepared by the CIA in November 1964 concluded that:

> The Indian nuclear energy programme, which was initiated in 1954, has thus far been limited to peaceful purposes. However, India now has three research reactors in operation, one of which can produce plutonium suitable for weapons and is not subject to stringent safeguards. In addition, India has sufficient uranium to provide reactor fuel and has a plutonium separation plant. Construction of a plant for plutonium metal production, which is necessary for weapon manufacture, is now under way and planned for operation in 1966; should the Indians so decide, it could be in operation in the fall of 1965.[22]

The report also mentioned that India was not only processing its domestic uranium reserves for use as reactor fuel, it had also imported uranium concentrate from France, Belgium and Spain without any safeguards. It also alluded to the fact that fuel from CIRUS was being removed after burning it to half of its designed burn up level. According to the report, India's first plutonium separation plant, that became operational in March 1964, had already processed 40 tons of uranium fuel from CIRUS by August 1964. It also stated that India already had about 20 kg of plutonium in the form of plutonium nitrate solution. India was also seeking assistance from Sweden in designing a pressurized heavy water reactor with a capacity of 200–300 MWe. This reactor would be similar in design to the Canadian supplied reactors being built in

Rajasthan but those reactors, as well as the US supplied reactors at Tarapur, were under safeguards. India obviously wanted to build 'indigenously designed' reactors which would not be subjected to safeguards.[23] All this information put together would have provided unambiguous evidence of the scope of India's nuclear activities to any objective analyst.

A special national intelligence estimate on 'India's Nuclear Weapons Policy', prepared in October 1965, concluded that India had the capability to develop nuclear weapons and already had enough plutonium for a nuclear device which could be tested within a year of the political decision to do so. Noting that the pro-bomb lobby had been strengthened by the recently concluded India–Pakistan War, it had also enhanced Prime Minister Shastri's political standing, giving him the ability to hold firm on his decision against a military nuclear programme. The estimate, however, ended with the conclusion that:

> ...we do not believe that India will hold to this policy indefinitely. All things considered, we believe that within the next few years India probably will detonate a nuclear device and proceed to develop nuclear weapons.[24]

Confirming that the CIRUS reactor has been operated in such a manner that it could yield weapon usable plutonium, the estimate added that:

> A plant for the production of plutonium metal......is scheduled for completion in 1966; in the meantime this task probably has been performed by a pilot facility which has enough capacity to process the plutonium the CIR can produce.[25]

The estimate also speculated that research and development work related to nuclear weapons technology may also have started. The intelligence analysts estimated that by 1970 India could produce about a dozen 20-kiloton (nominal yield) bombs, however, if it started using plutonium produced by its un-safeguarded power reactors, due to come on line in the near future it could substantially enhance its weapons production capability.[26] According to the NIE, the Indian military was not very keen to have nuclear weapons, instead it preferred to have sufficient funds to boost up its conventional capabilities.[27]

On 16 November 1965, addressing the Upper House of Parliament, Prime Minister Shastri hinted at the possibility of India developing nuclear weapons in response to the Chinese nuclear capability, saying that:

> While India stood for non-proliferation of nuclear weapons, if China developed her nuclear power and perfected the delivery system, 'then we will certainly have to consider as to what we have to do.[28]

However, he seemed to retreat from his earlier statement, saying on 3 December 1965 that, 'India has given up the idea of making an atomic bomb because it cannot afford it'.[29] It may not be easy to determine whether this was a genuine change of heart or was merely an effort to allay the concerns of the US officials, who were at the time highlighting the economic costs of an operational nuclear weapons programme in their interactions with their Indian counterparts.[30] However, the activities of the Indian nuclear establishment were clearly directed towards the development of a nuclear weapons capability in anticipation of the political decision to do so.

In March 1966, a US State Department cable to the American Embassy in New Delhi mentioned that:

> The fuel has reportedly been removed from the (CIRUS) reactor after an average burn up of only 450–600 MWd/t, which is significantly lower than the 900MWd/t burn up for which the reactor was designed. While this circumstance alone does not necessarily indicate that a decision has been made to develop nuclear weapons, it hints strongly that suitable material is being produced to permit the rapid implementation of such a decision.[31]

It was evident that if nothing else India was clearly taking steps to create a nuclear weapons option which could be converted into an operational capability at short notice, given a political decision in this regard. These unmistakable pointers caused the cable to begin with the statement that, 'Although there is no evidence that India has decided to develop nuclear weapons, a nuclear device could probably be ready for testing within a year following such a decision.' The cable acknowledging the easy availability in the open market in Europe of high quality detonators and electronic neutron generators likely to be used in the maiden Indian nuclear device, instructed the American Embassy to look for and report further evidence and information on the following technical parameters:

- Signs of activity in remote areas which might portend the construction of a nuclear test site.
- Indications that nuclear associated research facilities are being established surreptitiously or that security is being tightened at existing facilities.
- Evidence of continued operation of the Canada–India reactor at Trombay to produce relatively 'clean' plutonium.
- Procurement or development by India of small electronic neutron generators and high quality, electrically initiated, high explosive detonators.
- Testing of highly instrumented high explosive shapes or sections.

This was certainly a departure from the earlier conviction about the peaceful intent of India's nuclear programme and, it seems from the instructions sent to the American Embassy, that a serious concern was developing within the US administration based on the intelligence information on India's nuclear weapons related activities. This concern is clearly discernible from a memorandum for the National Security Council (NSC) meeting in 1966, by Acting Secretary of State, George Ball, which asserted that, 'India is almost certain to develop nuclear weapons', and argued that, 'efforts to influence India's decision...are not likely to achieve more than a short term delay'.[32]

While the US officials were trying to make Indian leaders conscious of the economic costs of a full-fledged nuclear weapons programme, senior Indian scientists were confirming the impression that they were indeed responsive to the American advice. Dr Sethna had for instance stated that, 'India cannot just detonate one or two devices and stop. Small nuclear bomb programme is worse than no programme at all because it would invite pre-emptive Chinese attack'.[33] In Sethna's reckoning India would need 150 bombs for a credible deterrent.[34] Dr Vikran Sarabhai, the newly appointed secretary of the Indian Department of Atomic Energy and chairman of the Atomic Energy Commission, in a June 1966 statement, seemed to reinforce Sethna's views by stating that:

> A prototype bomb would not be useful as a weapon and India could not become an effective nuclear power without developing its industrial and economic potential…mere possession of a bomb without a delivery system and a strong industrial base is a bluff.[35]

Sarabhai's statement must have sounded credible, given the fact that he came from a prominent industrialist family and obviously conscious of the economic costs of an operational nuclear deterrent.[36]

A memorandum forwarded by Acting Secretary of State George Ball to the US president, likely to be considered in the NSC meeting scheduled for 9 June 1966, entitled: 'The Indian Nuclear Weapons Problem; Current Issues', pointed out that due to a third nuclear test by China, domestic pressures for a nuclear weapons programme were building up in India, adding that, 'A pressure point is likely to be reached within a few years and unless there is some new development, India almost certainly will go nuclear'.[37] It also highlighted the consequences of such an Indian move on Pakistan, which was likely, out of its concern for its security, to seek the support of China or the US either in the acquisition of nuclear weapons or some kind of a security umbrella to deter possible Indian aggression. Such a step by India would also increase the possibility of Japan and Israel going down the same route and Germany might also feel the pressure to follow suit. There was also the obvious conclusion that should India go nuclear it would be less inclined to ask for US or Soviet assistance in defending itself against China. On the issue of threatening or imposing economic sanctions against India, the memorandum suggested that:

> The threat and certainly the cut off of aid, would greatly reduce American influence and enhance Soviet influence in India, and would subject India to heavy economic and political strains, which would threaten its viability as a democratic state and an Asian counterweight to China.[38]

It is interesting to note the similarity in the arguments presently being proffered to support India in building up its economic, military and political strength through the provision of civilian nuclear technology, among many other areas of cooperation to make it a 'strategic counterweight to a rising China.' It was also assumed that even if India decided to adhere to the anticipated non-proliferation treaty it would in all likelihood withdraw from it, should it feel that its national interest was at stake.[39]

Among the many courses of action proposed in the memorandum were suggestions such as a joint US–USSR guarantee to all non-nuclear states, including India, but since the Soviets were not agreeable to it at the time the alternatives proposed were a public declaration by the US, expressing its readiness to join with other nuclear powers to give such a guarantee or US assurances to India under the umbrella of a UN Resolution. US Ambassador to India, Chester Bowles, had more radical suggestions such as:

- US assistance to India in the installation of an effective early warning system and other defensive measures against manned bombers.
- Expansion of joint US–Indian efforts to monitor Chinese nuclear and missile capabilities.
- Secret scientific consultations on missile defences.
- Secret studies of integrated air defence against Communist Chinese nuclear attack to include the possibility of creating an

Indian manned bomber force for use against Chinese launching sites.[40]

The possibility of a US–Indian military alliance was ruled out, because the Indians would not wish to compromise their 'non-aligned' status, and also that such a development would mean a total break in US relations with Pakistan, which might force that country into a military alliance with China. A more radical course of action deliberated upon pertained to 'nuclear sharing'. The idea was to enhance Indian capability to deter a Chinese nuclear attack 'with its own delivery means, using American nuclear warheads' to be made available to India in the event of a Chinese attack. However, it was envisaged that crafting such an agreement would be a tricky and complicated affair in view of India's desire to retain its non-aligned status and the possible negative impact on Pakistan, Japan and other US allies in Asia. The US defence establishment was convinced that even such an agreement would at best delay an inevitable Indian decision to go nuclear. However, Mr Bowles thought that this was a price worth paying even for achieving a delay to the Indian decision. He also considered the possibility that, under pressure to demonstrate its nuclear technological capability, the Indians might opt for a peaceful ('ploughshare') explosion, but pointed out that such an explosion would be seen in Pakistan and elsewhere as the commencement of an Indian nuclear weapons programme.[41]

At a time when various ideas were being explored to deal with the 'Indian nuclear problem', the US Department of Defence did not agree with the recommendations of a study conducted by a working group, on 'Indian nuclear capability', constituted by the State Department. In a January 1967 memorandum for the Secretary of Defence, the Joint Chiefs of Staff expressing strong disagreements with the State Department study recommended that:

- No nuclear assurances be extended to India beyond those made by the President in 1964.

- No action be taken in regard to India which could alienate US allies, especially Pakistan.
- The United States avoid creating any impression that it is willing to broaden its commitments to India.
- The United States retain maximum flexibility for future US action in response to CHICOM (Chinese Communists) nuclear attack or blackmail.[42]

The Joint Chiefs of Staff were of the view that, while the US concern with Indian security was serious enough, it did not warrant provision of a NATO type nuclear umbrella to India. They also rejected the inclusion of Indian defence requirements in the US studies being conducted at the time for the deployment of an ABM system for the protection of the US. They further reiterated that intelligence estimates suggested that, irrespective of the guarantees offered, India was likely to detonate a nuclear device within the next few years.[43]

In April 1967 Mr L.K. Jha, secretary to the Indian Prime Minister Indira Gandhi, met President Johnson as her special emissary. He was on a mission to seek security assurances within the context of the NPT, which was being negotiated at the time and had already received a positive response from the Soviet Union on the issue. Johnson assured Mr Jha that the US would look at the Soviet Draft very carefully and would follow it up, reiterating the earlier US interest in the subject.[44] Mr Jha had earlier met the Secretary of Defence, who expressed the view that Chinese nuclear capability would develop at a slow pace and there was a danger of India overreacting to the Chinese threat, adding that India's military forces were already too large and a drain on its resources. Jha retorted by saying that credible security assurances were important to offset the psychological impact of the Chinese nuclear threat, and to deter both a Chinese attack and Indian defence expenditure. The Indian Atomic Energy Commission Chairman, Dr Sarabhai, who was accompanying Jha, interestingly, raised the issue of the US decision to restore the supply of military spares to Pakistan, calling it an 'unfortunate new development'. Jha, reinforcing his point, added that this would have negative impact on Indo–Pakistan dialogue.[45]

The issue of assurances again came up in a meeting in June 1967 between US Secretary of State Dean Rusk and Soviet Foreign Minister Gromyko. While the Soviets expected a parallel US declaration to their statement, Secretary Rusk explained that due to constitutional constraints the US side could not issue such a declaration without the approval of a two-thirds majority of the Senate. It would, therefore, be easier for the US if the assurances were given in the form of a UN Resolution. Rusk also expressed his feeling that India had separated the issue of assurances from NPT. Gromyko, however, thought that declarations of assurances would be made in connection with the treaty.[46]

In May 1968, the American Embassy in New Delhi, referred to a conversation with Homi Sethna, a member of IAEC and Director of BARC, in which the Indian scientist was purported to have characterized the Indo–Soviet nuclear agreement as 'seventeen pages of crap', accusing the Soviets of not being forthright in their nuclear deals and liars. Sethna also believed that the only Soviet interest in entering into this agreement was to obtain Indian data on Chinese nuclear tests, and he went on to boast that the Indian data was more accurate than the US information and that the Indians were far ahead of the Soviets in fuel re-fabrication techniques.[47]

Apparently aware of the growing Indian interest in the so called Peaceful Nuclear Explosions ('PNEs'), the US government handed over an aide-mémoire to the Indian Atomic Energy Commission in Bombay on 16 November 1970. It clearly stated that:

> The American position, reflected in the NPT, is that the technology of nuclear explosives for peaceful uses is indistinguishable from that of nuclear weapons and that any nuclear explosive device, though it be intended for benign economic purposes, could be used for destructive purposes. The development of such explosives, therefore, is tantamount to the development of nuclear weapons. Any other position would be inconsistent with United States obligations under the NPT and the US Atomic Energy Act.[48]

Keeping in view the fact that at that time the only source of plutonium for a prospective Indian nuclear test was the Canadian supplied CIRUS reactor, the document citing the March 1960 contract under which the US had sold heavy water for the CIRUS reactor, made it clear that:

> The heavy water sold hereunder shall be for use only in India by the Government in connection with research into and the use of atomic energy for peaceful purposes....[49]

This aide-mémoire became the subject of much discussion recently when, in their effort to prove India's responsible nuclear behaviour, the State Department officials tried to argue that the CIRUS agreement was ambiguous and was subject to differing interpretations by the two sides. The document, however, clearly indicates that ambiguity, if there was any in the terms of the agreement, was unequivocally dispelled.[50]

In the meantime, India was busy entering into collaborative agreements in the nuclear field with other countries as well. In March 1972 it signed a protocol to receive financing worth 35 million francs from France and a supply of nuclear pumps worth 7 million francs in addition to the Swedish-made materials for the Madras Atomic Power Project.[51]

BUDDHA SMILES—INDIA'S FIRST NUCLEAR EXPLOSION

On 18 May 1974, the news of a successful underground nuclear test conducted by India shocked the world in general and India's South Asian neighbours in particular. The detonation with an explosive power of 10–15 kilotons was carried out at a depth of 100 meters, using plutonium extracted from the CIRUS reactor as the fissile material. The blast created a crater of 150 meters in diameter. According to Dr H.N. Sethna, the Chairman of the Atomic Energy Commission (AEC), aerial surveys carried out within minutes of the explosion at heights down to only 30 meters did not detect any significant increase in the level of radioactivity. The AEC's official announcement described it as a:

Peaceful nuclear explosion experiment using an implosion device. As part of the programme of study of peaceful uses of nuclear explosions the Government of India has undertaken a programme to keep itself abreast of developments in this technology, particularly with reference to its use in the field of mining and earthmoving operations.[52]

The Atomic Energy Commission stated that India had no intention, of producing nuclear weapons and reiterated its strong opposition to the military uses of the nuclear explosions. Prime Minister Indira Gandhi, declaring the peaceful intent of the explosion, said that, 'we do not intend to use the knowledge of this power for any other than peaceful purposes and our neighbours need have no fear'. In a similar vein Defence Minister Jagjivan Ram, in an interview to the press on 19 May 1974, pronounced that India did not intend using its nuclear capabilities for military purposes. The Indian foreign minister, while ruling out any intention of producing nuclear weapons described the explosion as an experiment in the development of nuclear energy for its peaceful and economic uses.[53] These declarations, however, were only meant to alleviate some the pressure and criticism by the international community. In more than three decades since that so-called 'PNE' test India has never even attempted to utilize the nuclear explosive technology for its stated peaceful uses. The pronouncements of peaceful intent by the Indian government officials did not carry much weight. This is because there is no difference in the nuclear explosive technology for peaceful purposes or weapons testing, as had been amply made clear by the US in the 'aide-mémoire'.[54] Therefore, technically speaking India had already qualified as a de facto member of the nuclear club. India, therefore, created for itself a niche in the nuclear hierarchy wherein it could neither be categorized as a nuclear weapons power as defined by the NPT, nor could it be included in the category of non-nuclear weapon states any more. A scrutiny of the technical specifications of India's 'PNE' indicates that weapons possibilities were deliberately incorporated into the experiment. Onkar Marwah, for instance, has pointed out that the Indian nuclear explosion had certain unique features such as:

- Initiation of the nuclear explosive programme with an underground test which no other nuclear power had done at early stages of development.
- Use of an implosion mechanism which is a sophisticated technology with possible weapons applications.
- Claimed yield of the explosion at 10–15 kiloton suggesting the size of a nominal yield fission bomb.
- Incorporation of special safety features to ensure a 'clean explosion'.[55]

A technical study carried out soon after the Indian test at Lawrence Livermore National Laboratory based on statistics announced by the Indians concluded that, 'All known facts appear to support the Indian statements that their nuclear test was carried out to further their PNE programme'.[56] A follow-up study by the laboratory based on more precise information revealed that the Indian device was placed in a chamber 7 meters high in an underground tunnel and its floor 110 meters deep. Assuming that the device was one metre above the floor, the calculations based on the size of crater produced by the explosion indicated a yield of 10 kilotons as opposed to the 15-kiloton yield claimed by the Indian scientists.[57]

The Indian government spared no efforts in trying to persuade the world to accept its nuclear explosion as a PNE. The justification provided for the test was that it was only aimed at mastering the nuclear explosive technology for its subsequent use for such purposes as the digging of canals and mining etc. The argument, was, however not very convincing and could be challenged on two counts. First, none of the established nuclear powers had thus far been able to exploit the potential of nuclear explosives for the purposes enunciated by the Indians. There are simply no proven techniques to follow in this particular field. A noted Indian strategic analyst K. Subrahmanyam tried to justify the 'PNE theme' saying that:

> …The Indian scientific community and the government are aware that it may take years for India as it will for the USA and USSR to master

the technique of nuclear explosive technology....When mastery over nuclear explosive technology is established and peaceful explosions become normally applicable to constructive uses Indians should not depend upon the Americans, the Russians, the Chinese, the French or the British to carry out such projects in their country. Knowing full well that this technology will take another 10–15 years to develop India has decided to make a beginning now.[58]

Secondly, by justifying its detonation of a nuclear explosive device India negated its own international stance on this issue adopted a decade before its 'PNE' experiment and expressed in various international forums. For instance, the Indian Prime Minister Nehru had appealed to the UN General Assembly for an agreement to halt all nuclear explosive tests to prevent the further development of nuclear weapons. India had always been a strong advocate of a Comprehensive Test Ban Treaty (CTBT). India made no distinction at that time between 'peaceful nuclear explosions' and those carried out for testing of nuclear weapons. As is evident from the Indian Ambassador Trivedi's proclamation at the Eighteen Nation Disarmament Committee (ENDC) in August 1965, that, 'We have maintained that all nuclear tests are basically evil; they encourage evil and the sooner the evil is dealt with the better.'[59]

INTERNATIONAL REACTIONS TO THE INDIAN EXPLOSION

International reactions to the Indian explosion were varied. US public reaction was mild, as expected, despite the fact that the US had made it known to the Indians that it did not accept a PNE as any different from a nuclear weapon test, but it seemed resigned to the inevitability of an Indian nuclear test. The Soviet Union was non-committal in its reaction. An assessment of the Indian test by the US mission to NATO pointed out that:

The Soviets share our concern about proliferation...they are wary of damaging their loose ties with India and have refrained from any public comment. Soviet news accounts have stressed the 'peaceful' character of the test.[60]

China seemed to downplay the Indian test by avoiding official comment. However, it was expected to take into account its effects on India–Pakistan relations and calibrate the pace of normalization of its own relations with India.[61] There was strong condemnation of India across the Japanese political divide and in the Japanese media. The strongest condemnation of the Indian action, however, came from Canada and Pakistan. Many in the West were surprised by the Indian explosion because they thought that the cost of such an experiment was beyond the capability of a poor and under developed country such as India. In fact, in India's case the explosion came as a spin off from the long-term civilian nuclear programme. The cost of exploding the device was, therefore, incredibly low. According to official Indian estimates about $400,000 were spent on the actual experiment including the cost of the plutonium and preparation of the test site.[62]

The superpowers' reaction was understandable. Despite their commitment to nuclear non-proliferation, neither of them wanted an outright condemnation of India that could result in loss of influence and could provide an opportunity to the other superpower to take advantage of the situation. Moreover, due to their common hostility against the Chinese, they did not really see an Indian nuclear test as a negative development. A nuclear capable India would obviously be in a better position to pose a more effective challenge to China, to the strategic benefit of both the super powers. The Indians were 'good guys' then, as they are now, and the US logic of propping up India through the civilian nuclear deal and support in other strategic areas is once again driven by the perceived need to check-mate China.

The US administration, however, did discontinue the supply of enriched uranium fuel for the US supplied Tarapur nuclear power plants. The supply was resumed during the Carter presidency but was again cut off by the Reagan administration. The US, however, encouraged France to step in to prevent the plants from closing down by providing the required amount of fuel. Similarly, the Soviet Union agreed to supply heavy water for the Canadian reactors after the suspension of the supplies by the Canadian government in 1976.

Those who condemned the explosion did so for two reasons: first, they saw it as a stimulant for further proliferation; and secondly, they thought that it would disturb the equilibrium and, therefore, the security of the subcontinent particularly with reference to Pakistan.

An article published in the *Washington Post* reflected these views stating that:

> India's Peaceful Nuclear Explosion Experiment is first of all the test of a bomb. Not only is there no real distinction between a military and peaceful explosion but even the United States with all its time and technology has yet to find a single feasible peaceful use for nuclear explosives. For India to call its explosion 'peaceful' and to abjure all military intent is in a word rubbish....The fact is that India, which has long had the capability to do so, has now gone nuclear in the political military sense....the Indian explosion is the height of irresponsibility. Whatever the supposed gains in national pride and governmental prestige and regional political standing, the blast can only further aggravate Pakistan's fears of Indian domination and slow the normalization process that had been unfolding recently in the South Asian subcontinent. In a wider orbit the Indian test will in effect license and strengthen various other countries—Japan comes quickly to mind—the internal forces partial to building national nuclear bombs.[63]

The strongest official reaction came from Canada obviously due to the fact that Canada had been the main supplier of technological as well as monetary assistance for India's nuclear research and development. Although the nuclear explosive device was assembled by the Indian scientists and technicians without any outside assistance it was widely known that the plutonium used for the explosion was extracted from the Canadian supplied CIRUS reactor. The Canadians naturally felt betrayed by the Indians, who may not have violated the letter, but surely violated the spirit of their agreements with Canada. Canada may also have felt responsible for unwittingly contributing to the Indian nuclear explosion by providing generous assistance. This technological support enabled the Indians to achieve the kind of expertise required to undertake a nuclear explosive experiment. In a statement on 22 May 1974, the Canadian Secretary of State for External Affairs, Mr Mitchell Sharp, gave vent to the frustration of the Canadian government in the following terms:

> First, we are concerned as to the effect that India's action, whatever its motivation, will have on international efforts to which Canada has been an active party to limit and control the proliferation of nuclear explosion technology for which there can be no distinction between peaceful and potential military application. For all intents and purposes, therefore, India now has developed the capability of producing a nuclear weapon. The development of this technology by India is bound to have serious and widespread repercussions throughout Asia and the world.

> Secondly, we are very distressed and concerned that this latest member of the nuclear club should be a country with which successive Canadian governments have carried on over the past two decades extensive cooperation in the nuclear energy field…Canada fully respects India's sovereignty and independence in all matters. It cannot, however, be expected to assist and subsidize directly or indirectly a nuclear programme which in a key respect undermines the position which Canada has for a long time been firmly convinced is best for world peace and security.[64]

Pakistani Prime Minister Zulfikar Ali Bhutto made a strongly worded public statement, in which he insisted that Pakistan would never be intimidated by the threat created by India's nuclear capability. He said that Pakistan would attempt to secure political assurances against India's use of such a nuclear threat and that the Foreign Secretary was being sent to China, France and the UK, while he himself would raise the matter with Soviet leaders and with officials in Canada. The Minister of State for Foreign Affairs and Defence has been instructed to raise the issue at the CENTO meeting in Washington and with US officials. Bhutto added that conclusion of a no-war pact, proposed by India in 1971, was out of the question because such a pact would amount to capitulation to blackmail.[65]

India's response to these criticisms was characteristically defiant. Mr K. Subrahmanyam, Director of Institute of Defence Studies and Analyses in New Delhi, and a leading proponent of the Indian bomb, came out with a strong rebuttal to the external criticism. In a lecture delivered to the Indian International Club on 1 August 1974 he did not make any attempt to disguise the long term objectives of the so called 'PNE', and in the process exposed the hollowness of official Indian claims of a purely peaceful intent. It may be worthwhile examining the following extracts from his speech:

> ...The Nuclear Non-proliferation Treaty does make a distinction between a nuclear explosion for weapon purposes and peaceful purposes. Deliberately peaceful explosions were prohibited by the treaty for non-nuclear weapon states on the ground that the technology underlying both peaceful and weapon explosions is the same....The question is raised: how credible is this declaration ('declaration by the Indian government that the explosion was for peaceful purposes and that India has no intention of developing nuclear weapons') and how much is this country committed to this policy? All declarations in international politics are contingent on the prevailing situation. To derive logically from Lord Palmerston's famous formulation that there are no permanent friends and permanent enemies but only permanent interests, it follows that there are no permanent policies while there might be permanent objectives....These may change not merely because the environment may change but also if there are changes in the government of this country.[66]

Subrahmanyam's views clearly raise questions about the credibility of the official undertakings that the explosion had no military implications whatsoever. True, India may not have immediately embarked on producing nuclear weapons at that time, but it had achieved the ability to pursue that option whenever it chose to do so. By adopting this ambiguous posture, India gained certain advantages. On the one hand, it was able to maintain its relations with both the superpowers by emphasizing the peaceful intent of its nuclear detonation. In fact, it provided a pretext to the super powers to take a benign view of the Indian test. On the other hand, by an explicit display of its technological ability in the nuclear field it had gained all the political advantages associated with the status of a nuclear weapon power. It gained in prestige amongst the third world nations and at the same time the superpowers also came to regard it as the pre-eminent regional power. As a result, India greatly enhanced its bargaining position vis-à-vis its regional archrival Pakistan.

While dealing with the question of credibility of the Indian government's stand on peaceful nuclear explosions, Subrahmanyam puts across the following arguments:

- India does not have un-safeguarded plutonium production facilities to sustain a reasonable weapons programme. Since the American and Canadian reactors at Tarapur and Kotah respectively are under IAEA safeguards while the Indian designed reactors will not be operational before 1977/78.
- If India intended to go nuclear in the near future it will require adequate command and control surveillance and early warning systems which are not within easy reach at the moment. Moreover, there will be the task of developing a nuclear doctrine for the armed forces which apparently has not yet been undertaken.
- India does not possess a credible nuclear delivery system and that its electronics industry was not sophisticated enough to meet the demands of an effective and credible nuclear posture.
- India's conventional preponderance against Pakistan is such that it does not require nuclear weapons in any future clash with that country while a few nuclear weapons will not be enough to deter a Chinese nuclear threat or to resist nuclear blackmail by a superpower.[67]

Interestingly, Mr Subrahmanyam, while talking of the un-safeguarded sources of fissile material did not make a mention of the CIRUS reactor which had provided the plutonium for the May

1974 explosion and had yielded enough plutonium by then for another 10–12 weapons. He could not have been unaware of these facts and in all probability he deliberately omitted any mention of CIRUS, which technically speaking was 'un-safeguarded', due to the controversy surrounding the differing Canadian and Indian interpretations of the possible uses of the plutonium produced by this plant. These arguments clearly illustrate that the Indians did not refrain from embarking on a programme to develop an operational military nuclear capability out of choice, but were forced to adopt this posture due to serious technological deficiencies in the associated delivery, and command and control systems. It is also obvious that the possibility of India opting to exercise its nuclear weapons option at some future date was not ruled out. Rather, it appeared to have been deferred to allow sufficient time for the development of the necessary infrastructure for a deployable nuclear force.

Dr Vikram Sarabhai tried to justify the Indian action by arguing that India aims at alleviating its state of economic backwardness by taking quantum leaps in the way of technological achievement, telescoping the time frame of this change to a few decades, rather than centuries. To achieve this goal, industrialization of the country by establishing traditional industries like steel production, shipbuilding, fertilizer and machine building plants and oil refineries etc is not enough. India wants to venture into more sophisticated fields such as electronics, aerospace, nuclear technology, computers and automation, and in this regard PNE technology is considered to be of vital importance. It was argued that India was colonized due to its technological backwardness and the Indians are determined not to let it happen in future.[68]

Domestically, all major political parties in India welcomed the explosion and the Indian press in general tended to accept, at face value, the government's pronouncements with regard to the peaceful intent of its nuclear capability. Amongst the advantages of the PNE cited by the media and the public were, 'greater respect for India abroad', 'an opportunity to remove the inequities of the NPT', 'greater respect for India's position on disarmament related issues' and a 'proof of India's ability to achieve results through efficient utilization of resources'.[69] There were, however, sceptics as well. For instance, a ruling Congress Party MP doubted the official claims of peaceful purposes of the test and believed that many other colleagues thought likewise. Similarly, military officers at the National Defence College had no doubt that India would develop a nuclear weapons capability, and a Ministry of External Affairs official worried about loss of credibility in case India was unable to find peaceful uses for nuclear explosives. The extremist right wing party Jana Sangh, the predecessor of the modern day Bharatiya Janata Party (BJP) accused Prime Minister Indira Gandhi of acting against India's national interests by denouncing the weapons option and demanded that the government develop nuclear weapons.[70] A US assessment of the domestic Indian reactions concluded that efforts by the aid donors to punish India by curtailing economic aid or by slowing down its nuclear development programme would further strengthen the domestic support for more nuclear tests in the future.[71] This line of argument suggested a tendency to condone Indian action fearing adverse reaction by the Indians. Consequently, the softer approach adopted did not work and, in fact, encouraged India to proceed with its nuclear ambitions without fearing any penalties.

There are different views with regard to the timing and the circumstances, both internal as well as external, which led the Indian government to take such a momentous decision. It is generally believed that the decision was taken sometime in 1972, in the aftermath of the Bangladesh crisis. It is also argued that the role played by China, and in particular the United States, in this episode enhanced the feeling of vulnerability in India against superpower blackmail. This argument is however very superficial and tends to ignore some important facts to the contrary. First, it totally ignores the role played by the USSR in support of India, which had a profound effect on the outcome of the 1971 military conflict with Pakistan. The Soviet Union not only provided large quantities of sophisticated military hardware before the outbreak of hostilities but also during the war itself. Then, on the political and diplomatic front, the Soviet role in blocking all attempts at the UN to implement an early ceasefire, which could have prevented the ultimate collapse of the Pakistani forces in the Eastern Wing, is well known. This provided India with ample opportunity to achieve its objective of dismembering Pakistan by the use of military force. Secondly, this thesis tends to exaggerate the extent of the American tilt in Pakistan's favour. In fact, the US administration did not take any practical steps of any significance, for instance the provision of the much-needed military supplies. It did not even allow Jordan, a country friendly to Pakistan, to transfer four F-104 aircraft to Pakistan as a gesture of friendship and solidarity.[72] The dispatch of the Enterprise Task Force to the Bay of Bengal is generally viewed as an explicit action in support of Pakistan. Even this appears to have had an adverse effect on the morale of the beleaguered Pakistani garrison in the east, as they were led to believe that the American task force was coming to their rescue either by intervening on their side or by helping in their evacuation to the Western Wing. When none of these eventualities materialized the resistance of the forces, particularly the high command, crumbled.

The Indian political leaders as well as their strategic community never tire of mentioning the US intervention on Pakistan's behalf during the 1971 war by sending a naval task force. They however, never mention a similar US naval task force dispatched to the Bay of Bengal during the 1962 Sino–Indian War at Prime Minister Nehru's request.[73] It is another matter that the task force had not reached its destination when the Chinese announced a unilateral cease fire to the hostilities. The Indian leaders should, in fact, have felt more confident after the 1971 war, that if the Americans did not have the will to physically intervene to prevent the dismemberment of one of their long term partners in defence and security arrangements, there was no likelihood of their doing so in any future crisis in South Asia. At the same time the limitations of China's ability to militarily intervene on Pakistan's behalf were also thoroughly exposed. It was evident that the Chinese were not in a position to risk a direct confrontation with the Soviet Union through their meddling in the affairs of the subcontinent. This development was a direct outcome of the long term 'Treaty of Friendship and Cooperation' signed between India and the USSR in August 1971. During the war itself, once the Indians felt anxious due to the news of the dispatch of the US Naval Task Force to the battle zone, the Russians assured them that they would not allow the Americans to intervene.

Rodney W. Jones, then Director of Nuclear Policy Studies at the Center for Strategic and International Studies, Georgetown University, Washington, D.C. while analyzing the Indian decision to conduct a nuclear explosion argued that:

> Authorization to prepare a nuclear explosive device may have been proposed and considered earlier but was probably not granted until late 1969 or early 1970. Reports at that time of a successful Chinese long-range missile test provoked fresh pressure from Parliament. The split of December 1969 in the ruling Congress Party probably gave Indira Gandhi an incentive to seize the initiative and remove the nuclear issue from inner circle contention. About the same time in May 1970 Vikram Sarabhai announced a ten-year programme (the so called 'Sarabhai profile') to accelerate nuclear energy and space technology development.[74]

This argument implies that there was no direct link between the 1971 crisis and the Indian decision to detonate a nuclear device. The decision appears to have been taken much earlier probably under the domestic political compulsions or as a response to the Chinese developments in the field of long-range ballistic missiles, as argued by Rodney Jones. In fact, Homi Bhaba had claimed, in the wake of the Chinese nuclear test in 1964 that India could produce a bomb of its own within eighteen months, a claim which he had been making since the late 1950s. Accepting that claim, the implication is that India could have detonated its nuclear device sometime in 1966. It can, however, be assumed that this possibility could not materialize due to the sudden deaths of Prime Minister Shastri and Dr Bhaba in quick succession in the same year.

Jones also presented an alternative thesis apparently inspired by Indian sources. He contended that:

> The one development between late 1971 and the following year that might have served as a specific stimulus to initiate (or rather confirm) a project for a nuclear explosive test would have been evidence which Indian intelligence probably picked up that Z.A. Bhutto had deliberately launched an active programme in Pakistan for the development of a nuclear weapons capability shortly after he assumed control of the government. This would coincide with (and perhaps explain) some Indian opinions conveyed to the author that the official decision to prepare for the nuclear demonstration occurred in the early autumn of 1972.[75]

This idea is clearly based on conjecture. India enjoyed a substantial technological lead over Pakistan in the nuclear field. The state of Pakistan's economy immediately after the 1971 disaster did not allow the sort of financing required to bridge the technological gap with India. It was, therefore, almost impossible for Pakistan to catch up with, or overtake India in the nuclear race overnight. A CIA analysis of the event stated that, 'The decision to go ahead at this time, was probably made in order to boost India's sagging international prestige and to divert public attention from the government's mounting domestic problems...'[76]

In the aftermath of the test a 'Post Mortem Report', prepared for the Director of the CIA, to analyzing the performance of the intelligence community prior to the Indian test had, among its major conclusions, the following:

- In the months prior to the Indian test, the intelligence community failed to warn US decision makers that such a test was being planned. This failure denied the US government the option of considering diplomatic or other initiatives to try to prevent this significant step in nuclear proliferation.
- The intelligence community had long known that India was capable of producing and testing a nuclear device. It had also estimated as far back as 1965 that India would 'in the next few

years' detonate a nuclear device. Its inability to predict the actual event was due essentially to two factors: inadequate priority against an admittedly difficult target, and lack of adequate communications among those elements of the community, both collectors and producers, whose combined talents were essential to resolving the problem.

• Most importantly, success against the nth country intelligence problem will require that the community accord it a higher priority than it has received to date.[77]

This evaluation of the failure of the intelligence community and the measures adopted consequently helped the intelligence agencies to pick up India's imminent preparations for another nuclear test in December 1995, in time for the US administration to put diplomatic pressure on Narasimha Rao government to abandon the test.[78] However, it also provided the Indians with the insights into the US intelligence methods which helped them to deceive the US intelligence once again in May 1998. The other fall-out of this post mortem was the heightened intelligence focus on Pakistan's nuclear programme and its procurement activities.

POST-1974 DEVELOPMENTS

In the immediate aftermath of the Pokhran explosion the Indian government asserted that it had no intention of producing nuclear weapons. However, the possibility of further PNEs for 'research purposes' was never ruled out. A relatively long period of 24 years elapsed after India's first nuclear explosion, before it conducted further nuclear explosive experiments. Apparently, there were no visible signs to suggest that India was somehow engaged in the production of nuclear weapons. The question then arises as to why the Indians took such a major step in May 1974, if they did not have to follow it up with more concrete actions. There is, however, enough evidence to suggest that the Indians had, in no way abandoned their nuclear ambitions. In fact, they were moving in a very deliberate manner to broaden their technological base. In the mid-1970s India lacked a credible delivery system, a sophisticated command and control system and requisite surveillance and early warning systems. In the absence of these important prerequisites India's nuclear deterrent could never achieve credibility. It was because of this realization that the Indians invested heavily in the fields of electronics, space and missile technologies beginning in the early 1970s. It appears with hindsight that India wanted to develop its delivery and support systems, so that whenever it decided to cast aside its ambiguous nuclear stance and become a declared nuclear weapon power, its nuclear warheads could be readily deployed. India embarked upon a dedicated military missile programme through the initiation of an ambitious Integrated Guided Missile Development Programme (IGMDP) in 1983 with the declared objective of developing five missile types namely: 'Nag'—an anti-tank guided missile; 'Trishul'—a short range surface to air missile; 'Akash'—a medium range surface to air missile; 'Prithvi'—a short range battlefield support missile and 'Agni'—an intermediate range ballistic missile.[79]

India's space programme was initiated in 1967 and by 1972–73 the first indigenously developed two stage rocket 'Rohini-560' was test fired. The space programme was sharply upgraded in the early 1970s. The space programme was closely integrated with the nuclear programme in the famous Sarabhai profile, the ten-year programme announced in 1970, and adopted by the Indian government a year later. In the first half of the 1970s the space research establishments in India developed and tested various components including the inertial guidance system, on board computers, rate integrating gyroscopes, heat shields, nose cones and different types of solid and liquid propellants for use in the space rockets. In July 1974, the director of the Indian Space Commission claimed that the country already possessed the ability to produce medium range missiles with locally developed solid fuels and guidance systems. In early 1975 a scientific satellite was launched from a Soviet Cosmodrome.[80]

In view of the importance of a sophisticated electronics base for both nuclear, as well as the space programmes, important policy decisions were also taken in this field. In 1972 the newly created 'Electronics Commission' and the 'Department of Electronics' were assigned objectives and schedules similar to those fixed for the nuclear and space activities. In the electronics field India already possessed a broad civilian base, and the decision makers were mainly concerned with integrating the activities of the public and private enterprises in this field.

Despite some advances in the development of strategic as well as tactical delivery systems India, however, was not able to declare itself a nuclear weapons power. Some commentators are of the view that India's nuclear programme had been faced with various technological problems ever since the Pokhran test. These difficulties were partly due to the withdrawal of nuclear cooperation by Canada, as a reprisal to the Indian 'PNE'. Restrictions were also imposed by the other nuclear suppliers on the supply of sensitive components in the aftermath of the Indian nuclear explosion. At the same time India's efforts to achieve self-sufficiency in important areas such as the production of heavy water for the existing, as well as the projected, nuclear power plants did not keep up with the anticipated schedules. As a result India was forced to enter into an agreement with the Soviet Union in 1976 for the import of heavy water. The Soviets, however, insisted that the agreement should be covered by stringent IAEA safeguards. This meant that any power plant using the Soviet supplied heavy water would be subject to IAEA monitoring and inspections. Ironically, the Indians who had always resisted subjecting their nuclear installations to inspections by the IAEA officials, were forced to accept these conditions to keep their plants running. However, the agreement with the USSR implied that the Indians would not be able to divert the spent fuel from the plants using the Soviet supplied heavy water for reprocessing, thus depriving them of considerable quantities of fissile material, which they were hoping to extract from these power plants had these installations remained un-safeguarded.[81]

Bhabani Sen Gupta an Indian strategic analyst has described this dilemma in a book written under the auspices of the 'Centre for Policy Research' New Delhi:

...An embargo placed on the supply of nuclear components, technology and know how by the countries that later constituted the London Club severely constrained India's peaceful nuclear energy development programme. Any possible military programme was handicapped because the components required for such a programme were banned. For example, without the R5 special plutonium reactor a military programme is not sustainable because India lacks the needed quantities of safeguard free plutonium. The embargo affected the completion of this reactor. Serious mishaps and other factors have delayed the completion of India's heavy water plants; without un-safeguarded heavy water R5 cannot be operated. These mishaps led to doubts such as whether interested foreign powers had tried to cripple, damage or inordinately delay India's nuclear programme.[82]

In Gupta's opinion the CIRUS reactor had a very limited output of 9.4 kg of plutonium a year, which was too little to support a nuclear weapons programme because 10 kg of plutonium is required for a single fission bomb [This was an incorrect assumption since the amount of plutonium required for a nuclear device can be as low as 4.5 to 5 kg depending on the sophistication of the design]. The plutonium produced by CIRUS was also required for research purposes and to divert all available plutonium to a bomb programme would amount to crippling the research programme. In Gupta's view the bomb programme would have to wait for the commissioning of the R5 reactor with an estimated output of 23.4 kg of plutonium per annum. This reactor was originally scheduled to be commissioned in 1978. However, this date was put off by five years to 1983. According to Gupta's estimate the first Indian nuclear weapons might not be available till the late 1980s or mid 1990s.[83] The R5 reactor mentioned by Gupta eventually went critical in 1985 and is now known as the 'Dhruva' reactor.[84]

Professor S.S. Mehdi on the other hand felt that India had already piled up sufficient stocks of plutonium to sustain a nuclear weapons programme. He claimed that:

India hopes to achieve a high level of demonstrated confidence in fast breeder technology and in increasing manifold its potential nuclear un-peacefulness through plutonium accumulation. According to an estimate India had already produced 220 kilograms of plutonium by 1980 and is projected to have 2531 kilograms on hand by 1984.[85]

Mehdi's estimates are based on a study by David K. Willis entitled, 'On the Trails of the Atom Bomb Makers', which appeared in the *Strategic Digest* of March 1982. India had only one dedicated plutonium production reactor, the 40 MW CIRUS, which did not have the capacity to produce the amounts of plutonium mentioned by Mehdi, even with an uninterrupted operation at full capacity. These figures are certainly exaggerated and appear to have taken into account the plutonium produced by the un-safeguarded nuclear power reactors as well. Mehdi, though, acknowledged that because of the agreement with the Soviet Union for the supply of heavy water for the 'Rajasthan Atomic Power Plant' and the acceptance of the IAEA safeguards, this plant has been rendered inconsequential for military purposes. However, the commissioning in July 1983 of the first unit of the Indian built 'Madras Atomic Power Plant', which is moderated by indigenously produced heavy water, could have some military implications. The Indian plans envisaged that all future power plants would be Indian made and would use heavy water produced in the country.[86] However, after years of glitches, there appeared to be a major change in the Indian approach, and through the civilian nuclear cooperation agreement signed with the US in March 2006, India would now import most of its power plants of the more advanced Light Water type. It would also be importing fuel for many of its existing heavy water reactors and would, therefore, have to place these reactors under IAEA safeguards. Something, which India had assiduously avoided for decades. This decision clearly indicated that the Indians had seen the limits of indigenization and, also, that there is an acute shortage of uranium in India.

Mehdi did not seem to be impressed by the idea that India's nuclear programme was aimed at harnessing the potential of the atom for peaceful purposes, such as nuclear power production. He felt that the true objective of India's nuclear endeavours was to attain the capability to produce nuclear weapons, and argued that if India had required nuclear energy so desperately it should have opted for large-scale acquisition of peaceful nuclear technology by accepting IAEA safeguards. He also pointed out that if India really wanted to harness the potential of nuclear energy it would not have carried out a nuclear detonation around the same time as OPEC had raised the prices of oil, thereby depriving itself of the civil nuclear cooperation of countries like Canada and facing increasingly tougher restrictions on the import of nuclear technology.[87]

This point of view is supported by the statistics contained in a 1978 World Bank report dealing with the economic situation and prospects for India. According to this report by 1971–72 the total electricity production in India amounted to 66,385 GWh of which 3,171,228,024 and 1,190 GWh were produced by thermal, hydro and nuclear sources respectively. By 1976–77 the amount of electricity through nuclear power amounted to 3,252 GWh while thermal and hydro electricity production rose to 50,245 and 34,836 GWh respectively out of a total output of 95,573 GWh. In 1982–83 the share of electricity produced through the employment of nuclear power was an insignificant 2 to 3 per cent of total production.[88]

India had mapped out very ambitious plans to install 10,000 MW of nuclear energy capacity by the year 2000, which meant that nuclear energy would constitute 5 per cent of the total projected commercial energy production. Achievement of this target depended on the smooth execution of these plans according to the laid down schedules. Bhabani Sen Gupta, expressing his scepticism, pointed out that, 'No one takes seriously the Atomic Energy Commission's plan to install 10,000 MW of nuclear energy capacity by 2000 AD'.[89] Ravindra Tomar also criticized the overall performance of India's nuclear establishment, and viewed the execution of India's nuclear programme as an attempt to superimpose a highly advanced technology over a collaboration-dependent industrial economic infrastructure. He felt that the planning suffered from indifference and a lack of attention to detail, which resulted in a large-scale revision of estimates soon after the initial plans were announced. Such practices have been encouraged by lack of public debate on various aspects of nuclear energy planning, and the autonomous style of functioning of the scientist bureaucrats of the Atomic Energy Commission. These AEC officials are, however, reluctant to admit a lack of satisfactory progress despite huge investments. This has resulted in increasing dependence on foreign supplies and acceptance of stricter safeguards, despite the frequently proclaimed goal of achieving self-reliance and indigenization.[90]

In line with the track record of the Indian nuclear establishment, the results fell far short of the objectives and by 2005–6 the percentage share of nuclear power in India's overall energy profile remained a miserly 3 per cent or less with an installed capacity of 3,750 MW. With all the currently under-construction and projected plants coming on stream the total output of nuclear energy is expected to rise to 8,530 MW by 2011. India plans to have 20,000 MW of nuclear capacity by 2020, and long term projections suggest that nuclear power will constitute 20 per cent of India's power production by 2050.[91]

By the early 1980s India was trying to pursue the following competing foreign policy objectives:

- Recognition as a major power not aligned with the super powers.
- Military power sufficient to protect its borders from Pakistan and China.
- Leadership of the subcontinent.[92]
- The reputation as a major proponent of nuclear disarmament.

Since its border conflict with China in 1962 and the Chinese nuclear detonation in 1964 India had perceived China as a more serious long term threat than Pakistan. That perception, however, was undergoing change due to the Chinese gradually increasing warmth toward the West, and its focus on the modernization of its economy and refurbishment of its military forces. Nevertheless, India accelerated its nuclear weapons-related research and development, ostensibly due to the growing prospect of facing two nuclear-armed neighbours, China and Pakistan. Any Indian decision to undertake measures to match a Pakistani nuclear effort was bound to sour its relations with the US and other nuclear suppliers, and by provoking China would reverse the trend of improving relations with that country. India had to respond to any Pakistani actions, in order to maintain its primacy in the region, but faced the dilemma of losing its image of a major power by appearing to be reacting to the policies of a comparatively smaller country. At the same time, India continued to insist on the merits of PNEs, as was evident from a large number of papers on the subject appearing in Indian publications. This approach provided India with a convenient hedge to cover the continued pursuit of its nuclear weapons programme.[93] During the same period Indian scientists were also publishing technical papers on issues which could only be of interest to the nuclear weapon designers. For instance, in June 1980 B.K. Godwal, S.K. Sikka and R. Chidambaram, of the neutron physics division of BARC, published a paper entitled 'Model for the Equation of State of Condensed matter in the Intermediate Pressure Region'. These calculations, which were carried out for aluminium and molybdenum, were clearly related to the Indian nuclear explosives programme.[94]

In the early 1980s, India also initiated research in uranium enrichment technology. A group of scientists from BARC were experimenting with the Laser Isotope Separation (LIS) method of enrichment, and although they succeeded in separating sulphur isotopes, they did not make much headway.[95] However, in November 1986, the Department of Atomic Energy Chairman, Dr Raja Ramanna claimed that BARC scientists had succeeded in mastering the centrifuge enrichment process using an experimental centrifuge based on the 'Zippe' centrifuge.[96]

In November 1986 the US Defence Advisor in New Delhi reported to the Defence Intelligence Agency on the Indian nuclear programme. According to the report, the Indian nuclear programme continued to be faced with some technical problems, especially the shortfalls in heavy water production, the running of Rajasthan Power Station and the repeated shutdowns of the Dhruva reactor, while the domestic debate on whether or not to acquire nuclear weapons was intensifying. Responding to several reports on Pakistan's nuclear weapons development, Indian Prime Minister Rajiv Gandhi, while addressing a gathering of senior military officers, stated that, 'Although India does not want to produce a nuclear weapon, the GOI will have to reconsider its defence options if it were faced with nuclear weapons across the border'.[97]

The Soviet Union had offered to provide two VVER-440 light water enriched uranium fuelled nuclear power reactors to India, to enhance its power production capacity. The offer, however, became a subject of criticism in the Indian press for two reasons. First, the induction of light water reactors would have gone against the Indian policy of standardizing its nuclear power programme on heavy water reactors. Secondly, India had no indigenous capability to produce enriched uranium fuel for these reactors, which would mean a perpetual dependence on the Soviet Union. The latter argument carried a lot of weight, in view of India's bitter experience with regard to the termination of the fuel supply for the Tarapur Nuclear Power Station by the US. However, Dr Ramanna claimed at a Press Conference that, 'India is in a position to produce as much enriched uranium as might be required to support these two reactors'.[98]

This claim, like many other claims made by Indian nuclear scientists in the past, would turn out to be exaggerated, as borne out by later events. A June 1994 US defence intelligence agency report alluded to the fact that India was facing problems in fuelling the Tarapur plant. Finding it difficult to import the fuel due to stringent NSG controls, India announced its intention to fuel the plant with mixed oxide fuel (MOX) using some of the plutonium extracted from the spent fuel from the Tarapur plant. Beside the technical problems in fabricating MOX fuel, and modifying the reactor design accordingly, there were also legal issues. Since part of the plutonium generated by the plant was based on the US supplied fuel, it would have attracted US sanctions. India would appear to have abandoned this option. The fact remains that twenty years later India is still not able to produce fuel for the Tarapur power station and has recently purchased the fuel from Russia to keep the plant running.[99]

Around December 1995, the US intelligence picked up what appeared to be imminent preparations for a nuclear test at the Pokhran test site. The US administration confronted the Narasimha Rao government with the evidence and put sufficient pressure on him to abandon the test.[100] This sharing of intelligence information, which helped avert the test in 1995, was however to become the bane of the US intelligence community, since it gave the Indian scientific community the ability to work out the gaps in satellite coverage and to camouflage the activities most likely to be picked up by American intelligence resources. This is one of the most significant causes of the failure of US intelligence, termed by Senate Intelligence Committee Chairman, Richard Shelby, as a 'colossal failure' by the CIA to detect the event in time.[101]

On 4 February 1998 the BJP, widely expected to emerge as the single largest party in the national elections, announced its election manifesto in which it stated in clear terms its intention to test and induct nuclear weapons, should it come to power. Under the rubric of 'external security' the manifesto outlined the party's commitment to:

- Establish a National Security Council to constantly analyze security, political and economic threats and render continuous advice to the Government. This council will undertake India's first ever strategic defence review to study and analyze the security environment and make appropriate recommendations to cover all aspects of defence requirements and organization.
- Re-evaluate the country's nuclear policy and exercise the option to induct nuclear weapons.
- Expedite the development of the Agni series of ballistic missiles with a view to increasing their range and accuracy.
- Increase the radius of power projection by inducting appropriate force multipliers such as battlefield surveillance system and air to air refuelling.

- Enhance the traditional and technical capabilities of our external intelligence agencies and also to increase the interaction and coordination with user departments.
- Place paramilitary forces in sensitive border areas under the full control of the army.[102]

A spokesperson of Pakistan's Ministry of Foreign Affairs, expressing serious concern about BJP's manifesto, cautioned that Pakistan might have to review its policy in line with the demands of its national security and sovereignty. On 7 February 1998 the US Ambassador to New Delhi, Richard Celeste, commented that Washington would have profound concern if India were to overtly declare itself a nuclear weapons state.[103] Many observers, however, were inclined to believe that this was merely an election rhetoric, and once in the government and faced with the realities of power, the BJP would back down. This conclusion was further reinforced by the general softening of the BJP stance on various other political issues, and its nationalist image on assuming office. This was also manifested in the BJP government's reaction to the Pakistani testing of its Ghauri missile in April 1998. It was also expected that the BJP would, as outlined in its manifesto, constitute a National Security Council to review the policy options. This would give time to the leadership to take cool, calculated and rational decisions on national security issues. The expectation that the BJP government would wait for the National Security Council to formulate its recommendations, before taking any major policy decision with far reaching consequences, seems to have deceived the US administration as well as the intelligence agencies sufficiently for them to be surprised by the timing of the Indian nuclear tests on 11 and 13 May 1998.

Buddha Smiles Again

Within little more than a month of its taking up the reins of power in New Delhi, the BJP government made Buddha smile again in the desolate wilderness of the Rajasthan desert, though the grin was much wider this time around. The tests were named the 'Shakti' series of tests. Manvendra Singh, an Indian journalist, wrote;

> Buddha today smiled for the second time at Pokhran, and grinned three times on his birth anniversary which coincided with India's triple nuclear test...The triple tests included a simple fission device, a low yield device and remarkably a thermo-nuclear device.[104]

Paul Laventhal of the Nuclear Control Institute in Washington remarked that, 'This whole exercise is quite likely an exercise to showcase India's thermonuclear capability. It is the one test that India needed to do to show they have a Hydrogen Bomb.'[105] However, the analysis of the seismographs carried out around the world, suggested much lower yields than those claimed by India, and its claims of a successful hydrogen bomb test were seriously questioned. Experts were of the view that, while the primary stage of an attempted thermo-nuclear bomb may have worked, its secondary stage was merely a fizzle. On 13 May 1998 India claimed to have conducted two more 'low yield tests'. However, the seismic signatures of these tests were not picked up by any seismic station around the world, not even by some of the closest ones including one at Nilore near Islamabad in Pakistan. It cannot be said with any degree of certainty whether India actually conducted this second set of tests or their attempt to carry out these tests was a botched one.

The tests however, created a strong nationalistic fervour within India and, except for an insignificantly small anti-nuclear lobby, there was widespread rejoicing in the streets of major Indian cities. As many as 91 per cent of the population approved of the tests in one of the polls conducted immediately after the tests. The tests were presented and seen as a 'showcase of technological leap by Indian nuclear establishment'.[106] Parallels were drawn with J. Robert Oppenheimer's famous quotation from the Bhagwat Geeta after witnessing the first nuclear test in 1945, 'Now I have become death, destroyer of the worlds'.[107] Two former Indian foreign secretaries, J.N. Dixit and S.K. Singh, called the tests a 'positive step'. Mr Dixit said that, 'the tests sent a clear signal that we are a confirmed nuclear power',[108] adding that the tests were in keeping with India's national security interests and would consolidate not only India's regional political status but lead to a strategic equilibrium in the region.[109] While Mr Singh was of the view that there would be no long-term negative fallout, and repercussions such as economic sanctions would be short lived.[110] His assessment was quite correct, as the European Union, Russia and France refused to impose sanctions and the US sanctions also did not last long.

Prime Minister Vajpayee wrote personal letters to President Clinton as well as the G-8 heads of state, explaining India's rationale for carrying out the nuclear tests.[111] His letter to President Clinton, which was published by *The New York Times,* became contentious, since he cited the Chinese threat to India's security as the primary reason for India's decision to conduct nuclear tests. However, he did not miss the opportunity to target Pakistan as well. Vajpayee wrote:

> We have an overt nuclear weapon state on our borders, a state which committed armed aggression against India in 1962. Although our relations with that country have improved in the last decade or so, an atmosphere of distress persists mainly due to the unresolved border problem. To add to the distress, that country has materially helped another neighbour of ours to become a covert nuclear weapon state. At the hands of this bitter neighbour we have suffered three aggressions in the last fifty years. And for the last ten years we have been the victim of unremitting terrorism and militancy sponsored by it in several parts of our country, specially Punjab and Jammu & Kashmir.[112]

The China card was ostensibly used to soften the impact of sanctions, by appealing to the American sensitivities to growing Chinese power, by presenting India as the potential strategic counter weight to China. China bashing was then taken up by Defence Minister George Fernandes, who declared China as India's enemy number one. In the frenzy created by the tests, Home Minister L.K. Advani, and some other BJP leaders, started hurling threats at Pakistan. Advani issued a series of inflammatory statements which were condemned by the State Department spokesman James Rubin who said that, 'We call upon India to exercise great caution in its statements and actions at this particularly sensitive time, with emotions running high'.[113] He termed Advani's posture to be 'foolish and dangerous'.[114] One cannot definitively state that Advani had adopted a genuinely aggressive posture towards Pakistan, sensing an opportunity created by India's nuclear tests, especially if Pakistan failed to respond in kind. It could also have been an attempt to egg on Pakistan to follow suit, so that the focus of international opprobrium heaped on India could be diverted towards Pakistan, or at least its effect could be mitigated by bringing Pakistan into the dock as well. Realizing the folly of antagonizing China unnecessarily, the Indian leadership quickly changed course and initiated measures to limit the damage.[115] A CIA intelligence report analyzing the situation created by India's nuclear tests pointed out that:

• Although the BJP failed to win a majority in the general election, the party is riding a tidal wave of popularity from the tests and is now signalling that resolving Kashmir on India's terms will be next on its agenda.
• New Delhi is claiming that its nuclear tests were for national security and to counter China. Nonetheless, last week Home Minister Advani declared publicly that Pakistan must 'roll back its anti-India policy immediately' or 'it will prove costly' for Islamabad.
• Pakistan's decision to conduct nuclear tests is being portrayed by the BJP government as confirmation that its 'get tough' policy towards its neighbour was justified.[116]

The Indian leadership also seemed to be developing a direct linkage between its newly acquired nuclear capability and its Kashmir policy. For instance, at a press conference held with Kashmir Chief Minister, Farooq Abdullah, Advani declared that, 'the nuclear tests have ushered in a new era in India–Pakistan relations', and he warned Islamabad that New Delhi would respond to provocations in Kashmir in a manner 'costly for Pakistan'.[117] Advani did not rule out 'hot pursuit' operations across the Line of Control and indicated that Indian forces would adopt a more aggressive posture, while refusing to hold talks with the Kashmiri militants.[118] In a symbolic move, Vajpayee also indicated a linkage between the nuclear tests and India's Kashmir policy, by taking along Kashmir Chief Minister Farooq Abdullah during his visit to the Pokhran test site.[119] Abdullah was the only state chief executive accompanying the Indian Prime Minister to the nuclear test site. However, the belligerent rhetoric and threatening tone of statements by Advani and other BJP leaders was distinctly toned down after Pakistan conducted its own test, in response to the Indian tests.

A HINDU BOMB?

The BJP portrayed its decision to go ahead with the nuclear tests as a means of claiming recognition for 'Hindu civilization's rightful place in the world'[120] and a clear message to India's neighbours to accept its primacy in the region.[121] An Indian journalist wrote:

> Already, the first whisper of the Hindu Bomb is being heard. Many writers and analysts have attributed the tests as much to the BJP's domestic political compulsions and instinct for survival than India's security needs or strategic foresight. The result: A spate of editorials, analyses and cartoons with a 'Hindu' touch.[122]

Not unlike that of 1974, the international response to the Indian tests remained feeble and muted, and while President Clinton termed the tests a 'terrible mistake'[123] and slapped mandatory sanctions under the 'Nuclear Proliferation Prevention Act 1994', also known as the Glenn Amendment, the EU, Russia and France refused to apply sanctions. In a statement made in London prior to a G-8 meeting, while advising Pakistan to reconcile with India, Clinton said that he understood India's security concerns in undertaking nuclear tests.[124] The speaker of the Lower House of the Russian Parliament, Gennady Seleznyov expressed his support for India's decision to test, saying that, 'I believe that India acted correctly. In this respect, it acts very consistently and it was a correct decision not to curtail its research programme halfway despite US pressure. I can only admire their national pride'.[125] The G-8 failed to agree on any punitive measures against India. It appeared that the major powers were inclined to accept India's status as a nuclear weapon power as a fait accompli.

Motives Behind India's Decision to go Nuclear

There are differing perspectives and views with regard to the ultimate goals and objectives of India's nuclear policy. It may be instructive to review some of these, to provide an insight into the motives underlying India's nuclear programme and policy. A pro-nuclear bomb lobby has always existed in India. It was initially led by the architect of India's nuclear programme, Dr Homi Bhaba himself until his death in 1966. The cause was later taken up by K. Subrahmanyam and others, who had influential voices in the Indian strategic community. Subrahmanyam argued that:

> In the current global strategic environment in which against our opposition, nuclear weapons have been made an international currency of power and surrounded by the three nuclear weapons powers of the world it is absurd for a country of India's size, population and resources to talk of non-alignment and keeping her options open by renouncing nuclear weapons. Without India going nuclear she will not be able to normalize relations with China—just as China could not exercise its US options without going nuclear first.[126]

Subrahmanyam was convinced that China had earned its rightful place in the comity of nations only after it had gone nuclear. He thought that India could also gain recognition in the corridors of power if it follows the Chinese example. However, while following this line of argument he did not seem to have reckoned that if India set that precedent, countries like Pakistan would also follow suit, thereby neutralizing the advantage sought to be gained by India.

Since the late seventies, or probably early eighties, a further factor entered into the calculation of Indian leaders with regard to their nuclear decision-making. This new factor was the perceived potential of Pakistan's growing nuclear programme. The Indian Prime Minister, Indira Gandhi, winding up a debate on defence appropriations in the Lok Sabha on 9 April 1981 declared that: 'It should be clearly understood that Pakistan's development of nuclear weapons will have grave and irreversible consequences for our subcontinent'.[127] She went on to add that: 'We shall respond in an appropriate way to any development'.[128]

According to Bhabani Sen Gupta, the Indian nuclear debate in the early 1980s focused almost entirely on the expected acquisition of nuclear weapons by Pakistan.[129] The Chinese nuclear explosion in 1964 did not lead to a perception in India of a nuclear threat to the country's security, nor did it lead to an immediate decision by India to embark on a nuclear weapons programme of its own. However, a Pakistani bomb, even a Pakistani PNE, would evoke an instant reaction from India. It would be considered a threat not only to India's security, but also a challenge to its regional as well as global influence and status.[130] Similar views were expressed by Mr C. Subramaniam, Indian Defence Minister in the Charan Singh government, in a speech at the National Defence College in October 1979. While outlining India's defence strategy in the next decade he declared: '...I am not naive enough to declare on behalf of all future generations and governments that India will not make nuclear weapons'. He listed seven possible factors which could have a bearing on India's decision to go nuclear, and at the top of the list was; 'whether or not Pakistan goes nuclear'.[131]

Gupta put forward three other plausible contexts in which India might decide to go nuclear, besides a possible Pakistan decision. These were: a deliberate decision to join the nuclear club; a protest against or defiance of the unjust and exploitative NPT regime by taking a deliberate step to break the non-proliferation barrier; and a belated response to Chinese nuclear power.[132]

However, a closer study of policies followed by successive Indian leaders and the overwhelming public perception the indications are that 'Prestige' has been a common denominator throughout, as amplified by the following discussion.

There is compelling evidence to suggest that right from the outset, the Indian nuclear scientists had pursued the development and retention of a military nuclear option, within the purview of an overall nuclear development programme, and successive political leaders went along wittingly or unwittingly. In a 1948 address to Parliament, Mr Nehru stated that, 'Of course if we are compelled as a nation to use it for other purposes, possibly no pious sentiments would stop the nation from using it that way'.[133] As far back as 1960, US Army Major General (retired) Kenneth D. Nichols, while on a visit to India as a consultant to Westinghouse to discuss plans for building India's first nuclear power reactor, briefed Prime Minister Nehru in the presence of Homi Bhabha. Nichols recounts that Nehru turned to Bhabha and asked:

> Can you develop an atomic bomb? Bhabha assured him that he could and in reply to Nehru's next question about time, he estimated he would need a year to do it. I was really astounded to be hearing these questions from the one I thought to be one of the world's most peace loving leaders. He then asked me if I agreed with Bhabha and I replied that I knew of no reason why Bhabha could not do it...He concluded by saying to Bhabha, 'Well don't do it until I tell you to.[134]

The 1971 war with Pakistan not only exposed the limitations of the American policy as well as the Chinese ability to intervene militarily on Pakistan's behalf, it cut Pakistan down to size and actually reduced the perceived threat from Pakistan. In these circumstances it is hard to believe that India felt more vulnerable in 1972 than in 1964. It may be fair to assume that in 1972 the Indian Prime Minister Indira Gandhi, riding on the crest of domestic popularity and enhanced prestige abroad, felt confident enough to try and consolidate India's predominance in South Asia through a display of India's nuclear potential.

Prime Minister Rajiv Gandhi, who is credited with the presentation of an action plan at the UN in 1988-89 for the elimination of nuclear weapons, had around the same time quietly given the green light to the Defence Research and Development Organization (DRDO) and the chairman of the AEC to develop an Indian nuclear deterrent.[135] Even the suave, and apparently docile, Inder Kumar Gujral is known to have seriously considered the possibility of conducting a nuclear test during his rather short period as the Indian prime minister, ostensibly to raise his domestic political standing.[136] Another abortive attempt was made in the spring of 1996, when Vajpayee was sworn in as the prime minister and was given 15 days, by President Sharma, to muster the required majority in the parliament. This he failed to achieve and had to quit on the expiry of the deadline. However, one the first things Vajpayee did in his rather brief stint in power was to give the go-ahead to Abdul Kalam and Chidambaram, who were in-charge of India's nuclear weapons programme, to proceed with nuclear weapon tests. The scientists immediately initiated the required steps in that direction and had reportedly emplaced at least one nuclear explosive in a test shaft. However, the execution of the intended tests was subject to the outcome of the 'confidence vote' and fell through when it failed to materialise.[137]

On the domestic front, a survey of public opinion polls conducted in the aftermath of the 1998 tests, 'self esteem' and 'pride' emerge as the pre-dominant themes. In a poll conducted by the Indian Market Research Bureau (IMRB), 91 per cent of the respondents felt a sense of pride at India's pronouncement of its nuclear status. The same argument was echoed by Prime Minister Vajpayee when he declared on the floor of the Indian parliament that, 'It is India's due, the right of one sixth of humanity'. In a 1994 poll, 49 per cent of those favouring weaponization of the nuclear option advocated the development of nuclear weapons by India to 'improve its bargaining position in international affairs', while another 38 per cent favoured the acquisition of nuclear weapons to enhance India's 'international status'. In two other opinion polls conducted in June 1974 and May 1998, the results were identical, with around 90 per cent of people stating that they felt proud of this achievement and thought that it had raised India's stature in the comity of nations.[138]

Statements by various Indian leaders also betray this self-consciousness of India's status. For instance, Foreign Minister

Jaswant Singh, in an interview with National Public Radio in the United States said that, 'All that we have done is given ourselves a degree of strategic autonomy by acquiring those symbols of power...which have universal currency'.[139]

The issue of viewing nuclear weapons as the means of acquiring power and prestige is a recurring theme elsewhere. To quote former Prime Minister I.K. Gujral:

> An old Indian saying holds that Indians have a third eye. I told President Clinton that, when my third eye looks at the door into the Security Council Chamber it sees a little sign that says, 'only those with economic wealth or nuclear weapons allowed.' I said to him, 'it is very difficult to achieve economic wealth. The implication was clear; nuclear weapons were relatively easy to build and detonate and could offer an apparent short cut to great power status.[140]

A CIA analysis in the aftermath of the Indian tests also concluded that by demonstrating its nuclear capability, India was reckoning that it could no longer be ignored by the international community, and it would not only win a permanent seat in the UN Security Council, but would also be accommodated at the high table in various regional forums.[141] Other than their failure to gain a place on the UN Security Council, the developments of the past eight years bear testimony to the fact that Indians were not wrong in their assumptions. Over the years India has been very assertive in demanding its right to have access to nuclear technology and has been consistent in the pursuit of its nuclear objectives. The US and the Western world have, on the other hand, been vacillating in their non-proliferation policies and, after initially aiding and abetting India's nuclear programme through technical assistance, financial support and training of personnel, tried for a while to contain India's nuclear ambitions. They soon gave up their efforts and became reconciled to a nuclear India. Having failed in their efforts to restrain India, they directed all their energies to stifling Pakistan's nuclear endeavours, only to be frustrated at the end of the day.

NOTES

1. 'India Conducts 3 Nuclear Tests', *The Financial Express*, 12 May 1998. Also see 'Road to resurgence', Shekhar Gupta, *The Indian Express*, 12 May 1998.
2. SIPRI Yearbook 1975, The MIT Press, Cambridge Massachusetts and London, p. 16.
3. Ibid., p. 17. Also see K Subrahmanyan; 'India's Nuclear Policy', in Onkar Marwah and Ann Schulz (eds.), *Nuclear Proliferation and Near Nuclear Countries*, Ballinger Publishing Company, Cambridge Massachusetts, 1975, p. 141 and Onkar Marwah, 'India's Nuclear and Space Programmes: Intent and Policy', *International Security*, Vol. 2, Fall 1977, p. 98.
4. Subrahmanyam, p. 141; also see SIPRI Yearbook, 1975, p. 17.
5. SIPRI, p. 16.
6. Marwah, p. 98.
7 Ibid., p. 98.
8. Andrew Koch, *Selected Indian Nuclear Facilities*, Center for Non-proliferation Studies, Monterey Institute of International Studies, 1999, p. 3. Also see Central Intelligence Agency, Scientific Intelligence Report, 'Indian Nuclear Energy Programme', 6 November 1964; 'US Intelligence and the Bomb', National Security Archive Electronic Briefing Book No. 187, Washington, D.C.
9. Ibid.
10. Ibid.
11. Prime Minister's suo moto statement during discussion on 'Civil Nuclear Cooperation with the US: Implementation of India's Separation Plan', *The Hindu*, New Delhi, 7 March 2006.
12. Scientific Intelligence Report, Indian Nuclear Energy Programme, op. cit. Also see Andrew Koch, *Selected Indian Nuclear Facilities*, op. cit., p. 3.
13. SIPRI, 1975, p. 17. Andrew Koch, op. cit.
14. CIA, Scientific Intelligence Report, 'Indian Nuclear Energy Programme', 26 March 1958. National Security Archive Electronic Briefing Book No. 187, Washington, D.C.
15. Department of State telegram to American Embassy, New Delhi and American Embassy, London, 24 May 1966. Also see Department of State, telegram to American Embassy, New Delhi with information to American Embassy, London, American Consulate, Bombay and American Embassy, Rawalpindi, 28 July 1966.
16. Department of State, Airgram No. A-253, 29 April 1964 from American Consulate, Bombay, to the Department of State, 'Inauguration of Indian Plutonium Separation Plant'.
17. SIPRI, p. 18. Also see Marwah, p. 101.

18. CIA, Scientific Intelligence Report, 'Indian Nuclear Energy Programme', 6 November 1966 and CIA, Directorate of Science and Technology, Scientific Intelligence Digest, December 1965.
19. Department of State Telegram No. 15545, 27 February 1965, 'For Governor Harriman from the Secretary'.
20. Memorandum for the President, NSC Meeting, 9 June 1966, prepared by Acting Secretary of State George Ball, 7 June 1966, p. 4.
21. CIA, Intelligence Information Cable, No. 99143, 24 October 1964.
22. Ibid.
23. Ibid.
24. Special National Intelligence Estimate Number 31-1-65, 'India's Nuclear Weapons Policy', Directorate of Central Intelligence, 21 October 1965.
25. Ibid.
26. Ibid.
27. Ibid.
28. Scientific Intelligence Digest, December 1965, op. cit.
29. Ibid.
30. Department of State Telegram No. 26616, 28 July 1966, addressed to American Embassy, New Delhi.
31. Department of State Airgram, No. A-256, to American Embassy, New Delhi, 'Possible Indian Nuclear Weapons Development', 29 March 1966.
32. Memorandum for the President, 9 June 1966, op. cit.
33. Department of State Telegram No. 13982 of 24 May 1966 addressed to American Embassy New Delhi with information to American Embassy, London.
34. Ibid.
35. CIA, Office of Scientific Intelligence, Weekly Surveyor 20 June 1966.
36. Ibid.
37. Memorandum for the President, op. cit.
38. Ibid.
39. Ibid.
40. Ibid.
41. Ibid.
42. Memorandum for Secretary of Defence—JCSM-2-67 of 4 January 1967; 'The Indian Nuclear Weapons Problem: Security Aspects'.
43. Ibid.
44. Memorandum of Conversation between President Johnson and L.K. Jha on 19 April 1967.
45. Memorandum of Conversation between Secretary of Defence and Mr L.K. Jha on 18 April 1967, prepared by Assistant Secretary of Defence.
46. Department of State; Memorandum of Conversation between Secretary of State Dean Rusk & Soviet Foreign Minister Gromyko, 23 June 1967.
47. Telegram No. 13839 from US Embassy, New Delhi to the Secretary of State, 12 May 1968.

48. US Government Aide Memoir, presented to the IAEC in Bombay on 16 November 1970.
49. Ibid.
50. Ibid.
51. National Security Agency; Communication Intelligence Report No. 3/00/ QOC/R668-72 of 31 August 1972. [NSA/DTA NSA/HCF-ZPCA].
52. SIPRI, p. 16.
53. Ibid.
54. US government 'Aide-Memoir' to IAEC, op. cit.
55. Marwah, p. 104.
56. 'The Indian Explosion', Lawrence Livermore National Laboratory, Memorandum, 29 May 1974, prepared by Milo D. Nordyke.
57. Lawrence Livermore Laboratory, Memorandum, 1 October 1974, addressed to Roger E. Batzel, from Milo D. Nordyke.
58. Subrahmanyam, op. cit., pp. 141–2.
59. Rodney W. Jones, 'India', in Jozef Goldblat (ed.), Non-Proliferation: The Why and the Wherefore, Taylor and Francis, London & Philadelphia, 1985, p. 102.
60. 'Assessment of Indian Nuclear Test', US mission to NATO, 5 June 1974.
61. Ibid.
62. SIPRI, p. 19.
63. Ibid., p. 20.
64. Ibid., p. 21.
65. CIA, Central Intelligence Bulletin, 20 May 1974.
66. SIPRI, pp. 21–2.
67. Subrahmanyam, pp. 138–9.
68. Ibid., p. 143.
69. Dept of State; Intelligence Note, 13 June 1974.
70. Ibid.
71. Ibid.
72. Robert Jackson, South Asian Crisis, Chatto & Windus, London, 1975, p. 226.
73. US Department of State Telegram No. 15545, to American Embassy at Tel Aviv with information to embassies at New Delhi, Moscow, Hong Kong and Karachi, from Secretary of State Governor Harriman.
74. Jones, p. 113.
75. Ibid.
76. CIA, Central Intelligence Bulletin, 20 May 1974.
77. 'Post Mortem Report—An Examination of the Intelligence Community's Performance Before the Indian Nuclear Test of May 1974', for the Director Central Intelligence, July 1974.
78. Amitabh Mattoo, 'India's Nuclear Policy in an Anarchic World', in Amitabh Mattoo (ed.), India's Nuclear Deterrent—Pokhran-II and Beyond, New Delhi, Har Anand Publications, 1999, p. 18.

79. *Indian Defence Review Digest*, Vol. IV, Lancer Publications, New Delhi, 1992.
80. Marwah, p. 103.
81. Jones, in Jozef Goldblat (ed.), op. cit., p. 114.
82. Bhabhani Sen Gupta, *Nuclear Weapons? Policy Options for India*, Sage Publications, New Delhi, Beverly Hills, London, 1983, p. 9.
83. Ibid., p. 10.
84. Andrew Koch, op. cit., p. 3.
85. S.S. Mehdi, '*India's Nuclear Programme: How much Peaceful?*' *Pakistan Horizon* (Pakistan Institute of International Affairs, Karachi), 1983, pp. 130–33.
86. Ibid., p. 35.
87. Ibid., pp. 116–17.
88. Ibid., p. 118.
89. Ibid.
90. Ravindra Tomar, 'The Indian Nuclear Power Programme: Myths and Mirages', *Asian Survey*, Vol. XX, No. 5, May 1980, pp. 529–31.
91. Government of India, Department of Atomic Energy, Annual Report 2005–06.
92. CIA, National Foreign Assessment Center, 'Indian Nuclear Policies in the 1980s,' An Intelligence Assessment, 10 September 1981.
93. Ibid.
94. CIA, *Science and Weapons Daily Review*, National Foreign Assessment Center, 17 November 1981.
95. CIA, Directorate of Intelligence, 'India's Nuclear Programme—Energy and Weapons: An Intelligence Assessment', July 1982.
96. CIA, Directorate of Intelligence; 'India's Potential to Build a Nuclear Weapon—An Intelligence Assessment', July 1988.
97. Report from US DAO, New Delhi, to JCS, DIA, CIA, 'An Update on Government of India Nuclear Programme', November 1986.
98. Ibid.
99. 'India to get nuclear fuels from Russia', Dawn, Karachi, 15 March 2006.
100. Mattoo, op. cit., p. 18.
101. 'Hide'n Seek': CIA Muse over N-Tests, Associated Press, *The Indian Express*, 18 May 1998.
102. Disarmament Diplomacy, Acronym Institute, Issue No. 23, February 1998. Also see http://www.bjp.org/manifes/chap8.htm.
103. Ibid.
104. Manvendra Singh, 'Showcase of technological leap by Indian Nuclear Establishment', *The Indian Express*, 12 May 1998.
105. Ibid.
106. Manvendra Singh; *The Indian Express*, 12 May 1998.
107. Chidanand Rajghatta, 'The Hindu Bomb', *The Indian Express*, 21 May 1998.

108. *The Asian Age*, 12 May 1998.
109. Ibid.
110. Ibid.
111. 'Prime Minister Writes to G-8 Heads on Tests'; *The Times of India*, 14 May 1998.
112. Arati R. Jerath, 'Govt Flashes China Card at the West', *The Indian Express*, 14 May 1998.
113. 'US Rebuttal has Advani fuming', *The Indian Express*, 21 May 1998.
114. Ibid.
115. Arati R. Jerath, 'Damage Control begins as Government wakes up to high cost of China card', *The Indian Express*, 28 May 1998.
116. Intelligence Report, Office of Near Eastern, South Asian and African Analysis, CIA, 29 May 1998.
117. Ibid.
118. Ibid.
119. Ibid.
120. Ibid.
121. Ibid.
122. Chidanand Rajghatta, 'The Hindu Bomb', *The Indian Express*, 21 May 1998.
123. *The Indian Express*, 17 May 1998.
124. Chidanand Rajghatta; 'Patch up with India, US tells Pak', *The Indian Express*, 20 May 1998.
125. 'Hide 'n' seek: CIA muse over n-tests', *The Indian Express*, 18 May 1998.
126. K. Subrahmanyam, *Nuclear Myths and Realities—India's Dilemma*, ABC Publishing House, New Delhi, 1981, pp. vi–vii.
127. Ibid., p. i.
128. Ibid.
129. Gupta, p. 39.
130. Ibid., p. 17.
131. Ibid., p. 17.
132. Ibid., p. 20.
133. Zia Mian, 'Homi Bhabha killed a Crow', in Zia Mian and Ashish Nandy (eds.), *The Nuclear Debate: Ironies and Immoralities*, Colombo: Regional Center for Strategic Studies, July 1998, p. 12.
134. George Perkovich, *India's Nuclear Bomb*, Berkeley, University of California Press, 1999, p. 36.
135. K. Subrahmanyam, *'Indian Nuclear Policy—1964-98'*, in Jasjit Singh (ed.), *Nuclear India*, New Delhi, Knowledge World, 1998, p. 44.
136. Amitabh Mattoo, 'India's Nuclear Policy', op. cit., p. 18.
137. Perkovich, op. cit., pp. 374–5.
138. Mattoo, op. cit., pp. 11–15.
139. Perkovich, p. 441.
140. Ibid., p. 400.

141. Intelligence Report, Office of Near Eastern, South Asian and African Analysis, CIA, 29 May 1998.

3

Pakistan's Nuclear Programme

PREAMBLE

Pakistan, when compared with India, was a late entrant into the nuclear field. Pakistan took the nuclear road by a coincidence of events, accentuating an already adverse security environment. The development programme was predominantly security driven and, based on the statements of its leaders and senior government officials, India-centric. Pakistan has claimed that it does not harbour any pretensions to either a regional or global power status, or a permanent seat in the Security Council, by leveraging its nuclear capability. Since the mid-1970s Pakistan's nuclear programme has been at the centre of one controversy after another, and has been the subject of much concern in the international media and academic publications alike. The primary reason for the programme becoming controversial and suspect in public perception around the world was its characterization by many Western as well as Indian authors and the Western media as the so-called 'Islamic Bomb'.[1] Secondly, following India's first nuclear test in May 1974, the major powers seemed to have reconciled themselves to the inevitability of a nuclearized India, and to have thought that it was still possible to restrain Pakistan's nuclear ambitions, since its programme was still in its infancy. The focus of international non-proliferation efforts, therefore, naturally shifted towards Pakistan.

Pakistan had initiated a modest peaceful nuclear programme in the 1950s, but had been slow and tentative in taking it forward due to bureaucratic inertia and a lack of interest at the highest levels of leadership. It only started thinking seriously about developing a military nuclear option in the aftermath of the traumatic experience of the loss of its Eastern wing in the 1971 war, largely through active Indian military intervention. Pakistan realized that the gap between its conventional military capability and that of India was widening all the time, and that before long conventional military balance with India would become untenable. It had also learnt, through its bitter experience in the 1971 war, that in any future crisis it would have to defend itself and could not realistically rely on any intervention on its behalf by friendly powers.

The search for an equalizer logically led to the decision in early 1972 to pursue the nuclear weapons option. However, the effort had hardly been initiated before India carried out its first nuclear explosion, which it preferred to call a 'Peaceful Nuclear Explosion' (PNE) at the time, though the architect of that project, Dr Raja Ramanna, later acknowledged that it was indeed a nuclear weapons test.[2] Whilst the gullible international community was willing to take the bait and accept the Indian nuclear test as a 'PNE', it started tightening the export controls on nuclear related technologies.[3] Pakistan had, therefore, to overcome many obstacles and challenges in its nuclear pursuits, and had to pay for the sins committed by others. Pakistan also was forced to contend with layer after layer of sanctions imposed by the US, some of which were Pakistan specific due to its nuclear activities which were seen to be inimical to the US non-proliferation policies. From a Pakistani perspective, a successful conclusion of its national nuclear programme was critical for its very survival, and therefore no cost was considered too high towards this end. There was also a unique national consensus on this issue, cutting across the political divide and enjoying the support of all segments of society.

In the aftermath of the Indian test the Nuclear Suppliers Group (NSG), initially known as the London Suppliers Group (LSG), was constituted by technologically advanced countries, in order to restrict the export of not only nuclear, but also dual use technologies. These export control and technology denial mechanisms made things difficult for Pakistan. India's nuclear programme had by then advanced to the extent that it could be sustained with little outside help. Pakistan, however, being a late entrant into the nuclear field, was trying to catch up. It therefore had to improvise, find ways around the restrictive technology denial regimes, and use unconventional means to procure the necessary materials and equipment to pursue its programme. This necessarily unconventional approach to the development of nuclear capability also led to some potentially dangerous practices, which subsequently were to haunt Pakistan and damage its credibility.

Pakistan maintained that, despite having achieved the technological wherewithal to test or produce nuclear weapons by the mid-1980s, it refrained from conducting a nuclear test in deference to international norms.[4] From a different standpoint, however, the political and economic costs of a stand-alone test would have been too prohibitive, and Pakistan was not in a position to pay that price. On 11 and 13 May 1998, India carried out multiple nuclear tests and declared itself a nuclear weapon power. The tests were followed by highly provocative and threatening statements by the Indian Home Minister, Mr Advani, and the senior leadership of the ruling Bharatiya Janata Party (BJP). These developments created a situation in which Pakistan had no other option but to respond to the Indian tests. However, this was a blessing in disguise, as it also provided Pakistan with the long awaited opportunity to test the efficacy of its nuclear weapons and to demonstrate its nuclear capability. Pakistan responded with its own nuclear tests on the 28 and 30 May 1998. The events of 9/11 and the commencement of US military operations in neighbouring Afghanistan brought in new and potentially destabilizing factors. With the backdrop of known desire and reported efforts by the international terrorist organizations to acquire WMDs, sometimes misplaced and largely exaggerated concerns were raised about the safety and security of Pakistan's nuclear weapons and materials. Pakistan, on its part, assured its American allies and the world at large that it had institutionalized its nuclear command and control from the beginning of 2000[5] and had in place adequate security arrangements to deal with any threat to its sensitive installations/ sites. The US media, however, continued to build all kinds of scenarios ranging from the Taliban/Al Qaeda attacking Pakistani nuclear facilities and getting away with nuclear weapons or fissile materials, to suggestions of moving Pakistani nuclear assets to China for safe custody, or even sending in US forces in an emergency situation to secure and take physical control of Pakistan's strategic assets. Seymour Hersh, a senior American journalist known for his sensational stories, even went so far as to suggest that the US and Israeli special forces were already carrying out joint training exercises to meet such an eventuality. More recently Pakistan has had to contend with the fall-out of the A.Q. Khan episode. This played into the hands of those who had been expressing doubts about Pakistan's ability to safeguard its strategic assets in a responsible and fail-safe manner. Consequently, all positive steps Pakistan had taken to enhance the command, control, safety and security of its nuclear assets were overshadowed by this controversy, which refuses to die down.

It is, therefore, a natural corollary of these decades old controversies that any mention of the words 'nuclear' and 'Pakistan' together sends alarm bells ringing around the world. One can justifiably raise the question as to why Pakistan has been singled out for the scorn of the Western media and has been subjected to political, economic and diplomatic pressures by Western countries, particularly the USA, while there is a willingness to accommodate India's status as a de facto nuclear power as is evidenced by the US–India nuclear deal. In Pakistan's case, part of the blame must lie with the Pakistani government, media and intelligentsia for their failure to project their point of view with the same vigour and conviction as is apparent in the case of India. For instance, given the power equation in South Asia against the back drop of perpetually hostile relationship between India and Pakistan, it was perfectly justifiable for Pakistan to seek a nuclear deterrent against India, even if that country did not have a nuclear weapons programme. Once India started to move down the nuclear path Pakistan had no choice but to follow suit, because its very survival was at stake. However, Pakistan never tried to articulate the 'raison d'être' for its nuclear programme, but adopted a defensive approach and always used India's nuclear programme as a hedge.[6] There has also been a lack of informed domestic debate on nuclear issues, especially in the pre-1998 era, which could have helped educate national as well as international public opinion regarding the rationale of Pakistan's nuclear programme. There has been a greater public discourse on nuclear related issues post-1998, but even now no authentic and comprehensive account of Pakistan's nuclear programme and policies has been written by any Pakistani scholar. In the event, most of the literature available to researchers and analysts is based on the writings of either Indian or Western writers. These publications are obviously coloured by their ethno-centric and political biases, and lack objectivity. A credible Pakistani narrative is, therefore, hard to find, which leaves a wide-open space for all kinds of speculation and misconceptions.

There have been many myths and controversies surrounding Pakistan's nuclear programme. Before attempting to separate the myth from reality, however, it may be pertinent to look at the salient aspects of the evolution of the nuclear programme from its inception to the present day, in order to gain some insight into the objectives of Pakistan's nuclear policy.

The history of Pakistan's nuclear development can be divided into three phases. Phase 1, spanning the period from the inception of the programme in 1954 and leading up to 1974, was the beginning of a modest programme for purely peaceful purposes.[7] The second phase encompasses post-1974 developments in the wake of the Pokhran test and culminating in the May 1998 nuclear tests, while the third phase covers post-1998 developments. Some people may argue that the beginning of the second phase may be reckoned from 1972 when, on assuming power, Z.A. Bhutto took the decision to initiate a programme designed to create a military nuclear option, and reinvigorated Pakistan's nuclear programme. However, the fact of the matter is that, despite the decision to go ahead in 1972, nothing concrete had been done in this regard until 1974, when the Indian nuclear test gave the real flip to Pakistan's nuclear pursuits and, therefore, 1974 constitutes a major landmark.

PHASE 1: NUCLEAR DEVELOPMENT 1954–1974

In comparison with India, Pakistan was slow to venture into the nuclear field. Dr Homi Bhaba had embarked on a programme of training nuclear scientists and technicians under the auspices of the 'Tata Institute for Fundamental Research' in 1945, and an Atomic Energy Commission had been established in India in 1948. However, in Pakistan no such steps were taken until in 1954, when an American exhibition under the auspices of President Eisenhower's 'Atoms for Peace' programme toured Pakistan, and aroused interest in the potential of this new technology for national development.[8] As a result, following some initial spadework, the government of Pakistan appointed a 12-member Atomic Energy Committee to prepare plans for 'the promotion of peaceful uses of atomic energy in Pakistan'. Based on the recommendations of the committee, a high-powered 'Atomic Energy Council' was set up by the government in March 1956. The council had a governing body, comprising two ministers and two federal government secretaries, besides the chairman of the Atomic Energy Commission. The commission was the second component of the Atomic Energy Council and in turn consisted of six scientists under the chairmanship of Dr Nazir Ahmad. In addition to this, an advisory committee comprising thirty scientists, doctors, industrialists, agriculturists, and educationists was also set up.

The Atomic Energy Council was assigned the task of planning and developing the peaceful uses of atomic energy. In this regard attention was to be paid to the exploration, procurement, and disposal of radioactive materials; the establishment of nuclear research institutes; the installation of research and power reactors; nuclear cooperation agreements with international atomic energy organizations; the creation of a cadre of trained personnel and the application of radio-isotopes to agriculture, health and industry.[9]

To begin with, the allocation of funds for nuclear research was fairly modest, amounting to 2.5 million Pakistani rupees for the year 1955–56, which was doubled for the fiscal year 1956–57. However, the total allocation for the 'First Five Year Plan,' covering the period 1956–60, came to a total of 23.5 million Pakistan rupees.[10]

The major obstacle to the execution of the Pakistan Atomic Energy Commission's (PAEC's) plans was the absence of a core of specially trained nuclear scientists and technicians. The absence of indigenous training facilities meant that arrangements had to be made to send a number of scientists abroad for training elsewhere including Britain, France, Canada and the United States. At the same time the PAEC was busy evaluating available reactor technology, in order to choose a suitable research reactor. The PAEC finalized its plans in 1957, and hoped that, even if these plans were approved by the government in 1958, the research reactor would, in all probability, go critical in early 1960, if not by the end of 1959. However, lack of interest and conviction at government level, coupled with other bureaucratic impediments, meant that the plans for the research reactor did not take off as anticipated. The situation was further complicated by the fact that many of the scientists sent abroad for training did not return to Pakistan on completion of their training.[11]

The situation improved with the entry of Z.A. Bhutto into President Ayub Khan's cabinet as Minister of Fuel, Power and Natural Resources, towards the end of October 1958. Bhutto provided the badly needed impetus to the atomic energy programme. He was later to claim that:

I have been actively associated with the nuclear programme of Pakistan from October 1958 to July 1977, a span of nineteen years...when I took charge of Pakistan's Atomic Energy Commission it was no more than a signboard of an office. It was only a name. Assiduously and with granite determination, I put my entire vitality behind the task of acquiring nuclear capability for my country.

...I negotiated the agreement for the 5 MW research reactor located in PINSTECH. In the teeth of opposition from Finance Minister Shoaib and Deputy Chairman of Planning Commission, Said Hassan, I negotiated with success to obtain from Canada the 137 MW Karachi nuclear power plant.[12]

Another important development was the appointment of Dr Usmani, a member of the elite Indian Civil Service, a physicist by training and a graduate of Imperial College of Science and Technology, London, as the chairman of the PAEC. Dr Usmani, with his bureaucratic background, was certainly better qualified than his predecessor to implement the research and power reactor programmes of the PAEC, and to lay the ground work for Pakistan's nuclear infrastructure. Professor Ashok Kapur has, for instance, highlighted the key role played by Dr Usmani, stating that: 'More than any other person, he (Usmani) set the direction of Pakistan's peaceful nuclear programme...' Not only did Pakistan's nuclear power programme get off the ground during this period, but this was the high point in the development of nuclear energy in Pakistan.[13] Together with Dr Abdul Salam, the chief scientific adviser to the president and a renowned physicist, who was to become the first Pakistani to win a Nobel Prize in physics, and Z.A. Bhutto, Usmani formed a winning partnership, and argued the case for nuclear energy, despite the inadequacy of hydro sources as well as fossil fuels in Pakistan. However, he did have some reservations as is quite apparent from his statement that, 'What the future of atomic energy will be no one can guess. Its potential for good is immense; for evil it is equally great'.[14] Usmani's strong views against the use of nuclear technology for weapons purposes were diametrically opposed to Bhutto's thinking and led to his ultimate downfall in the early 1970s.

The US supplied 'swimming pool' type research reactor was finally set up at PINSTECH (Pakistan Institute of Science & Technology) in 1963 under the IAEA safeguards. The reactor went critical in 1965, six years behind schedule. In the meantime, the estimated financial allocation for the atomic energy development programme in the Second Five-Year Plan 1961–65 was projected as 46.5 million Pakistani rupees, almost double the amount allocated in the First Five-Year Plan. Between 1960 and 1968 the expenditure on the nuclear development programme amounted to 290 million rupees. This was besides an allocation of 400 million rupees for the Karachi Nuclear Power Plant (KANUPP), most of which was shown in the financial estimates as expenditure for fuel and power development programmes. Parallel to these developments the PAEC proposed the setting up of two centres each in West and East Pakistan, now Bangladesh, for the employment of radio-isotopes in agriculture and food preservation. In addition, PAEC proposed the setting up of eight nuclear medical centres for the diagnosis and treatment of diseases including cancer. These plans are indicative of a genuine interest in the peaceful application of atomic energy.[15]

According to Dr P.B. Sinha, an Indian academic/security analyst, India's procurement of an atomic power reactor from Canada in 1962 prompted Bhutto, then Minister of Industries, Natural Resources and Atomic Energy, to press for a similar deal. The PAEC started negotiations with Canada in 1962 and agreement was reached in 1965. Canada provided a soft loan of $23 million and a credit of a further $24 million to cover the foreign exchange component of the cost, besides providing training facilities to Pakistani personnel. Japan assisted by providing credit of $3.6 million to cover the cost of the turbo-generator and its installation. Pakistani technicians returned from Canada in December 1968, after the completion of their training, to work for the commissioning of the KANUPP reactor with the help of Canadian experts.[16]

The plant went critical in 1971 and was formally inaugurated in 1972. This plant is covered by IAEA safeguards under a trilateral agreement involving Pakistan, Canada and the IAEA.[17] Sinha also claims that in 1965 Bhutto asked President Ayub Khan to sanction a sum of 300 million Pakistani rupees for the purchase of a reprocessing plant, but the request was turned down, the reason given being that Pakistan's economy was not in a state to bear such a heavy burden.[18] Sinha's assertion clearly implies that Bhutto was trying to keep pace with India, who had already commissioned a reprocessing facility in 1964.

During early and mid-1960s, Pakistan entered into agreements with France, Great Britain, Denmark, Italy and Spain for the supply of nuclear materials and equipment, provision of training facilities and cooperation for peaceful research purposes. In May

1970, a ten-year agreement was signed with the Soviet Union for the exchange of scientists, technical know-how and atomic equipment between the two countries. Agreements for collaboration in the field of atomic energy were also signed with Turkey and Poland.[19]

In the meantime, efforts were being made to discover uranium and other radioactive materials within Pakistan, and by the late 1950s the presence of such materials had been established in the sands of the river Indus and in the foothills of the Sulaiman mountain ranges in the Dera Ghazi Khan area. Although substantial quantities of uranium had been recovered in the first half of the 1960s, the potential of these reserves was not fully exploited. In 1969 Australian experts employed by the PAEC had reported the discovery of uranium in Gilgit, and other materials used in the nuclear industry such as zirconium and titanium were located in the coastal belt near Cox's Bazaar in former East Pakistan. Consequently, a pilot uranium extraction plant was set up at the Atomic Minerals Centre, Lahore. In 1971, at the Pakistan government's request, the IAEA started large-scale exploration for uranium in the Dera Ghazi Khan area, with the financial assistance of the United Nations' Development Programme. This exploratory effort, by indicating the presence of several hundred tons of uranium in the area, yielded encouraging results, confirming Pakistan's rich potential in the basic raw materials required for atomic power production.[20]

When Z.A. Bhutto assumed power in Pakistan, towards the end of December 1971, his former nuclear aspirations were rekindled, with the difference that Pakistan was now faced with a greatly deteriorated security environment. He had, however, assumed the requisite authority to implement his plans. Bhutto embarked on his ambitious nuclear power programme. To begin with he carried out a reorganization of the nuclear establishment and took personal charge of atomic energy affairs. As a next step, a separate Ministry of Science and Technology was established. The chairman of the Atomic Energy Commission was made directly answerable to Bhutto in matters concerning procurement and administration.

This gave more freedom of action to the scientists and relieved them of bureaucratic impediments. A comprehensive programme was launched to create a 'talent pool', both by organizing the training of personnel in local training facilities, and by attracting expatriate Pakistani nuclear scientists back home. In March 1972, Munir Ahmad Khan, who was in charge of the Nuclear Power and Reactor Division of the IAEA, and had been working there as a nuclear power specialist for over 13 years, was appointed Chairman of the PAEC, replacing I.H. Usmani.[21] It was because of the same 'talent hunt' programme that another Pakistani scientist, Dr Abdul Qadeer Khan, was persuaded to return to the country in 1975. Dr A.Q. Khan, a brilliant metallurgist, with hands-on experience of working in Urenco's Gas Centrifuge Plant at Almelo in Holland, was to lead the effort to establish Pakistan's own gas centrifuge uranium enrichment facility at Kahuta.

In 1972 the IAEA, in collaboration with the PAEC, carried out a study to determine Pakistan's long-term energy requirements. The IAEA report based on this study was released in October 1973. It stated that in IAEA's opinion, Pakistan would have an appreciable nuclear power generating requirement by the 1980s. The report outlined Pakistan's requirement for eight 600 MW nuclear units between 1982 and 1990, and nine 600 MW and seven 800 MW units from 1990 to 2000. In 1973 a PAEC report envisaged the beginning of the implementation of the projected plans in accordance with the IAEA recommendation, to be completed over the next 12 years. The building of a 500 MW power plant, later modified to 600 MW, was planned for a site near Chashma, in Punjab province. This project was approved by the National Economic Council in July 1973. It was expected that the work on 'CHASNUPP' would begin sometime in 1978, and that the plant would be operational by 1983 at an estimated cost of $25 million.[22] The projected capacity of this plant was later revised to 900 MW, but the work on the project could not commence mainly due to the refusal of the American and British suppliers to provide the necessary equipment, and the reluctance of other potential suppliers, under pressure from the United States, to bid for the supply of the plant.

There were critics however, among them Charles Ebinger, who criticized the 1973 and 1975 IAEA assessments regarding Pakistan's nuclear energy generation requirements on two counts. First, in his opinion, the IAEA assessments were heavily biased in favour of increasing power generating capacity, while ignoring the effects of reduced transmission losses on Pakistan's electric utility sector. Secondly, he believed that 'the IAEA reports continue to rely on historically high levels of electric power demand growth and do not adequately consider the impact that the worldwide recession would have in reducing energy demand'.[23] Interestingly enough, Ebinger persisted with this criticism, despite acknowledging the fact that Pakistan's oil import bill soared from $64.9 million in 1973 to over $400 million in 1974, and that the price of oil for power generation had become prohibitively high. He also acknowledged Pakistan's 'severe lack of fossil fuel resources' and the shortage of hydroelectric potential in the southern parts of the country, which could easily justify a sizeable nuclear power programme. But he insisted that Pakistan had not made any serious efforts to promote nuclear development until after the Indian nuclear explosion in May 1974,[24] implying that Pakistan's nuclear development programme was not a consequence of domestic energy shortage compulsions, but was propelled by a sense of competition with India. His argument, however, cannot be dismissed lightly and has some merit because competition with India was definitely a factor, but it happened to coincide with the energy crisis, and therefore provided a compelling economic justification, aside from the security considerations, for the expansion of the nuclear programme. Pakistan's growing interest in nuclear power generation to alleviate its energy deficiencies was, in any event, not an isolated case. It was, in fact, part of a prevailing view throughout much of the world at the time, that an expansion of nuclear power generation capacity was the best answer to meet the global energy predicament, brought about by the oil crisis in the wake of the 1973 Arab–Israeli war. The nuclear alternative was obviously more attractive to countries like Pakistan, possessing limited fossil fuel reserves.[25]

P.B. Sinha and R.R. Subramaniam, however, were supportive of Pakistan's decision to embark on a large scale nuclear power generation programme, observing that: 'Thus for reasons of intrinsic economy as well as on grounds of domestic fossil fuel resources and the possibility of finding enough uranium reserves within the country, Bhutto was right in allotting high priority to the development of nuclear technology'.[26]

However, until December 1974, when Pakistan's long-term development plans for nuclear power generation were unveiled, no practical steps seem to have been undertaken by way of planning and the preparation of the necessary infrastructure. This factor alone was enough to stoke suspicions with regard to Pakistan's real intentions.

DEVELOPMENT OF A NUCLEAR WEAPONS OPTION, 1974–1998

By the mid-1970s the international nuclear picture was fairly confused, with at least a dozen countries considered to be pursuing or harbouring nuclear ambitions. Among these, India had already demonstrated its nuclear capability through a nuclear explosive test in May 1974, while Israel, which had not conducted a nuclear test, was widely believed to have developed nuclear weapons. Other threshold countries included Taiwan, Argentina and South Africa. In the opinion of US Air Force and Naval Intelligence officials Japan was likely to consider going nuclear, if it felt that it was essential in order to achieve its rightful place in the emerging Asian balance of power. Other potential candidates included Spain, Iran, Egypt, Pakistan, Brazil and South Korea. However, an October 1974 US Special National Intelligence Estimate (SNIE) assessed that these countries would need at least a decade to implement their respective nuclear weapons development programmes. However, it was added that acquisition of materials or foreign assistance could speed up the process. Among the motives ascribed to these countries were concerns about their neighbours and antagonists already pursuing nuclear weapons development, or having already achieved a nuclear weapons' capability. While Egypt and Brazil were considered comparatively less likely to go all the way, Pakistan and Iran were expected to feel the 'strongest impulses' to join the nuclear club.[27]

By 1975, Pakistan's perceived nuclear intentions were causing some concern in Washington, as is evident from a background brief prepared by Robert Gallucci of the Policy Planning Group in the State Department. Prepared on the eve of Prime Minister Z.A. Bhutto's visit to Washington, the paper pointed out that though at that point in time Pakistan's nuclear infrastructure was not 'worrisome', 'the intentions of the Pakistani government once it achieves a significant capacity are cause for concern'.[28] Pakistan's ongoing negotiations to procure a heavy water production facility, a Canadian fuel fabrication plant and a French reprocessing plant, along with the existing heavy water reactor, it was thought, would provide Pakistan with all the elements of a complete nuclear fuel cycle. This would provide the wherewithal to separate enough plutonium to build a nuclear weapon. The paper also concluded that because of the Indian nuclear explosion, Pakistan had a strong incentive to build a bomb of its own. It was also thought that, although, Pakistan was ready to proceed down the nuclear path, it would confront political and technical hiccups along the way. Interestingly, the paper recommended that in case Bhutto tried to develop a linkage between Pakistan's compulsions to go nuclear and the US readiness to supply conventional arms, he should be discouraged by the counter argument that any effort on Pakistan's part to move in the nuclear direction would lead to a denial of any conventional military supplies.[29]

Interestingly, the fact that the Karachi Nuclear Power Plant (KANUPP) the only possible source of plutonium was under trilateral safeguards between Pakistan, Canada and the IAEA was simply brushed aside. Nor was the information that the proposed reprocessing plant would be under trilateral safeguards involving Pakistan, France and the IAEA given due consideration. These safeguards were among the most stringent at the time. Should Pakistan abrogate its safeguards agreement, its nuclear intentions would have come out in the open prematurely, and would have made the procurement of critical nuclear equipment and materials almost impossible, along with extremely negative politico-diplomatic repercussions for the country. Alternatively, if Pakistan cheated on its obligations, and tried to divert material from KANUPP, it would again be putting its credibility on the line besides facing the possibility of international opprobrium if it was caught in the act. Moreover, the diversion route would have taken a very long time to yield even the bare minimum amount of fissile material. Most of the analyses, which are based on the presumption that Pakistan would have diverted burnt KANUPP fuel for reprocessing and would thus have obtained fissile material worth a weapon or two, seem to be divorced from reality. They take a narrow view and focus on the non-proliferation aspect of the issue, completely ignoring the fact that mere possession of one or two weapons does not bestow a country with a credible operational nuclear capability.

A noted Indian analyst, Ravi Rikhye, however did not find the 'diversion' theory convincing enough. Rikhye pointed out that, in its annual reports for 1980 and 1981, the IAEA clearly said that there was no evidence of diversion of nuclear fuel from KANUPP. Pakistan could not possibly divert fissile material from its US supplied research reactor because that reactor was fuelled only twice a year, in the presence of the IAEA inspectors, and in any case ran on low enriched uranium fuel. He also asserted that following the Indian nuclear test in 1974, the IAEA had been extra vigilant regarding KANUPP. The Canadian withdrawal in 1976, and the availability of indigenously produced fuel rods, must have caused the IAEA to be even more careful. Rikhye went on to claim that:

> Shortage of fuel rods, spare parts and heavy water, have led KANUPP to be operated at efficiencies of less than 15 per cent as opposed to the 60 per cent plus of a commercial reactor. That means Pakistan would have to divert fissile material for two years for one bomb. Two successive years of diversion is a bit much to assume.[30]

In April 1975, in an informal State Department memorandum for the US Embassy in Islamabad, reference was made to a debriefing related to a March 1975 visit by a US Energy Research and Development Administration (ERDA) team to India, Pakistan and other potential nuclear countries. The visiting team, besides other observations, presented a ranked list of countries likely to produce nuclear weapons. Their list had India, Taiwan, South Korea, Pakistan, Indonesia and Iran in descending order. However they did not make mention of either Israel or South Africa. In their view they had hard evidence pointing to the fact that Prime Minister Bhutto had ordered the PAEC Chairman, Munir Khan, to produce a PNE in four years time. This was viewed as an indicator that, once Pakistan had achieved that initial objective, it would possibly have a crude first generation nuclear device after another year or so. It was pointed out that all the potential nuclear weapon states were at that time trying to either acquire or expand their nuclear fuel reprocessing facilities.[31] Both Pakistan and South Korea were negotiating with France to acquire reprocessing plants. The South Koreans were projecting themselves as the 'regional re-processors', while the IAEA and the US were also exploring the possibilities of promoting the concept of regional reprocessing centres. The memo also referred to PAEC's intention to invite bids for the planned nuclear power plant at Chashma, but it appeared that the US government by then had not issued any clear-cut guidelines for US companies that might be interested in participating in the bidding.[32]

The US anxiety over Pakistan's efforts to acquire the full nuclear fuel cycle capability was growing, as is evident from the summary of a US change of attitude toward Pakistan circulated in a Department of State letter in January 1976. Of particular concern was Pakistan's negotiation with France to acquire a pilot scale reprocessing capability with a potential to produce several kilograms of plutonium annually.[33] Subsequently, negotiations were undertaken to obtain a commercial scale reprocessing plant. The US experts did not find any plausible utility for the plutonium separation, other than producing nuclear devices, since KANUPP runs on natural uranium fuel and the reactors PAEC planned to build in future were likely to be light water reactors, which run on low enriched uranium fuel. This was very different from the Airgram sent by the American consulate in Bombay, in April 1964, on the inauguration of India's first reprocessing facility by Prime Minister Shastri. The American consulate stated that the purpose of the plant was to 'extract plutonium', which it described as a 'material and atomic fuel for future reactors besides being valuable fissionable material'.[34]

While controversy over the reprocessing deal was gathering steam, the first practical manifestation of PAEC's nuclear power programme became known with the allocation of funds in the budget for the fiscal year 1975–76. This was for a 600 MW light water reactor (later upgraded to 900 MW) to be set up at 'Chashma'. At the same time, PAEC embarked on drawing up blueprints for an additional twenty-three reactors, planned to be constructed by the turn of the century. The western critics pointed out that, due to the long lead times involved in the construction of nuclear power reactors and the huge financial expenditure, which in their view Pakistan's economy was not in a state to meet, it would be impossible to achieve the ambitious goals set by PAEC. PAEC, on its part, was firm in its belief that its nuclear power programme was the only long-term solution to Pakistan's looming energy crisis. The PAEC officials could always refer to the 1973 and 1975 IAEA reports, which supported Pakistan's need for nuclear energy, to justify their long-term plans.[35] In hindsight, these appear to have been unrealistic and over ambitious. It is evident that there was some disconnect between PAEC's declared developmental goals and its apparent technology acquisition efforts. Had PAEC built a few more CANDU type reactors, following the Indian example, there would have been a technical rationale for setting up a large reprocessing facility. Acquisition of a commercial scale reprocessing plant to support a single, and relatively small, power plant made neither economic nor technical sense. It raised suspicions about Pakistan's real motives and resulted in reluctance of international suppliers to supply even the materials and equipment meant for purely peaceful applications of nuclear technology. Consequently, this input paid to the ambitious plans to expand nuclear power production. In a May 1976 meeting at the State Department, chaired by Secretary of State, Dr Henry Kissinger, the suggestion arose of using the influence of the Shah of Iran to dissuade Bhutto from his efforts to acquire reprocessing technology. It was pointed out that an Iranian official had told the US officials in Washington that the Shah was concerned and suspected that Bhutto was seeking nuclear weapons. The proposal to build a regional reprocessing facility also came up, and the participants appeared to be inclined towards setting up such a facility in Iran, rather than Pakistan. However, it was expected that Pakistan would prefer to have it in Pakistan. The Secretary was informed of the passage of the Symington Amendment in the US senate, which would cut off all military and economic assistance to countries that either exported or imported reprocessing facilities, unless the facility was under multilateral control and the recipient country agreed to accept IAEA safeguards on all its nuclear facilities. Dr Kissinger pointed out that Pakistan had accepted IAEA safeguards on the CHASHMA facility (reprocessing plant built with French assistance), but was told that the Symington Amendment required full-scope safeguards, at which he asked whether India and Iran had such agreements. The reply was that India is not a party to the NPT while Iran is an NPT party, simply overlooking the fact that Pakistan, like India, was not a party to the NPT. The Secretary of State commented that it would be 'a little rough' on the Pakistanis to expect them to do what Indians are not expected to do. He also dismissed the whole notion of regional reprocessing plants, and said that in case Pakistan came up with the idea of a joint reprocessing project with Sri Lanka or Iraq it would obviously not be acceptable to the US. On the issue of suppliers' involvement also he was sceptical, and remarked that, 'We are the only country which is fanatical and unrealistic enough to do things which are contrary to our national interests. The Europeans are not so illogical'.[36]

India's 1974 nuclear explosion had highlighted the fact that peaceful nuclear technology can be manipulated for potentially military applications, once a certain degree of technological proficiency has been achieved. As a result, the nuclear supplier states imposed stringent regulations on the export of sensitive nuclear components. Pakistan's efforts to achieve self sufficiency in the nuclear fuel cycle including the fuel fabrication, reprocessing and uranium enrichment and this was, therefore, bound to cause controversy. The major cause of this debate was, of course, Pakistan's agreement with France for the procurement of a reprocessing plant, since till then its efforts to acquire enrichment technology were not known.

THE PAKISTANI–FRENCH REPROCESSING AGREEMENT

Negotiations for the supply of a reprocessing plant between France and Pakistan started towards the end of 1973. The agreement was finally signed in March 1976. The United States did not vigorously oppose the deal in 1974 and 1975 while the negotiations were in progress. However, immediately before the signing of the agreement in early 1976, the US stepped up its opposition. President Ford even sent a personal letter to the Pakistani prime minister, asking for the cancellation of the agreement. It was ironic that President Ford's letter was delivered on the same day that the successful conclusion of the tripartite agreement involving the IAEA, France and Pakistan was announced.[37]

In Ebinger's view the US attitude towards the Franco–Pakistan reprocessing deal hardened as a result of the failure of Pakistan to reach an accord with Canada. This breakdown of the negotiations was occasioned by Pakistan's refusal to accept the more stringent safeguards demanded by Canada in February 1976. It may be worth noting here that, after the Indian nuclear explosion, Canada and Pakistan had been discussing terms regarding stricter safeguards for any future supplies of nuclear materials by Canada. However, what was not palatable to Pakistan, was the Canadian demand that these new safeguards should also apply retroactively to all previous agreements between the two countries in the nuclear field. Another possible reason for the tougher American policy could be that the Ford administration was encouraged by its success in coercing South Korea into cancelling a similar reprocessing agreement with France.[38] Although both France and Pakistan apparently refused to bow to American pressure, because of this pressure France demanded tougher safeguards provisions. In meeting the French demands, Bhutto gave in on every point, and in doing so went out of his way to meet the non-proliferation concerns of the nuclear experts at the US State Department. He was, therefore, dismayed at the continued US demands for abrogation of the agreement.[39]

Secretary of State Henry Kissinger visited Pakistan in August 1976 with the Pak–French reprocessing agreement high on his agenda. During his press conference in Lahore, the questions asked by both Pakistani, as well as American journalists revolved around the reprocessing issue. It was clear from his response to the question posed, as to whether his visit had brought about any change in Pakistani attitude towards the reprocessing plant, that the two sides had failed to narrow down their differences. Dr Kissinger said:

> The issue of reprocessing…is an extremely complicated issue. Pakistan has been negotiating with France……for many years and has concluded an agreement…. That agreement has all the international safeguards that were considered appropriate at the time that those negotiations started. As far as the United States is concerned, we have….developed increasing concern about the spread of reprocessing plants, even with the safeguards that were considered appropriate several years ago. Our concern is not directed towards the intentions of Pakistan, but towards the general problem of the proliferation of nuclear weapons which can have, in our view, disastrous consequences for the future of mankind… We have agreed to continue these discussions in the weeks and months ahead…There will be no confrontation on that issue.[40]

When it was pointed out that apparently there was a dichotomy in the American approach to nuclear developments in Pakistan and India, Dr Kissinger responded that, 'we have deplored, we have greatly deplored, the Indian effort in setting off a nuclear explosive

device and we believe that what India has done is very inimical to
the process of proliferation and, therefore, to the problem of world
peace'.[41] This clearly was an afterthought, as the particularly mild
American reaction to the Indian nuclear explosion in 1974 had
come as a huge disappointment to Pakistan and the non-
proliferation protagonists around the world. Kissinger used a 'carrot
and stick' approach during the talks, offering 110 A-7 fighter
bombers as carrots, while the sticks were in the form of a warning
that the Democrats, who were expected to win the forthcoming
presidential elections, 'would adopt a tougher non-proliferation
approach and might make an example of Pakistan'.[42] Bhutto was
later to claim that, during his visit, the US Secretary of State had
threatened him that in case he did not back off from the
reprocessing agreement, 'we will make a horrible example out of
you'.[43]

In 1977 the political landscape saw radical changes. While the
Carter administration took office in Washington and the Janata
Party won an electoral victory in India ending Mrs Gandhi's
'authoritarian rule', General Zia had taken the reins of power in
Pakistan following his deposing of Prime Minister Bhutto. All these
developments combined to impact negatively on Pakistan–US
relations. The change became manifest when Indian Prime Minister
Morarji Desai was welcomed to the White House in July 1977, and
not long after, in January 1978, Carter paid an official visit to New
Delhi. However, unlike Eisenhower and Nixon, he did not make a
stop in Pakistan. It became clear that Zia was not about to change
course on nuclear policy when Joseph Nye, a nuclear specialist from
the State Department, visited Islamabad in September 1977. This
time there were no carrots, since the offer of A-7 aircraft had been
withdrawn. Nye warned his hosts that if Pakistan persisted with the
reprocessing project, the US would cut off economic assistance
under the provisions of the Glenn Amendment.[44] The American
experts did not seem to be convinced by the fact that Pakistan had
accepted stringent safeguards on the plant, and continued to believe
that Pakistan's ultimate objective was to achieve a nuclear explosive
capability to match India's capability. Zia told Nye that he did not

intend to abandon the project. The aid that was to be cut off was not likely to make much difference in any case since it had already been reduced to a paltry $50 million annually.[45]

Although the US failed in its efforts to dissuade Pakistan, it was able to bring about a change of heart in Paris. The French informed the US that they would be prepared to terminate the reprocessing agreement. Consequently, to avoid loss of face and credibility, the French government sent Andre Jacomet, a nuclear expert, to Islamabad, to offer a 'co-processing' plant instead of a reprocessing plant. The French knew that the proposed untested co-processing technology would be turned down by Pakistan. However, it provided them with a convenient means of backing out of their commitments. US officials saw it as a major success of their non-proliferation efforts, and probably the end of Pakistan's nuclear ambitions, enabling them to announce the resumption of economic aid. However, they were soon to find that, while they were focusing narrowly on the reprocessing issue, Pakistan had already embarked on a parallel effort to acquire uranium enrichment technology. Since Pakistan did not make an effort to acquire a complete enrichment plant, and instead adopted an unconventional approach of procuring small components separately from various European and North American suppliers assembling these in Pakistan, its effort was not detected for a while. In the summer of 1978 the issue of Pakistani attempts to procure electrical inverters from a British manufacturer was raised in the British parliament, bringing the issue out into the open. The US decided to ask its ambassador to Islamabad to confront Zia with the available intelligence. Zia, however, dismissed the intelligence as 'ridiculous' and offered to permit American experts to visit any site in Pakistan to verify the information.[46]

By late 1978 it appeared that Pakistan had either not abandoned the reprocessing project, or was possibly trying to create the impression that it had not, so as to keep the focus on reprocessing and away from its enrichment programme. This is evident from an October 1978 report by the American ambassador in France, relating to a private conversation he had had with Ambassador

Iqbal Akhund of Pakistan. During the discussion the Pakistani envoy had reportedly expressed Pakistan's determination to complete the reprocessing plant on its own. The Pakistani ambassador thought that, without French assistance, it would take much longer to complete, but in his view completion of the plant by Pakistan on its own would not be an infringement of the Glenn Amendment,[47] which applied only to transfers of equipment and technology. Mr Akhund also appeared to have alluded to the military purpose of the plant and argued that, in view of the situation in Afghanistan and relations with India, there was a need for the creation of a military nuclear option and capability, adding that it did not necessarily mean that Pakistan would explode a nuclear device. The US ambassador pointed out that Pakistan could better safeguard its security by having friends, and that it should not too closely follow the letter of the Glenn Amendment as the aid could still be cut off.[48]

By March 1979, the Americans had reached the conclusion that Pakistan was pursuing a covert uranium enrichment programme. As such Deputy Secretary of State Warren Christopher stopped over in Islamabad and warned General Zia that, unless the US president received credible assurances from Pakistan that it was not trying to develop a nuclear weapon, the US administration would be constrained to invoke the Symington Amendment to cut off assistance to his country. Although Zia reiterated that the Pakistani programme was 'entirely peaceful', he was not prepared to rule out the possibility of a 'Peaceful Nuclear Explosion', nor was he ready to accept international safeguards on Pakistani nuclear facilities. The Carter administration, therefore, decided to suspend aid for the second time within two years. In April 1979 the State Department formally announced that aid to Pakistan had once again been suspended due to concerns over its nuclear programme.[49]

By mid-1979 the Americans were becoming more concerned about what they saw as 'Pakistan's sensitive nuclear activities'. Ambassador Gerard Smith, accompanied by Ambassador Kirk and Robert Gallucci, met IAEA Director General Eklund on the sidelines of the IAEA Board meeting in Vienna, and briefed him confidentially on Pakistan's nuclear programme. Gallucci presented the evidence that had led the US to believe, 'Pakistan was pursuing a nuclear explosive programme, including activity in reprocessing, gas centrifuge enrichment and nuclear explosive design'. Eklund, while expressing his shock, asked as to where the Pakistanis would obtain their uranium and the facility to convert it into uranium hexafluoride. The IAEA DG seemed to be interested in learning about any possible misuse of uranium Pakistan had procured from Niger under an IAEA agreement, but was told by Gallucci that Pakistan had domestic sources of uranium. In response to another query, Gallucci stated that Pakistan had procured large quantities of critical centrifuge parts, and as such the project was well within the country's technical capabilities. Ambassador Smith added that he had been in contact with various suppliers, and had succeeded in closing down sales of centrifuge components. Dr Eklund sought another meeting with Ambassador Smith for further discussion of the Pakistani situation. In that meeting he expressed his doubts about the effectiveness of economic pressure on Pakistan, in view of the availability of what he termed the 'Moslem Oil Money', and commented that countries such as Libya would be ready to finance the Pakistani nuclear effort, and 'might want to use nuclear weapons in the Middle East'. Ambassador Smith thought that Pakistan would not be in a position to explode a nuclear device within the next two to three years. According to the American officials, Eklund saw a Pakistani nuclear weapons capability as a serious threat to future nuclear power programmes.[50] Interestingly, Mr Eklund did not show any concern over India's nuclear programme, which had exploited the peaceful nuclear technology provided to them by Canada and the US, to conduct their so called 'Peaceful Nuclear Explosion'. India's action had, in fact, resulted in the creation of technology control arrangements such as NSG and MTCR, thereby making the availability of nuclear technology for peaceful purposes ever more restricted and difficult for everyone. This fact is alluded to by the Assistant Director of the Arms Control and Disarmament Agency (ACDA), Mr Van Doren, during a General Advisory Committee meeting saying that: 'I think that the Indian explosion set back international nuclear commerce by many, many fathoms…. It was an extremely serious setback. It led to very restrictive legislation; it led to holding back by many, many suppliers of both uranium and equipment. It led to the shaking of public confidence'.[51] Nor did Mr Eklund seem to be perturbed either by the Israeli nuclear weapons development or that of South Africa. This kind of inequity and bias further hardened Pakistan's resolve to pursue its nuclear programme to its logical conclusion.

The Chairman of the PAEC, Munir Ahmad Khan, meanwhile continued to justify the need for the reprocessing technology, despite the fact that Pakistan's agreement with France had already fallen through. This was evident from his address to the Pakistan Engineering Congress in 1979, in which he highlighted the need for a reprocessing plant for Pakistan's nuclear energy programme, stating that:

> …The central role of a reprocessing plant can be understood from the following facts; A power reactor normally burns 1–3 per cent of uranium after which, because of fission products produced in the fuel, the reactor loses its ability to sustain chain reaction. The burnt fuel is, therefore, discharged and fresh fuel added. We can reuse this discharged fuel provided we remove the poisonous fission products and clean up the uranium and separate plutonium which is produced in the reactor. A reprocessing plant is used to perform this operation. Its advantages are:
>
> a. It enables one to recover un-burnt uranium which can be reused in new power reactors.
> b. It yields plutonium which is a known appropriate fuel for breeder reactors.
> c. Without plutonium there can be no efficient breeder reactor and without breeders the full potential of nuclear power cannot be realized.[52]

Munir Ahmad Khan went on to elaborate the problems faced by Pakistan consequent to the unilateral withdrawal of technical assistance by Canada from KANUPP, adding that Pakistan could no longer afford to depend on anyone for critical supplies of nuclear fuel. 'A power reactor is a billion dollar project and cannot be left at the mercy of others, who may stop fuel supplies any time without any notice and thereby jeopardize a country's entire economic development programme'.[53] Munir Ahmad Khan's motives behind this statement could have been manifold. He appeared to be using the arguments similar to those employed by India's Homi Bhabha decades before to justify the expansion of India's nuclear infrastructure. However, despite his reference to breeder technology, Pakistan is not known to have actually pursued a 'breeder programme'. On the one hand, it could be argued that Munir must have been concerned that if the reprocessing route was abandoned PAEC would have to depend for fissile material on A.Q. Khan, who had by then been given complete charge of the Kahuta enrichment project and made independent of the PAEC. On the other hand, it could well be that he was deliberately pointing up the reprocessing issue to keep the focus as far as possible away from the fledgling Uranium Enrichment programme.

In a briefing at the State Department to the General Advisory Committee on Arms Control and Disarmament in September 1979, the Assistant Director ACDA pointed out that, 'the obvious case of greatest concern is Pakistan'. Elaborating the point he stated that, in the aftermath of the Indian test in 1974, Pakistan had been seeking plutonium from various sources and had gone on to sign an agreement with France for the acquisition of a reprocessing plant, adding that the agreement had been 'wisely' terminated by the French. His contention with regard to Pakistan's attempts to procure 'plutonium' is unsubstantiated and naïve. He did not mention the sources from where Pakistan was trying to obtain plutonium. He went on to talk about Pakistan's ongoing efforts to procure enrichment technology, claiming that the Americans had persuaded the other suppliers to control the export of even the smaller components, and as a result had succeeded in slowing down Pakistan's acquisition efforts. He conceded though, that 'we may have been a little late', which meant that Pakistan had already obtained the bulk of the critical equipment and components.

In analyzing the approaches used so far to deal with the problem, it was concluded that the tightening of export controls would at best be a delaying instrument, while the imposition of sanctions on the supply of military and economic assistance, which had already been reduced to insignificant levels, was also going to be ineffective and may even have proved to be counter productive. It was believed that in the case of Pakistan conducting a nuclear explosion, it would inevitably be termed a 'peaceful nuclear explosion', as the Indians had claimed. It was obvious that benign neglect, and the readiness to accept the Indian claim with regard to the peacefulness of its nuclear test at its face value, would come back to haunt the Americans. Van Doren stated in response to a question that, 'This is a railroad train that is going down the track very fast, and I am not sure anything will turn it off.' When Mr Paul Dotty, one of the participants, asked if there were any pre-emption plans, Van Doren responded that it had been categorically denied that they were discussing any pre-emption plans.[54]

On a query about whether the Chinese had been asked to help the US, Van Doren replied that the Chinese did not intend to become actively involved in halting the Pakistani programme, but 'they are not in favour of a Pakistani nuclear explosive programme, and I don't think they are doing anything to help it'. He added that the Chinese were advising the US to augment Pakistani conventional military capability against the Soviet threat. This remark clearly contradicts the general perception that the Chinese had been assisting the Pakistani nuclear weapon programme. Mr Dotty remarked that amongst America's friends, the Israelis were the 'most highly motivated' to do something, as he had gathered from informal discussions. Van Doren agreed that the Israelis were concerned, but wondered as to what they could do, to which Dotty responded that the Israeli's were talking about 'Entebbe Two'. To another participant, Ms Pfeiffer's, suggestion that 'Entebbe Two' was the answer, Doren explained that, 'We are a bit hindered in that by the fact that Mr Burke of *The New York Times* thought of that solution, dreamed it up and put it in the New York Times article which played in the Pakistani press very hard and led some in the (US) government to immediately deny that that was under consideration'. Among other drastic measures considered were an embargo on items such as oil.[55]

The deliberations of this particular meeting of the General Advisory Committee have been discussed in some detail, since they clearly reflect the thinking and hostile attitude of those responsible for providing the intellectual basis of the US non-proliferation policy. No consideration appeared to have been given to the fact that Pakistan was not a signatory to the NPT, and it was well within its sovereign rights to develop a nuclear capability, based on the assessment of any threat to its national security, just as it was the right of India or Israel to develop their nuclear capabilities. In doing so, Pakistan had not violated any international law or treaty obligations. Of course its actions went against the grain of US non-proliferation objectives, and were in contravention to US national laws, but the mere fact that measures such as a military strike to destroy Pakistan's key nuclear facilities by the US, or by the Israelis, was being seriously considered, smacks of duplicity, arrogance and short sightedness. It is also indicative of how far the Americans were prepared to go, circumstances permitting, to prevent Pakistan from attaining a nuclear capability. Ironically, the possibility of such an attack was considered well before a similar strike was carried out by the Israelis against the Osirak reactor in Iraq in 1981, and that is why the term 'Entebbe Two' was used instead of 'Osirak Two'. One wonders what would have happened to the 'Great Jihad' which the US waged against the 'Evil Empire' for ten years, with the active help from Pakistan, had such an attack been carried out in 1979, irrespective of its failure or success.

Meanwhile President Ziaul Haq was trying to alleviate some of the concerns regarding Pakistan's nuclear activities. In a letter to the Indian Prime Minister Desai, Zia suggested a Joint Statement by India and Pakistan, renouncing nuclear weapons. Desai, however, proposed unilateral statements by both countries to the same effect.[56] On 17 January 1980, while speaking to American journalists, General Zia stated, in response to a question as to whether he would consider some sort of American inspection of Pakistani nuclear facilities, that a unilateral inspection was not possible. However, he said that if the US could make India agree to inspection of its nuclear facilities, he would go out of his way to subject his nuclear facilities to inspection either by the US or any international agency. This was a very shrewd ploy by Zia, knowing that the Indians would never concede any ground on this issue. In his reply to another question he categorically denied that Pakistan was making a bomb, while openly acknowledging that uranium was being enriched, stating that, 'Yes we are enriching uranium. I have said so on top of my voice. But it is very humble modest experiment.' In an obvious reference to the situation in Afghanistan, following the Soviet invasion of that country in December 1979, he suggested that the nuclear problem could be kept to one side, to be discussed later, in view of the more serious issues confronting everyone at that moment.[57]

The Soviet military intervention in Afghanistan compelled President Carter, who had twice suspended military and economic assistance to Pakistan, to change his policy and for once make non-proliferation take a back seat. The US offered $400 million in military and economic aid. However, General Zia was unhappy at the public announcement of the aid package without having obtained his consent, and dismissed it as 'peanuts' during an interaction with the press. He explained that the amount was inadequate to bolster Pakistan's security and would rather earn it the greater animosity of the Soviet Union. Foreign Minister Agha Shahi's talks in Washington failed to narrow down the differences, as the Americans had turned down the request for the supply of F-16s, and Washington was also not ready to reduce the importance it attached to non-proliferation, despite the fact that the administration was already seeking authority from the Congress to waive the non-proliferation-related sanctions imposed on Pakistan. President Carter, in what came to be known as the Carter Doctrine, reaffirmed the security commitment to Pakistan in his State of the Union message, declaring that, 'The United States will take action—consistent with our laws—to assist Pakistan resist any outside aggression'.[58] During October 1980, while Zia was in New York to address a session of the UN General Assembly, he was invited by Carter to the White House. Zia, conscious of his new found importance, did not show much interest in the US aid package, despite the fact that Carter had revoked his earlier decision with regard to the F-16s, and politely declined to make any commitment by pointing out that, since the US President was deeply committed in the election campaign, they could defer these matters to a later date.[59] It is instructive to see how General Zia played his cards. He took his time and did not show any undue eagerness to accept a US assistance package. He patiently waited for over a year after the Soviet military intervention in Afghanistan, and so was able to obtain a more substantive deal than the 'peanuts' offered by Carter. Zia and his advisors had correctly appreciated the outcome of the US Presidential elections and were willing to bide their time to see off the last few months of the Carter presidency, despite the fact that Carter had shown greater flexibility towards the end, as is evident from his change of heart on the F-16 question. However, the covert cooperation between the respective intelligence agencies continued.

REAGAN—WILLING TO LIVE WITH THE PAKISTANI NUCLEAR PROGRAMME

When President Reagan assumed office in January 1981, he declared his commitment to a more forceful foreign policy in response to the Soviet expansionism in Asia and Africa. In this context, developing an intimate relationship with Pakistan, as a key partner in resisting the Soviet presence in Afghanistan, was high on his national security agenda. Secretary of State Alexander Haig, Secretary of Defence Casper Weinberger and CIA Director William Casey were all in favour of offering a far more substantive aid package to Pakistan than the one offered by Carter. As a result, in consultation with the US ambassador in Islamabad, a $3.2 billion five year military and economic assistance package was put together.

Zia still wanted to move cautiously, and sent Foreign Minister Agha Shahi and his Chief of Staff General K.M. Arif to Washington, in order to reach an understanding with the US leadership on issues of concern to Pakistan, before committing himself to the aid package. Amongst these was the nuclear issue, on which Shahi and Arif were unequivocal in telling Secretary Haig that Pakistan was not prepared to compromise on its nuclear programme. In response Haig made it clear that the nuclear issue would not be the 'centrepiece' of US–Pakistan relationship. He did, however, strike a note of caution, that in case Pakistan were to conduct a nuclear test, the Congress would not allow the Reagan administration to cooperate with Pakistan in the manner in which it intended. The implication was very clear, and was understood by Deputy Assistant Secretary of State Jane Coon, to imply that, 'there was, in effect, a tacit understanding that the Reagan administration could live with Pakistan's nuclear programme as long as Islamabad did not explode a bomb'.[60]

However, the non-proliferation lobby on Capitol Hill did not yield easily, and resisted the six years waiver to the Symington and Glenn Amendments to allow Pakistan to receive assistance to the bitter end. In the bargaining procedure, Congressman Solarz was able to secure approval for an amendment that would trigger an aid cut off to any country that detonated a nuclear device. The tacit understanding reached between the administration and the Pakistani interlocutors was, therefore, solemnized in the form of a US law.[61] The Reagan administration did not believe in the use of sanctions to dissuade Pakistan from going down the nuclear route, as was evident from Deputy Assistant Secretary of State Coon's statement before the House Foreign Affairs Committee, declaring that: 'We certainly cannot claim that sanctions have been successful...Our interest would be better served by addressing the underlying security concerns of countries such as Pakistan and by developing more useful and cooperative relations which could engage us with them in a positive fashion'.[62] Similar sentiments were expressed by Under Secretary of State James Buckley in an August 1981 letter to the New York Times stating that the US was trying to address the security concerns forcing Pakistan to seek nuclear capability by strengthening its conventional defence capability.[63]

By then the US did not have detailed intelligence information about Pakistan's nuclear programme and, although it was known that Pakistan was actively engaged in a nuclear weapons effort, the US did not know how much progress Pakistan had made.[64] Many experts in the US as well as in India were sceptical of Pakistan's technical ability to achieve a nuclear weapons capability. No country prior to Pakistan had ever produced weapons grade fissile material through the Gas Centrifuge Enrichment technology, though the joint Dutch, German and British Consortium (URENCO), Japan and Germany were using this technology for producing low enriched fuel for their power plants. All other countries which had developed weapons based on enriched uranium had employed the Gaseous Diffusion process for enriching uranium to the bomb grade. There were also detractors within the Pakistani scientific community. One probable reason for Munir Ahmad Khan's persistence in advocating the reprocessing technology may well have been doubts about the efficacy of the gas centrifuge enrichment technology. A senior Pakistani diplomat once mentioned in a conversation with the author that the former PAEC Chairman, Dr Usmani, visited him while he was serving at the Pakistani mission in Brussels. Usmani expressed serious doubts about the prospects of achieving a nuclear weapons capability via the centrifuge enrichment route, and suggested that Pakistan should not squander resources and time on this technology.[65] The technical demands of the enrichment process are no doubt formidable, and it took Japan a highly industrialized country, ten years to surmount the problems. This point has also been made by Rodney W. Jones saying that:

> There may be reason to doubt that the technology Pakistan has imported can be successfully used to produce large quantities of HEU (highly enriched uranium). First, measures were put into effect, albeit belatedly, to restrict sensitive Pakistani purchases, and these measures probably have limited the number of centrifuge units that can be

readily assembled in Pakistan. Second, the technical requirements for successful operation of uranium centrifuges are by no means trivial.[66]

Despite the fact that the need to resist the Soviet military presence in Afghanistan had trumped the non-proliferation objectives for the time being, and that the US was prepared to live with the Pakistani nuclear programme, concerns continued to surface from time to time. In the wake of US intelligence reports leaked out to Senator Alan Cranston, and the news appearing in the Indian press pointing towards India's preparations for another nuclear test in May 1981, Cranston demanded that all aid to India and Pakistan should be cut off in case either of them conducted a nuclear test. Already upset over the trajectory of the US-Pakistan relationship, the Indians tried to deflect the debate and to galvanize the anti-Pakistan lobbies in the US, as is evident from *Indian Express* correspondent, T.V. Parasuram's 'Letter from America', which appeared in the newspaper on 5 May 1981. Complaining of the US inspired intelligence leaks and discriminatory attitude towards India, he asserted India's right to carry out nuclear tests, lamenting that the current US policy seemed to be to prevent India from conducting its second nuclear test and to stop Pakistan after conducting its first. Parasuram was, in fact, implying that the US was encouraging Pakistan to gain parity with India in the nuclear field. He therefore raised the bogey of the so called 'Islamic Bomb', and in an apparent attempt to provoke the powerful and influential pro-Israeli and Jewish lobbies in the US, suggested that Israel was worried that a nuclear-armed Pakistan, along with Egypt, Syria, Jordan, Saudi Arabia and Morocco, would assail Israel with a view to 'wipe it out' or 'drive it into the sea', adding that the Israelis were not worried about India's nuclear capability.[67]

When President Zia visited Washington in December 1982, President Reagan raised US concerns about Pakistan's nuclear programme in his private conversations with the Pakistani leader. However, it appeared that the US president was prepared to accept Zia's assurance that Pakistan's programme was purely for 'peaceful purposes' at face value. Zia also reassured the members of the

Senate Foreign Relations Committee that his country was not seeking nuclear weapons.[68]

At around the same time the American Embassy in Beijing sent a series of telegrams to help State Department officials prepare talking points for Secretary of State Shultz' forthcoming visit to China. There were some specific references to the nuclear issue, such as one which stated that while the Chinese were still opposed to the NPT, they had said in private interactions that, 'they have not assisted and will not assist any country in developing nuclear weapons'.[69] However, in another telegram it was claimed that, 'the Chinese have refused to give us an unequivocal answer that they are not assisting Pakistan's reported efforts to manufacture a nuclear explosive device'.[70] In an effort to use Chinese influence to dissuade Pakistan, it was suggested that the Chinese should be clearly told that if Pakistan exercised a nuclear weapons option, it would invoke relevant US laws, resulting in the cutting off of military and economic assistance. Additionally, a Pakistani nuclear capability would degrade its security by provoking India either to attempt a pre-emptive strike, or to launch a full-fledged nuclear weapons effort of its own. It would also provide an opportunity to the Soviets to extend their influence beyond Afghanistan.[71] In yet another communication the American Embassy alluded to the suspicions that Chinese nuclear cooperation might have facilitated Pakistan's development of nuclear weapons-related knowledge.[72]

Meanwhile, stories based on information ostensibly leaked by official sources continued to malign Pakistan. One such story appeared in the 20 December 1982 issue of *Newsweek,* blaming Pakistan for having gone around the world to covertly procure nuclear technology related to reprocessing and enrichment. The report also alleged that a Pakistani scientist had stolen enrichment technology from a nuclear installation in Holland, and that China had not only supplied 'raw uranium' to Pakistan but blueprints for a bomb as well. Pakistan denied these charges while a State Department Advisory note to the American Embassy in Islamabad instructed the US diplomats to offer 'no comment' on this report.[73] It was obvious that the US did not want to dispel such allegations, and used them to maintain pressure on Pakistan on the nuclear issue.

In a January 1983 dispatch, the American Embassy in London sent the text of an article by Indian Journalist Shyam Bhatia, published in the *London Observer* on 2 January 1983. Bhatia, quoting 'highly placed sources' and Western diplomats based in Islamabad, asserted that during his December 1982 visit to Washington, Zia had succumbed to American pressure and had pledged not to conduct a nuclear test. He also alleged that, according to some Japanese scientists, China had sold sensitive nuclear material, i.e. 'enriched uranium' to Pakistan the previous year, also mentioning that China had since denied selling any sensitive nuclear item to Pakistan. It is instructive to note how the *Newsweek* story about the Chinese transfer of 'raw uranium' to Pakistan had become transfer of 'enriched uranium' within two weeks. This is how many of the myths surrounding Pakistan's nuclear programme were created. Bhatia also thought that another factor, which might have discouraged Pakistan from conducting a nuclear explosion, was the possible Indian response. According to him, Mrs Gandhi had seriously contemplated a pre-emptive strike against Pakistani nuclear installations in 1982 as reported by *Washington Post*, but had held back due to fear of Pakistani retaliation against Indian nuclear facilities. He believed that concerns about a possible Indian strike had prompted PAEC Chairman Munir Khan to call on his Indian counterpart, Raja Ramanna, in his Vienna hotel room, to assure him of Pakistan's peaceful intentions. He also alluded to the secret discussions between Indians and Israelis regarding Pakistan's nuclear development, and quoted a statement by an Indian politician, Subramaniam Swamy, on his return from a visit to Israel. Swamy reportedly asked the Israelis whether they would consider a pre-emptive strike against Pakistani nuclear targets, as they had done in Baghdad. The Israelis replied in the affirmative, if the Indians would provide them with refuelling facilities at their forward air base at Jamnagar in Rajasthan near the Pakistani border.[74]

A June 1983 State Department assessment entitled: 'The Pakistani Nuclear Programme' concluded that there was enough evidence to suggest that Pakistan was pursuing a nuclear weapons programme, aiming in the short term to develop a capability to conduct a nuclear explosive test, if it was seen as feasible and advantageous from the politico-diplomatic point of view. In the longer term, the aim was to create a nuclear deterrence against possible Indian aggression. The report mentioned that Pakistan was following a dual track approach, that was to acquire both reprocessing as well as enrichment capabilities. In this regard construction of a small scale reprocessing facility called 'New Labs', with the help of European assistance in design and equipment, was well under way near Rawalpindi. However, the report acknowledged that since Pakistan had no other source of spent fuel than KANUPP, it would have to abrogate its agreements with Canada and the IAEA, in order to use the material from this plant. The US assessment also mentioned the Kahuta enrichment plant, for which, according to the report, Pakistan had obtained European technology through a network of procurement agents, front companies and European suppliers. It also alleged that Pakistan had been facing difficulties in running the enrichment plant and had sought Chinese help to overcome these problems.[75] This was a strange and illogical accusation, since the Chinese had no experience in gas centrifuge enrichment technology. Their own enrichment plants were based on gaseous diffusion technology. It could well have been that the Chinese took technical information from Pakistan with regard to gas centrifuge enrichment rather than the other way around. Rodney Jones has dismissed these allegations arguing that:

This author is inclined to discount reported allegations that China knowingly transferred nuclear weapons design information to Pakistan. It would not be surprising, however, to discover that Chinese technologists who developed their own gaseous diffusion technology for uranium enrichment, were also curious about the potentially more efficient centrifuge technology of European origin that Pakistan had tried to replicate.[76]

The State Department Report also challenged the rationale for the enrichment plant being presented by Pakistan as being intended as a source of fuel for the planned light water reactors to be installed by Pakistan in future. This justification for the enrichment plant was, in fact, far more plausible than the one given by the PAEC for the reprocessing plant in the mid-1970s. The authors of the report thought that it was too big to be an R&D facility, and too small to be a source of fuel for even a single light water reactor. However, alluding to Pakistan's efforts following the 1974 Indian test, made in nuclear explosive design and development, including 'implosion hydrodynamics', 'neutronics', 'high explosives testing', 'metallurgy' and 'electronic triggering circuits', they conceded that Pakistan had achieved the capability of producing a 'workable package of this kind'.[77] A mention was made of the US approaches to the Pakistani government to express concern over its procurement efforts, and a shift in emphasis was believed to have taken place from procurement of equipment to procurement of machinery, and later to the manufacture of these requirements indigenously. The usual issue of Chinese assistance was also raised. Though there might be some truth in Chinese assistance in operating the KANUPP following the Canadian withdrawal of technical support, it was speculated that the Chinese might well have helped in fissile material production and 'possibly' in nuclear device design.[78] This was despite the fact that the report had earlier acknowledged that through years of effort, Pakistan had already achieved the capability of putting together a workable nuclear weapon design.

In July 1983 during a visit to Pakistan, Secretary of State George Shultz raised the issue of continuing American concern about the Pakistani nuclear activities. However, the Pakistani leaders reassured him that they were not trying to develop a nuclear weapon. Shultz was followed a few months later by Secretary of Defence Caspar Weinberger, who stated that Pakistan had a 'strong military and we are trying to strengthen it all the more'.[79] Although Weinberger did not make any mention of the nuclear issue, his statement clearly implied that the US policy was aimed at alleviating Pakistan's security concerns by strengthening its conventional defence capabilities. It was hoped that this would act as a disincentive for seeking a nuclear capability.

The issue of past Chinese assistance to Pakistan came up during Chinese Premier Zhao's visit to Washington, while the two sides were strenuously negotiating a nuclear cooperation agreement between the US and China. However it appears, from a background brief sent by Paul Wolfowitz for US Commerce Secretary's meeting with the Chinese leader, that the assurances and clarifications provided by the Chinese negotiators were able to satisfy the American concerns.[80] On 12 January 1984 the *People's Daily* published the text of Prime Minister's Zhao's statement at the US president's banquet in Washington. During his statement the Chinese Premier had elaborated the Chinese Nuclear Policy. Underlining the Chinese policy of 'no first use' and its criticism of the NPT, the Chinese leader also elaborated China's non-proliferation policy stating that, 'We do not advocate or encourage nuclear proliferation. We do not engage in nuclear proliferation ourselves, nor do we help other countries develop nuclear weapons'.[81] This however, did not discourage India from creating misconceptions and spreading unsubstantiated stories of so-called China–Pakistan nuclear cooperation. The Indian press carried an associated press story, quoting Indian Foreign Secretary M.K. Rasgotra, claiming that Pakistan had already produced a bomb and expressing his 'hunch' that China might have helped Pakistan in conducting a nuclear test at its Lop Nor test site. The Indian Ministry of External Affairs categorically denied the story, and stated that the Indian Foreign Secretary was misquoted. Interestingly, the American journalists present at the 'background briefing' confirmed to the American diplomats that Mr Rasgotra had said that he had a 'feeling' that Pakistan already had a nuclear bomb.[82] Interestingly, the senior Indian official had spread this misinformation based on unsubstantiated press reports and a mysterious feeling, despite the fact that the Russians had discounted the rumours about the Chinese going as far as allowing a Pakistani test on their soil. This was similar to the situation in which a lawyer makes a provocative comment and on being asked by the judge withdraws his statement. The statement lingers on in the minds of the members of the jury, however. Such statements are then quoted and re-quoted in news items and academic articles, and nobody seems to take into account the denials. This pattern is unfortunately being repeated even today.

The State Department, in response to the telegram, issued a Press Advisory to the US Embassy in New Delhi. In the event that they were asked to comment on the Indian Foreign Secretary's statement about Pakistan's possession of a nuclear bomb and the alleged Chinese assistance to Pakistan in exploding a nuclear device, the US diplomats were to state that:

> We understand that the Indian Ministry of External Affairs has described the story as 'a total distortion' of an informal conversation between the foreign secretary and a group of journalists....we do not believe that Pakistan has acquired nuclear weapons capability, indeed Pakistan has repeatedly stated that it has no intention of developing explosives of any kind. We certainly have repeatedly made clear to the government of Pakistan at the highest level the adverse effects of development of a nuclear explosive capability would have on our bilateral relationship.[83]

When Vice President Bush visited Pakistan in May 1984, the nuclear issue came up during a luncheon meeting between Bush and Zia. President Zia assured Bush of the peaceful intent of Pakistan's nuclear programme and declared that, 'As long as he was head of State, Pakistan would have no intention of acquiring a nuclear device'. Bush, while appreciating Zia's personal assurance, emphasized that, 'exploding a device, violating safeguards, or reprocessing plutonium would pose a very difficult problem for the Reagan administration' and that the nuclear issue continued to be a very sensitive topic in the United States.[84] A closer look at the Bush statement indicates that there was no mention of 'uranium enrichment' amongst the list of forbidden actions. The message was clear, that the Americans knew about Pakistan's enrichment effort, and were prepared to live with it, as long as Pakistan did not detonate a nuclear explosive device.

However, various press reports and 'leaked intelligence reports', in contradiction to Zia's assurances, were causing consternation amongst the non-proliferation proponents in the US Congress. In February 1984 a report was published in the London Times, entitled: 'Hint of Pakistani Atom Bomb'. This news item was based on an interview by Dr A.Q. Khan with an Urdu daily Nawa-i-Waqt, in which he was purported to have claimed that, 'Pakistan has broken the western countries' monopoly on the enrichment of uranium' and that, 'if in the interest of the country's solidarity, the President of Pakistan were in extreme need and gave the team of scientists an important mission it would not disappoint the nation'.[85] It was believed that Dr Khan ostensibly revealed Pakistan's capability of producing nuclear weapons. President Ziaul Haq immediately moved to quell the rumours. Talking to reporters in Islamabad on the eve of his departure to Moscow he said that, 'his government's stand on the issue had been quite clear: Pakistan wanted to acquire nuclear technology for peaceful purposes only'.[86] Despite Zia's efforts at damage limitation, Senator Cranston in a June 1984 statement harshly criticized the State Department for deliberately misrepresenting the facts about Pakistan's nuclear programme.[87] Cranston's statement was immediately picked up and made front-page headlines in major Indian newspapers. Based on a 22 June report by its Washington correspondent, the Times of India quoted Senator Cranston as claiming that 'disgruntled' government officials had informed him that, with Chinese assistance, Pakistan had already acquired the capability of making nuclear bombs. He accused the State Department of hiding the facts from Congress in order to maintain the ongoing $3.2 billion assistance package to Pakistan. Cranston also claimed that Pakistan was estimated to have the capability of manufacturing at least a dozen nuclear weapons within the following 3–5 years. He demanded immediate cessation of all aid to Pakistan and, playing the anti-Muslim and pro-Israeli card, pointed out that, 'This increases the danger that extremist forces may employ nuclear threats in a holy war against India, Israel or other nations. This weakens America in the Third World'.[88] He also used the opportunity to take a pot shot at the Chinese, and blamed the Reagan administration for signing a nuclear cooperation agreement with China without comprehending its implications.[89]

The Times of India story, quoting 'usually well informed' sources, also alleged that Pakistan has already made a crude bomb based on Chinese designs, and was now trying to build a lead shell to protect its personnel from radiation. The story added that Pakistan would use the US supplied C-130s as the means of delivery, since the Pakistani bomb was too heavy to be carried by F-16s.[90] There are numerous contradictions in the story. On the one hand, it claimed that the Pakistani bomb was based on tried and tested Chinese designs, and on the other, it said that the weapon was so unwieldy that it could only be delivered by transport aircraft. Should one assume that even the proven Chinese designs were so crude that weapons based on these were virtually undeliverable, or could it be that the stories of Chinese assistance were mainly based on fiction rather than facts. Senator Cranston and other Indian lobbyists were opposed to the supply of F-16s to Pakistan, on the basis that these would ultimately be used as nuclear delivery platforms, so now, when it had dawned on them that the Pakistani bomb could not be carried by the F-16s, why was Cranston demanding immediate stoppage of delivery of F-16s?

This was a classic example of how news stories are recycled and re-circulated back and forth across the globe. On this occasion Senator Cranston made a statement in Congress, the story was picked up and published by newspapers in India, with the addition of some spice of their own. These stories were, in turn, picked up by the US embassy in New Delhi, which duly reported it back to Washington, thereby completing the full cycle. Another such example was a request made by the American Embassy in Islamabad in August 1984 to the US Embassy in London, referring to a story that appeared in the *Financial Times* with regard to US concerns about 'Chinese scientists working at a Pakistani nuclear facility'. It also cited a 5 August BBC news item, quoting sources linked to the *Guardian* newspaper, which had claimed that 'two' Chinese scientists were working at a nuclear plant in Pakistan. The US

Embassy asked its colleagues in London to share any such report appearing in the British press, with details such as names and location of the facility at which the Chinese were allegedly working.[91] It defies comprehension that the American Embassy, with its CIA Station Chief and elaborate electronic and human intelligence sources at its disposal, was asking the US Embassy in London to provide it with very specific details, based on 'press reports', about Chinese collaboration with Pakistan. How could it be that a British newspaper knew about the number of Chinese 'scientists' and the plant at which they were working, while the US Embassy located in Islamabad, with all its intelligence collection assets, was unable to find it out. It is hard to believe that only two Chinese scientists were able to help run a plant which otherwise needs thousands of scientists and technicians.

At about the same time a study entitled 'India-Pakistan: Pressures for Nuclear Proliferation', conducted by Robert Hardgrave of the University of Texas for the Bureau of Intelligence and Research of the US Department of State, analyzed the prospects for nuclear proliferation in South Asia. Hardgrave was of the view that though Pakistan's covert nuclear activities were creating pressure for India, a pro-bomb lobby also existed in India, which was pressing for a nuclear capability for the sake of prestige and technological development. He recommended that US should use its leverage over Pakistan by withholding the supply of conventional arms, in order to exert pressure against the exercising of the nuclear option by Pakistan.[92] This recommendation was exactly opposite to the official US policy at the time, which was aimed at alleviating Pakistan's security concerns by augmenting its conventional capabilities, with the intention of reducing its incentive for going nuclear.

Nevertheless, taking note of the growing concerns in Congress, President Reagan wrote a letter to President Zia on 12 September 1984, in which he warned him of 'serious consequences' in the event that Pakistan tried to enrich uranium beyond 5 per cent, the level required for producing fuel for nuclear reactors. Zia in his reply, delivered by Foreign Minister Sahabzada Yaqub Khan in

November 1984, was non-committal and did not make any specific commitment.[93] This was the first time the US president had drawn a clear line which specified the limits within which Pakistan could continue to pursue its enrichment programme. Up to that point the understanding appeared to have been that Pakistan could continue its enrichment activity, but would refrain from detonating a nuclear explosive device. It is also evident, from Ambassador Dennis Kux's account, that this so called 'red line' was arbitrarily and unilaterally drawn by the US president and was not based on any mutual agreement, nor did Zia make any clear commitment to this effect. In any case, in the absence of an intrusive verification arrangement, there was no way to determine the level to which uranium was being enriched at Kahuta. From a technological point of view, maximum effort is expended in enriching the uranium from its natural 0.7 per cent of U-235 to 5 per cent of U-235, and it is relatively quicker and easier to enrich it further to the weapons grade level. Had Pakistan continued to enrich uranium at the 5 per cent level and accumulated large stocks over the years, these could be rapidly upgraded to the weapons grade within weeks at a later stage. This was, therefore, no more than a psychological barrier.

An opportunity to raise the nuclear issue with Zia in person was provided by the funeral of Mrs Indira Gandhi in November 1984, where Secretary of State Shultz and Senate majority leader Howard Baker broached the issue with him. Zia replied that, 'We support your non-proliferation policy and we implement it. But the difference for us is happening around here (i.e. India)'. In response to a query by Senator Moynihan, a former US ambassador to India, as to whether Pakistan had a bomb, Zia stated that, 'We are nowhere near it. We have no intention of making such a weapon. We renounce making such weapons'.[94]

Whilst there was lingering unease in Congress, and Zia's pronouncements were not seen as credible, the Reagan administration was preparing to seek congressional approval for a new $4 billion six-year package for Pakistan. This provided an opportunity to non-proliferation protagonists, such as Senator John Glenn, to criticize the administration for allowing Pakistan a free hand to develop its nuclear programme by using the waiver to sanctions it had obtained in 1981. Glenn tried to raise the bar by proposing an amendment to the foreign assistance act, obliging the US president to certify annually that, 'Pakistan neither possessed nor was developing a nuclear weapon'[95] to allow the assistance to continue. However, the administration was able to reach a compromise on a slightly toned down version, which would require certification to the effect that, 'Pakistan did not possess a nuclear device and that the US assistance was advancing non-proliferation goals'.[96] This amendment came to be known as the 'Pressler Amendment', enacted in 1985, after its sponsor Senator Larry Pressler.[97] This was, however, not an amendment to the nuclear non-proliferation act but to the foreign assistance act and, unlike the Glenn and Symington amendments which had universal application, Pressler was a Pakistan specific amendment which caused a lot of heartburn and bickering in Pakistan when it was invoked in October 1990. However, at the time the Pakistani government did not protest, probably in the hope that it would never be applied, which in hindsight appears to have been a very cavalier and shortsighted approach. Whether this oversight was due to lack of understanding of the working of the American system or based on an assessment that the Soviet occupation of Afghanistan would continue indefinitely is difficult to determine.

In July 1985 Indian newspapers published reports and editorials on the basis of an ABC TV report with regard to the alleged testing of nuclear triggers by Pakistan. The reaction of the Indian press was mixed, with some newspapers highlighting Pakistani denials while others pointed at Pakistani duplicity and blamed the US for complicity. In response to these news items Pakistan's Minister of State for Foreign Affairs, Zain Noorani, speaking in the upper house of the Pakistani parliament, expressed Pakistan's willingness to sign a bilateral agreement with India, or a regional or global agreement with other non-nuclear weapon states, to renounce nuclear weapons. He also reiterated that Pakistan had no intention of producing nuclear weapons.[98]

The Indian media, however, used this opportunity to raise the spectre of a Pakistani 'Islamic Bomb', which they contended posed a real danger to India and not to the US. *The Hindustan Times*, in its editorial, also cited an incident wherein some years ago an Indian journalist had asked an Israeli general, a former head of Mossad, as to what his country would do in the case of Pakistan acquiring an atomic bomb, and whether it was contemplating a pre-emptive attack like the one it had carried out against an Iraqi nuclear complex. The General responded that, 'the Pakistani nuclear bomb is your headache. How you go about it is your business. Why drag in Israel to do your dirty work'? The left leaning Indian newspaper *Patriot*, in its editorial, blamed the US for complicity in Pakistan's nuclear effort, and lambasted Reagan and Zia for working to undermine Afghanistan's 'independence' and 'sovereignty'.[99]

In November 1985 the story, 'based on his hunch', cleverly planted by the Indian Foreign Secretary Rasgotra in March 1984, with regard to the alleged testing of a Pakistani nuclear device at the Chinese test site, Lop Nor, came to life again when the baton was picked up by Jack Anderson. Consequently, the State Department was compelled to issue an advisory note to US missions in Delhi, Islamabad and Beijing, stating 'unequivocally that it is our judgment that Pakistan does not possess a nuclear device', in line with the presidential certification and added that, 'this conclusion takes into account all relevant information'.[100] In the same month Reagan met President Ziaul Haq and Indian Prime Minister Rajiv Gandhi in New York, where they had come to attend the fortieth anniversary session of the UN. While Reagan, in his meeting with Zia, discussed the prospects for India–Pakistan relations, National Security Advisor McFarlane in a separate meeting with him brought up the nuclear issue. McFarlane did not see any need for Pakistan to seek a nuclear weapon and, pointing to the growing congressional pressure epitomized by the Pressler Amendment, cautioned the Pakistani president that his country should stop short of producing or testing a nuclear device. Zia responded that Pakistan's modest nuclear programme was necessitated by its security compulsions, adding that no Pakistani leader could afford to abandon the nuclear programme and compromise national security. He assured McFarlane that Pakistan would do nothing that would be embarrassing for Pakistan–US relations.[101] As Dennis Kux has pointed out, Zia very clearly understood the threshold of 'embarrassment', and knew that any activity short of a nuclear explosion would be tolerated by the Americans, in view of the importance they assigned to the ongoing fight against the Soviets in Afghanistan.[102]

The US believed that, by periodically confronting Zia with intelligence information about Pakistan's nuclear programme, they would keep him on guard and under pressure, and in this connection a former CIA Deputy Director, General Vernon Walters, made several trips to Pakistan. On one such visit General Walters showed President Zia a blueprint of a Pakistani bomb design, which the CIA had reportedly obtained, and on yet another visit he showed Zia a satellite picture of Kahuta plant. Far from being unnerved, Zia calmly remarked that, 'this can't be a nuclear installation. Maybe it is a goat shed'.[103] Munir Ahmad Khan, who was then the Chairman of PAEC, was of the view that this 'show and tell' exercise did not affect the nuclear programme in any way and, in fact, made the Pakistanis aware of what the Americans knew.[104] It is interesting to note that many years later A.Q. Khan told the Libyans that he would teach them the technique of making their enrichment plant look like a 'goat shed'.[105] One wonders whether Khan borrowed the idea from Zia or vice versa.

Prime Minister Junejo's visit to the US in July 1986 provided yet another opportunity for the American officials to reiterate the importance of Pakistani 'restraint' on the nuclear issue, in the context of the successful implementation of the recently announced $4.02 billion military and economic assistance package over the next six years. In his interaction with the *Washington Post*, Junejo unambiguously stated that Pakistan would not enrich uranium beyond the 5 per cent level mentioned in President Reagan's September 1984 letter, despite the fact that Zia had never made any explicit and specific commitment on this count. Junejo had clearly overstepped his brief.[106]

On 15 September 1986, the Pakistani Foreign Minister and the Chinese Minister for Science and Technology signed a peaceful nuclear cooperation agreement in Beijing. The agreement reportedly encompassed cooperation in nuclear power generation, nuclear medicine and agriculture, and envisaged exchanges of experts and information. Under the provisions of the agreement the sale of equipment and materials between the two sides would be under IAEA supervision, and the agreement would be registered with the IAEA. By codifying their nuclear cooperation under this agreement, and making it transparent through the IAEA's involvement, the two countries hoped that the frequent allegations of their surreptitious cooperation in nuclear weapons development would be addressed to a large extent. The signing ceremony was attended by the Chinese Prime Minister Zhao Ziyang, Foreign Minister Wu and PAEC Chairman Munir Ahmad Khan among others. After the ceremony Sahibzada Yaqub Khan, Foreign Minister of Pakistan, met the Chinese premier, and the occasion was used by Zhao to reiterate China's policy of 'neither advocating nor encouraging nor practicing the proliferation of nuclear weapons.' [107]

In October 1986 the certification, mandated by the Pressler Amendment was signed by President Reagan, to the effect that Pakistan was not in possession of a nuclear device and that the US assistance would delay such a development. This immediately spurred anti-Pakistan lobbies and elements within the US establishment who were unhappy with the administration for taking a benign view of Pakistan's nuclear programme into action. Media reports, based on leaked intelligence, indicated that Pakistan had tested a 'nuclear trigger' and that it had enriched uranium to weapons grade. An unnamed official was even quoted to have said that, 'Pakistan was barely 'two screw driver turns' away from putting together a nuclear weapon.' There was, however, no compelling evidence to force the administration to impose sanctions and in the words of Under Secretary of State Michael Armacost, 'there was no smoking gun'. There was also considerable difference of opinion amongst the intelligence community itself.[108] The issue of an alleged 'high explosive' test was drummed up by the Indian press, latching on to a 4 November 1986 *Washington Post* story by Bob Woodward. The newspaper articles built their arguments around the reported explosion conducted by Pakistan in September, whilst also citing reports that Pakistan had enriched uranium to 93.5 per cent. The Indian analysts argued that since Pakistan had allowed itself to be used as a conduit for operations against the Soviets in Afghanistan, the US was not serious in its efforts to halt the Pakistani nuclear weapons programme. Challenging the credibility of the presidential certification, they tended to give more credence to two claims made by Woodward to the effect that, 'Pakistan could assemble a bomb within two weeks' and, 'Pakistan is only two screw driver turns away from having a fully assembled bomb'.[109]

Though there are many unsubstantiated and flimsy claims in the inspired articles published both in the US as well as the Indian media, once these stories start going back and forth, and reinforce each other, they assume the status of a gospel truth. For instance, Woodward's claim that Pakistan could assemble a nuclear device in two weeks was at best speculative. Even with the best possible intelligence inputs one can never be so precise in making a judgment while the statement regarding 'two screw driver turns' was merely a cliché. Similarly, one could make a fair assumption that Pakistan was enriching uranium to a high level, but to estimate the level of enrichment to the decimal point, i.e. 93.5 per cent, is next to impossible, unless of course Pakistan provided samples to be subjected to sophisticated and intricate laboratory tests. Moreover, the report of an alleged explosive test by Pakistan was based on the reported seismic signals generated by that explosion and picked up by an Indian seismic station. Again, such seismic signals are generated by very powerful underground explosions, but no such signal could have been generated by the testing of the nuclear trigger.[110] Interestingly, the Director of the Bhabha Atomic Research Centre, Dr P.K. Iyengar, stated at a press conference that a signal was recorded on 19 September by the Indian seismic station near Bangalore with its epicentre in Pakistan. He categorically stated that the seismic station was capable of distinguishing between an explosion and an earthquake, and in this case it was certainly an earthquake.[111] However, no one seems to have taken note of this categorical statement and the media continued to peddle the theme of a Pakistani explosive test because saying otherwise would have taken the gloss away from their stories. This is how perceptions sometimes become more powerful than reality.

Toward the end of 1986, while Pakistan was being singled out for criticism over its nuclear procurement and development activities, West German Broadcasting (WDR) showed a documentary entitled 'Wanted...Bomb Business: Nuclear Aid for Pakistan and India'. The film was prepared by Egmont R. Koch, based on interviews and investigation conducted by journalists working for the German network in various European countries. It pointed out that since both India and Pakistan were not members of NPT, they were being denied access to nuclear technology by the industrialized countries. 'Both states had, however, found other ways to procure nuclear equipment including in West Germany'.[112] It also alleged that there were firms who were selling nuclear equipment from the Soviet Union to India for large sums of money. It was claimed that, 'India was, and currently is, dependent on illegal aid from abroad'. In this connection it cited India's requirement for large quantities of heavy water, and stated that in mid-July 1985, fifty-three stainless steel containers with a total of 6.8 tons of heavy water originating from the Soviet Union had been delivered to Bombay, through a network of front companies in Germany, Switzerland and Sharjah in the United Arab Emirates.[113] The documentary detailed activities and individuals involved in procuring nuclear related and dual use items for Pakistan in Europe, and especially in Germany. Interestingly, many of the European individuals named in the German film including the Dutchman Hank Slebos, Briton Peter Griffin, Gunes Cire a Turk, Germans Heinz Mebus and Albrecht Migule are some of the individuals whose names came up during the investigations into the A.Q. Khan network almost two decades later. It is evident that these individuals were never put out of business by their governments, and if any action was taken against them at all, it was merely cosmetic. Migule, for instance, was tried in 1985 and sentenced to eight months imprisonment, but was placed on probation and did not have to spend any time in prison.[114]

The producers of the German documentary, while acknowledging that Pakistan was trying to build a nuclear bomb out of fear of India's burgeoning nuclear capability, characterized Pakistan's prospective bomb as an 'Islamic Bomb', as was the fashion of the day. It also mistakenly and unjustifiably assumed that the Pakistani bomb would be used to threaten Israel. It is mainly due to such perceptions that Israeli intelligence became active in undermining Pakistani procurement activities, and targeted individuals known to be cooperating in this effort. For instance, Israeli intelligence sent a letter bomb to Heinz Mebus' home as an 'act of punishment'.[115] The documentary blamed the German government for not taking any action to stop this illicit trade and also alleged that a German firm had delivered 60 tons of enriched uranium worth 200 million DM to South Africa in 1981. The German network concluded from its investigations that:

> ...there can be no question that there is such a thing as a nuclear black market in the FRG. No question either that so far only the tip of the iceberg has become visible. India or Pakistan, Argentina or Brazil, Israel or South Africa, the examples are interchangeable....and that in the FRG, export takes political precedence over the non-proliferation of nuclear weapons.[116]

However, despite these damning conclusions, the international media remained obsessed with Pakistan, probably because of the so-called 'Islamic Bomb', and tended to overlook the nuclear procurement and development activities of countries like India, Israel and South Africa.

In February 1987 US Ambassador to Islamabad, Mr Dean Hinton in a speech entitled: 'Reflections on Nuclear Issues in South Asia', delivered at the Institute of Strategic Studies, Islamabad, publicly acknowledged that there were differences between the US and Pakistan on the nuclear issue. Clarifying the view that US non-proliferation concerns were not aimed solely at preventing the development of an 'Islamic Bomb', he stated that they were concerned with proliferation per se, be it Christian, Hindu, Jewish, Muslim or atheist. Chiding Pakistan for following a policy of ambiguity, he commented that:

> While Pakistan has publicly demonstrated a commitment to regional non-proliferation. I must add in all candour that there are developments in Pakistan's nuclear programme which we see as inconsistent with a purely peaceful programme. Indications that Pakistan may be seeking a weapons capability generate tension and uncertainty. Is ambiguity in Pakistan's interest? Would it not be better to reduce tension, to replace uncertainty with near certainty? To accept full scope safeguards, thereby assuring the world that nuclear programmes said to be peaceful are indeed peaceful.[117]

While conceding that Pakistan could not be blamed for the nuclear menace in South Asia, he also recounted Pakistan's efforts to resolve the regional nuclear problem through a series of bold proposals such as:

- Simultaneous signature of the non-proliferation treaty;
- Simultaneous acceptance of international inspection or full scope safeguards;
- Bilateral inspection of each other's nuclear facilities;
- A binding joint declaration by India and Pakistan renouncing the acquisition or manufacture of nuclear weapons;
- Agreement on a South Asian nuclear weapons-free zone.[118]

While acknowledging that India was the first to conduct a nuclear test in South Asia in 1974, he appeared to be more convinced of the Indian declarations, that it did not want to pursue a nuclear weapons option, stating authoritatively that successive Indian leaders had not converted their capability to a deployable nuclear weapon. He put the onus of any future nuclearization of South Asia squarely on Pakistan, advising it not to push India into producing nuclear weapons. He then patronizingly told Pakistan that India's capacity to produce fissile material was far greater than Pakistan as was its ability to sustain a nuclear conflict, and Pakistan should not entertain any ideas of competing with India in this field. He closed with the prayer that, 'May God grant you and Pakistan's other decision makers the wisdom to make the right choice for Pakistan, for South Asia, and for the world'.[119] This could of course be taken to mean that this wisdom was lacking and the Pakistanis were not capable of taking the right decisions. Hinton's public pontification not only annoyed Zia but also evoked a statement from a Pakistan government spokesman stating that, 'Pakistan will not be browbeaten or cajoled'.[120]

On 1 March 1987 the *Observer* in London published an interview with Dr A.Q. Khan, which he had given to an Indian journalist Kuldip Nayyar, at the height of a military stand-off between India and Pakistan that had resulted from a major Indian military exercise 'Brass Tacks', close to the Pakistani border. In this interview, A.Q. Khan had purportedly claimed that Pakistan had achieved nuclear capability despite the West's doubts about his capabilities. A.Q. Khan quickly denied any such statement and claimed that he had been misquoted. Since the interview was granted without any government clearance, and had been arranged by Mushahid Hussain, who was then editor of the English daily, *The Muslim*, Zia was obviously angered by Khan's propensity for seeking publicity and making irresponsible statements, and duly pulled him up. Consequently, Mushahid also lost his job. However, a month after the Khan interview, Zia declared in an interview to *Time* magazine that, 'you can write today that Pakistan can build a bomb whenever it wishes.' However, he clarified the statement by adding that Pakistan had no intention of making a bomb.[121]

A Pakistan government document published in 1987, justifying the need for an expansive nuclear programme, stated that: 'Pakistan's nuclear programme stems from the country's desperate need for energy, woeful deficiency in conventional energy resources and anxiety to achieve some independence in nuclear fuel supply for its present and future nuclear power plants'.[122] The document highlighted the seasonal fluctuations in the generation of electricity, as a result of which most parts of the country were subjected to hours of power cuts during the winter. The demand for electric power had risen by 12 per cent per annum since 1978, while the increase in power generation had been only 9 per cent during the same period, resulting in an ever-increasing gap in the demand and supply of electricity. It may be pointed out that the average per capita consumption of electrical energy, considered to be one of the measures of prosperity of a nation, in the late 1980s was 10,000 and 5,000 units per annum for the USA and Europe respectively. The world average was 1850 units, while that of the developing countries was 450 units per year. Pakistan's average consumption of 265 units of electricity per annum was very low, even by the standards of developing countries. Unfortunately, even this miserly supply of electrical energy was not assured. At that time hydroelectric power generation accounted for 55 per cent of the total power production. Hydel power however, is dependent on the river flow into the reservoirs of large dams, which in turn depends on the amount of rainfall in the catchment areas. Pakistan's proven fossil fuel reserves were estimated to be 34 million tons of oil, 16 million cubic feet of natural gas, and 85 million tons of coal. The large coal deposits in the Southern Thar desert had not been discovered at that time. All these put together came to about half a billion tons of coal equivalent (TCE). Pakistan's per capita fuel resources were 6 TCE as compared to the world average of 200 TCE. It was calculated that even after exploiting the full potential of hydel, as well as thermal power generation, there would be a shortfall of 5,000 MW of electricity by the turn of the century. This huge gap could only be filled through nuclear power generation, a fact duly acknowledged by the IAEA in its studies carried out in the early and mid-1970s.[123] However, due to the concerns about Pakistan's covert efforts to acquire nuclear weapons, PAEC's plans to generate substantial amounts of electricity through nuclear power failed to materialize, as the nuclear suppliers refused to sell any power plants to Pakistan, as described above.

Meanwhile, the controversy surrounding Pakistan's nuclear programme was kept alive in the US by a series of arrests and indictments of US and Canadian nationals of Pakistani descent for allegedly trying to procure sensitive materials used in the nuclear weapons and export them to Pakistan in violation of US laws. President Reagan used his waiver to avoid the invocation of the Symington Amendment related sanctions against Pakistan.[124] When President Reagan once again met Prime Minister Junejo in September 1987 on the fringes of the UN General Assembly session, he asked him to 'make it possible' for him to issue the certification to Congress, due in the following month.[125] The American president was in effect asking the Pakistani leader to avoid causing another controversy, as this would play into the hands of the opponents of continued US assistance to Pakistan.

The Indians on their part did not miss any opportunity to play on American anxiety about Pakistani nuclear intentions. During a visit to the US in October 1987, Indian Prime Minister Rajiv Gandhi reiterated that India did not intend to produce nuclear weapons unless it was forced to and that it did not want nuclear weapons in its neighbourhood and sought active American assistance to constrain Pakistan. Ironically, during the same visit the US had agreed to export super computers to India, with direct applications in nuclear weapons design and development. It is amazing to see the Indian duplicity and the gullibility of the US officials, as is evident from Under Secretary Armacost's background briefing to the press on the visit, in which he stated that, 'it is quite clear that from the Indian stand point, the thing they fear is a Pakistani decision to cross the nuclear weapons threshold'.[126] However, when it came to various Pakistani proposals put forward to prevent the introduction of nuclear arms in South Asia, he was quite willing to accept the Indian view that they were resisting these Pakistani proposals because they had to keep in mind the China factor.[127] It was apparent that while India wanted to keep its nuclear weapons option open, and to continue covert research and development activities in this regard, they wanted the Americans to exert pressure on Pakistan to abandon its nuclear ambitions. Depending on the circumstances, they would keep holding China and Pakistan responsible for forcing India down the nuclear path.

In Pakistan's case, given its late start after India had demonstrated its nuclear capability in 1974, it could not have been justifiably blamed for pushing India down the nuclear path.

Pakistani proposals for a nuclear weapons-free South Asia were elaborated in some detail by Pakistan's Ambassador to Washington, Jamsheed Marker, in a letter dated 20 January 1988 and addressed to Senator John Glenn. These proposals included:

- Establishment of a nuclear weapons free zone in South Asia, 1974.
- Joint Declaration renouncing the acquisition or manufacture of nuclear weapons, 1978.
- Mutual inspection of nuclear facilities, 1979.
- Simultaneous adherence to NPT by India and Pakistan, 1979.
- Simultaneous acceptance of IAEA Safeguards, 1979.
- Bilateral/Regional nuclear test ban, 1987.
- Conference on Nuclear Non-proliferation in South Asia, 1987.[128]

If India was genuine in its non-proliferation ideals, despite its doubts about Pakistan's sincerity, it could have called Pakistan's bluff. The South Asian nuclear map would surely be different today. India having already demonstrated its nuclear prowess in 1974, only wanted to shut Pakistan out and maintain its nuclear monopoly in South Asia. To justify its own nuclear pursuits and indiscretions it could always wave the China card, which has retained its currency with the Americans ever since the 1962 Sino–Indian border conflict.

On 15 January 1988 the White House issued a statement that President Reagan had signed waivers to the Symington and Solarz amendments to the Foreign Assistance Act, which would otherwise have required a cessation of aid to Pakistan because of its nuclear weapons development related activities. It was argued that cutting off aid to Pakistan would have been counter productive to US strategic interests, South Asian stability, and inimical for the achievement of the non-proliferation objectives desired by the authors of these amendments. It also clarified that the government of Pakistan was aware of US concerns about certain aspects of its nuclear programme, adding that there are 'crucial non-proliferation criteria which Pakistan continues to honour'.[129] The statement expressed the determination of the administration to 'continue to press Pakistan away from a nuclear weapons option' and mentioned the pledge made by the Pakistani government to tighten its procedures, with a view to bring to an end procurement activities in the United States, which would trigger otherwise sanctions under the provisions of the Solarz amendment.[130]

In June 1988, the US embassy in New Delhi sent a summary, based on Indian press reports, concerning a 'secret nuclear cooperation agreement' between Pakistan and Iran, to the State Department. The Indian newspapers had, in turn, picked up the news from a story published in the *Observer*, London. This was another instance of news circulating back and forth, each source in turn quoting the other, picking and choosing the information which suited their respective points of view, and adding their own interpretations to make the story look credible and coherent. According to the report, the so-called secret agreement, which apparently was the talk of the town even before the ink had dried, was purportedly signed in Vienna by PAEC Chairman Munir Ahmad Khan and his Iranian counterpart. The report raises many questions about its veracity. Firstly, if the Pakistanis and Iranians had to sign a secret agreement at all, why would they do it in Vienna, under the noses of western intelligence agencies, and not in Islamabad or Tehran. The *Observer* had even cited the number of Iranians training in Pakistan as six, and gave the names of a scientist and a technician. So much for the secrecy. The Indian media played up this story as another opportunity to malign Pakistan, but more surprising are the remarks of the US diplomats in Delhi, who commented that this news would enhance Indian concerns about collaboration between 'Fundamentalist Islamic States' in the region.[131]

It is amazing to note the underlying hypocrisy in these comments, because until then Pakistan was a frontline state in the fight against Communist expansionism, and the Afghan Mujahideen were the heroes whose leaders were frequently welcomed into the White House. Now that the Geneva Accords had been signed and the Soviet withdrawal from Afghanistan had begun, Pakistan had suddenly become a 'fundamentalist Islamic state' and lumped together with the Iranians. Incidentally, not long ago two Indian nuclear scientists, Y.S. Prasad and Surinder Chaudhry, were placed on the banned list by the US government for assisting the Iranians in their nuclear and missile programmes,[132] and there have also been reports of Iranian scientists working in the Indian laboratories, whereas the US embassy was describing this alleged cooperation between Pakistan and Iran as undermining Indian security. What the reports did not take into account was the fact that in 1988 Pakistan–Iran relations were far from being cordial, and General Zia, as the leader of the OIC Committee assigned to end the Iran–Iraq war, was not welcomed in Iran because of his refusal to declare Iraq as the aggressor. How could it be possible that the two countries, who also had considerable policy differences and competing interests in Afghanistan, would start secret cooperation in the nuclear field?

In December 1988 a Hanau prosecutor investigating into the illegal export activities of some German companies concluded that:

> The defendants, since 1982, had maintained business contacts with representatives of the Pakistan Atomic Energy Agency [Commission]. According to their own statements they delivered through summer 1988, among others, nuclear facility assembly parts to Pakistan without the required licenses of the Federal Agency for economic affairs.[133]

The parts exported to Pakistan included parts for the fuel elements, a facility for the production of tritium, tritium gas, and containers for transportation and storage of uranium hexafluoride. Additionally, cladding tubes, rods and plates of zirconium alloy, used in the manufacture of fuel elements, were also supplied along with a sintering oven, a vacuum oven for uranium melting and a pellet press.[134] He also added that the defendants had also delivered nuclear parts to India and South Africa without the requisite licenses. In India's case, 'the parts in question were reflector material as well as cadmium tubes'.[135] In South Africa's case it was the fuel element measuring machines.[136] However, while Pakistan's indiscretions continued to make headlines, similar import activities of the 'responsible nuclear power' were simply ignored.

Although President Reagan issued his third successive certification under the Pressler Amendment before leaving the office in January 1989, the signs of changing times were already becoming apparent. His transmittal letter to the Speaker of the House forewarned that in view of the current status of the Pakistani programme it might not be possible to issue another certification. However, while Reagan kept up his commitment with Pakistan, he literally forced the hand of his successor.[137] This was despite the fact that Zia had died in an air crash in August of 1988, and a democratically elected government with Benazir Bhutto as the prime minister had taken over in Islamabad. But the most surprising fact was the ignorance of the Pakistani leadership of this gathering storm on the horizon, while in their naiveté they continued to see the incoming Bush administration as a continuation of the Reagan administration. Had it been otherwise, they would not have been shocked when the Pressler axe fell upon them in October 1990.

Pakistani Army Chief, General Aslam Beg, visited the United States in early 1989. On Ambassador Oakley's recommendation, the outgoing National Security Advisor, General Colin Powell, as well as his successor, Brent Scowcroft, had separate meetings with General Beg. Scowcroft bluntly told Beg that the administration had no leeway on the nuclear issue and that President Bush would only certify if he was convinced, but he would not lie to Congress on Pakistan's behalf. When President Bush met Prime Minister Bhutto in Tokyo in February 1989, at the Japanese emperor's funeral, he too broached the nuclear issue and struck a cautionary note. Prime Minister Bhutto in turn reassured him that Pakistan was mindful of US concerns.[138] The change in US policy was clearly discernible against the backdrop of Soviet withdrawal from

Afghanistan and the cessation of the Cold War. The Americans were no longer prepared to look the other way and ignore Pakistan's nuclear activities, and they were conveying this message time and again in unambiguous terms. The fact that a democratically elected government was now in place in Islamabad did not make any difference. In Bush's 'New World Order' there seemed to be no confluence of interests between the US and Pakistan. A vast majority of people in Pakistan view interstate relations the same way they view inter personal relationships, and there is a lack of understanding of cold realism in international politics. This has time and again caused a feeling of betrayal by the American friends amongst the Pakistanis.

American intelligence reports indicated that after Beg's return from the US Pakistan had suspended the production of highly enriched uranium, which was the biggest irritant for the Americans. Bhutto was given to understand that Pakistan could continue getting US military and economic assistance, while retaining its nuclear capability, as long as it did not go beyond the current level. The decision to freeze the production of HEU was justified later, by both Bhutto and Beg, as voluntary and based on the assessment that Pakistan had already developed a nuclear weapons capability.[139] This was a far cry from General Beg's doctrine of 'strategic defiance', and a major concession without seeking any quid pro quo from either India or America.

Since this author was privileged to be part of the team of officers assigned the task of conceiving and establishing a nuclear command and control system, and to develop the contours of Pakistan's nuclear doctrine in the aftermath of the May 1998 tests, it is hard to understand how General Beg had arrived at the conclusion that Pakistan had achieved its 'minimum deterrence level'. No nuclear doctrine existed at the time, and the minimum deterrence level was quantified only after the National Command Authority had become operational, a few years after the nuclear tests.

Parallel to warning Pakistan off, the Americans were continuing to raise their concerns with the Chinese about their alleged nuclear cooperation with Pakistan. The talking points for President Bush's meeting with the Chinese president, in February 1989, included specific reference to Chinese assistance in Pakistan's nuclear weapons effort. The Chinese were also asked to refrain from exporting missiles with range/payload parameters exceeding those laid down by the Missile Technology Control Regime (MTCR), i.e. a range of up to 300 km and payload up to 500 kg.[140]

In May 1989 the US embassy in Beijing reported the details of a meeting with a senior official of the Chinese ministry of foreign affairs. The Chinese official reiterated their policy of neither encouraging nor assisting nuclear proliferation. Commenting on the lease of a nuclear powered submarine to India by the Soviet Union, he suggested that the US should be addressing its proliferation concerns in the region with that country, rather than China. The Chinese official also explained that China did not want any more nuclear countries than the five existing nuclear powers and, in a dig at the US and other western countries, he remarked on how some threshold countries such as India, Israel and South Africa had acquired their current capabilities. He dismissed the reports about Chinese assistance to Pakistan in developing its nuclear capability as rumours and factually incorrect, adding that any country that wants to have nuclear cooperation with China has to accept IAEA safeguards, and this applied to Pakistan, citing the Sino–Pakistan nuclear cooperation agreement which specifically included the safeguards clause. The Chinese diplomat also denied reports of any discussions between China and Pakistan on the issue of leasing a nuclear submarine to Pakistan, stating that China itself was most backward in nuclear submarine technology.[141]

Pakistani Prime Minister Benazir Bhutto paid an official visit to Washington in June 1989 where, in her address to a joint session of Congress, she said: 'Speaking for Pakistan I can declare that we do not possess, nor do we intend to make a nuclear device. This is our policy'.[142] Somehow an impression was created in Washington that the prime minister was not privy to the details of Pakistan's nuclear programme, and perhaps was deliberately kept out of the loop, and therefore her pronouncements might not have been factually correct. Nevertheless, her visit was a great success and

President Bush agreed to provide an additional sixty F-16 aircrafts to Pakistan, and to continue the annual assistance package amounting to $600 million. In this regard he also issued the Pressler certification, since there appeared to be no change in the status of the Pakistani programme from the previous year, and in addition it appeared that the Pakistani leaders had taken the US advice seriously.[143]

In early 1990 tensions were mounting between India and Pakistan over the expanding insurgency in Indian held Kashmir. Large-scale Indian troop movements into Kashmir and along the international border, and Pakistan's reciprocal redeployment of its own troops heightened international concern. This military activity was accompanied by sharp rhetoric from the leadership on both sides, and the Indian prime minister, V.P. Singh, even declared his willingness to go to war. The Americans were concerned over the prospect of a military conflict between India and Pakistan degenerating into a nuclear war. Though India had not carried out any further tests after its 1974 explosion, it was widely believed that in the intervening period they had worked on the development of a nuclear weapons capability, while Pakistan was also considered to have reached a stage where it could assemble a nuclear weapon in a short period of time. President Bush sent his deputy national security advisor, Robert Gates, as his personal envoy to South Asia to help defuse the crisis.[144]

This US concern regarding the prospects of a nuclear war in South Asia was highly exaggerated at best, and probably deliberately cranked up in some quarters within the establishment. Former army chief General Jehangir Karamat, who was at that time DGMO in the General Headquarters, has categorically stated that things were well under control, and the possibility of even a conventional war was remote. A meeting held at the Henry L. Stimson Center in Washington D.C. on 16 February 1994, which was attended by the US ambassadors at the time in Delhi and Islamabad, as well as their military advisors, also concluded that there was no nuclear angle to this crisis and that they 'knew of no credible evidence that Pakistan had deployed nuclear weapons during the crisis'.[145] American journalist Seymour Hersh, who claims to have extensive links in the intelligence community, in an article entitled 'On the Nuclear Edge', published in *The New Yorker* in March 1993, made an incredible claim that Pakistan was making preparations for a nuclear strike against India, which necessitated the Gates mission.[146] Many people in Pakistan believe, with some justification, that the nuclear angle of the 1990 crisis over Kashmir was deliberately trumped up by some elements in the US administration, to create a justification for the invocation of the Pressler sanctions in October of the same year.

According to Dennis Kux, US intelligence analysts had reached the conclusion by May 1990 that, 'Pakistan had taken the final step toward possession of a nuclear weapon by machining uranium metal into bomb cores. Washington no longer had any doubts that Pakistan had crossed the line'.[147] Gates raised the issue with President Ghulam Ishaq Khan and the army chief, but both insisted that there had been no change in Pakistan's nuclear capability in the past year. Gates threatened that, unless the Pakistanis melted down the uranium cores, Bush would be unable to issue the required certification for aid to Pakistan to continue. Pakistani denials did not make any impression and Gates remained adamant.[148] It was evident that the Americans were no longer asking the Pakistanis 'not to move forward', but were demanding a 'roll back'. There is no information to suggest that the Americans ever made such a demand on the Indians, despite the fact that they had conducted a nuclear test. In fact, after that test both super powers were competing with each other to appease India. The demand for a curtailment of the schedule was kept up by Ambassador Robert Oakley, who warned Benazir Bhutto that Pakistan was on a suicide course as far as its relations with the US were concerned, unless it agreed to roll back its nuclear programme. He also repeated this demand in his meetings with President Ishaq and General Beg. Oakley believed that Pakistanis were in a 'state of denial', and were probably under the illusion that, at the end of the day, the Americans would refrain from invoking the draconian Pressler sanctions.[149] What he appears to have missed was the intensity of public sentiment in Pakistan, and the fact that no leader in Pakistan could order a nuclear roll back and survive in his or her position, especially when there was no such pressure being exerted on India.

INVOCATION OF THE PRESSLER SANCTIONS

In August 1990 the Benazir Bhutto government was dismissed, the assemblies were dissolved by the President and a caretaker government was formed. Around the same time the intelligence community in the US gave its unanimous verdict to President Bush with regard to the 'possession' of a nuclear device by Pakistan, leaving no room for him to manoeuvre. President Bush, who had reportedly taken the decision to withhold certification with a heavy heart, made a feeble effort to delay the inevitable by suggesting to Congress that the imposition of sanctions might be delayed until after the new government took charge in Islamabad, but quickly retreated in the face of strong opposition from both sides of the aisle. Consequently, the $564 million economic and military assistance programme approved for fiscal year 1991 was frozen. This was a major setback when compared with the sanctions imposed by President Carter, when the volume of aid was merely $50 millions. Even the weapons and equipment already in the pipeline were blocked, and more importantly, the F-16s, for which Pakistan had already paid a substantial amount, were held up and remained an irritant between the two countries for many years. In mid-October 1990 Sahabzada Yaqub Khan, foreign minister in the caretaker government, came to Washington to meet his counterpart, James Baker. Yaqub made an offer that Pakistan was ready to freeze the nuclear programme in return for the lifting of sanctions. He did not evoke any sympathy from Baker, who curtly told him that this was not enough and the only way the President could issue a certification was for Pakistan to 'destroy its nuclear cores and roll back its nuclear capability to the other side of the line'.[150]

It was clear that the Americans were continuously changing the goal posts and making greater demands on Pakistan. It was obviously not possible for Pakistan to roll back its programme, and Yaqub Khan stated this in as many words.[151] There was now no way to avoid or delay the inevitable. The most surprising fact in this whole episode is the sudden and unanimous determination by the intelligence community about Pakistan's possession of a nuclear device. The whole case was built on the information that Pakistan had converted its enriched uranium into weapon cores, but the question arises as to how they could make such a judgment with such certainty since activities, such as the machining of uranium metal into weapon cores, do not lend themselves to detection by remote sensors. The only way they could be so sure about it was that they had some well placed moles in the sensitive areas of the Pakistani nuclear establishment. The American intelligence community admits to the fact that Pakistan may have had the nuclear cores before 1990,[152] a fact that can also be surmised from the statements by General Zia and A.Q. Khan that Pakistan had all the elements which put together would constitute a nuclear weapon sometime by the late 1980s. However, Pakistan refrained from carrying out a nuclear explosive test to avoid embarrassing the Americans, as Zia had continued to reassure them. In Pakistan the invocation of Pressler was seen as another proof of American fickleness as friends and allies. The general perception was that, as the Afghan war was now over the Americans did not need Pakistan any more, and therefore were under no compulsion to look the other way so far as Pakistan's nuclear programme was concerned, and had, therefore, let the Pressler axe fall.[153]

Alongside this, American officials continued to raise the issue of Chinese assistance to Pakistan's nuclear programme in their bilateral interactions with their Chinese counterparts. In April 1991, Under Secretary Bartholomew had extensive consultations with the Chinese on proliferation related issues. The Chinese, on their part, had repeatedly stated in their public pronouncements that they adhered to the three major goals of the NPT, that is to say: preventing the spread of nuclear weapons to non-nuclear countries, reducing nuclear arsenals worldwide and promoting peaceful uses of nuclear energy. The Chinese claimed to be following three basic principles in their nuclear dealings with other countries as under:

- They will only cooperate on the projects that fall under IAEA safeguards.
- They will not cooperate on projects geared towards weapons development.
- They will not cooperate on projects geared towards the transfer of technology to third countries.[154]

The Chinese insisted that these principles were equally applicable to their nuclear cooperation with all countries, including their cooperation with Pakistan and Algeria. In this regard they specifically mentioned that the nuclear power plant they had agreed to build in Pakistan would be covered by IAEA safeguards. The Chinese rejected the perception of their assistance in Pakistan's nuclear weapons programme. They also did not show interest in making any effort to prevent nuclear proliferation in South Asia. Though the Chinese did not want the Pakistani nuclear programme to provoke an Indian reaction, they believed that Pakistan's programme was a defensive response to India's 1974 nuclear test. They also rejected Indian claims that the existence of the Chinese nuclear arsenal made it difficult for them to enter into any bilateral non-proliferation arrangement with Pakistan, reiterating their policy of non-use of nuclear weapons against non-nuclear weapon states. On the issue of a multilateral effort to resolve the South Asian nuclear issue the Chinese were of the view that it was basically the responsibility of the two superpowers, that in any multilateral discussion on South Asian nuclear problem, Chinese weapons would not be the subject of discussion, and that the key to a resolution of the South Asian nuclear issue was held by India, but it was unwilling to give up its ambition to possess nuclear weapons.[155] Pakistan, meanwhile, was making progress in several areas. It had successfully acquired the capability to fabricate fuel for the KANUPP, was running the uranium enrichment plant at Kahuta, had made strides in other key areas of the nuclear fuel cycle and had, in November 1991, completed the redesigning and up-grading of the nuclear research reactor at PINSTECH. This 5MW swimming-pool type American-supplied reactor, which had become critical in 1965, had outrun its designed life and was now upgraded to 10 MW. The fuel for this reactor would be provided by China under an IAEA approved agreement.[156]

At the same time the Western countries such as Germany and France were tightening their export controls, and showed their unwillingness to sell nuclear power plants to Pakistan even under facility specific IAEA safeguards, demanding that Pakistan accept full scope safeguards, i.e. safeguards on all its nuclear facilities. When the Chinese approached a German firm for quotations for reactor cooling equipment for the reactor destined for Pakistan, the German company declined the request on the grounds that Pakistan did not accept full scope safeguards.[157]

The US also made a demarche on China for its decision to sell a 300 MW nuclear power plant to Pakistan, explaining that the US and most other nuclear suppliers had adopted a nuclear export policy requiring full scope safeguards. The Chinese, however, pointed out that they did not subscribe to that policy and that the NPT, which they were going to ratify shortly, also did not require full scope safeguards. They further declared that the nuclear power plant deal would be totally transparent and under IAEA safeguards, and that it was meant to help a friendly country in its economic development. The Americans, however, were insistent that such deals should not be made without full scope safeguards with countries of proliferation concern, such as Pakistan.[158] However, this last ditch effort to prevent the sale of the nuclear plant to Pakistan did not succeed. In February 1992, China and Pakistan signed a contract for nuclear cooperation, under which the agreement reached in November 1989 regarding the provision of a 300 MW nuclear power plant was formally ratified. Work on this light water reactor started in August 1993 and it was formally inaugurated in 1999.

The issue of Sino–Pak nuclear cooperation continued to be ritualistically raised by the Americans in all bilateral interactions on non-proliferation related issues with the Chinese. In August 1992 Ambassador Ronald F. Lehman, Director of Arms Control and Disarmament Agency (ACDA), on a visit to China to discuss matters related to the chemical weapons convention, solicited Chinese views on the proposal for a five-party conference to discuss the South Asian nuclear issue. The proposal had been made by the Pakistani Prime Minister Nawaz Sharif in June 1991, suggesting a meeting between India, Pakistan, US, Russia, and China to try and resolve the South Asian proliferation issue. Lehman, while appreciating the positive response of the Chinese on the proposal, reiterated continuing US concerns over possible Chinese involvement in Pakistan's nuclear programme. He did not elaborate any particular development or incident forming the basis of his concerns, and it appeared that the American officials routinely took up the issue with the Chinese interlocutors as a means of maintaining a constant pressure on China.[159]

In the United States itself Democrat Bill Clinton won the presidential elections held in November 1992, and given his rhetoric during the election campaign on non-proliferation issues, he sounded like a reincarnated Jimmy Carter. More trouble appeared to be in store for Pakistan with Warren Christopher, the deputy secretary of state in the Carter administration, taking over as the secretary of state in the new administration. In practice, however, it appeared that the Clinton administration's policy was going to be more pragmatic, as was clear from the written testimony submitted to the House Foreign Affairs Sub-committee on Asia and Pacific, by John Malott, Interim Director, Bureau of South Asian Affairs. In his testimony, Malott outlined the administration's objectives as under:

- To prevent war and the spread of weapons of mass destruction and their means of delivery.
- Our goals of reducing tension, increasing regional stability and promoting non-proliferation are closely intertwined.
- Our ability to achieve our goals with India and Pakistan requires that we pursue an even-handed approach.

- India and Pakistan have advanced programmes to acquire weapons of mass destruction and ballistic missile delivery systems…outbreak of armed conflict has the potential to escalate to a nuclear exchange with devastating consequences for the region and global non-proliferation efforts.
- We continue to advocate Indian and Pakistani adherence to NPT, but our efforts are on more immediate goals.[160]

An analysis of these stated objectives indicated the following key elements:

- Adoption of an even-handed approach with both India and Pakistan.
- Acceptance of the fact that reduction of tensions and enhancement of regional stability could not be achieved without addressing the issue of nuclear proliferation in the region.
- Recognition of the reality that non-proliferation efforts must be directed at both India and Pakistan if the region was to be saved from devastating consequences of a nuclear exchange between the two countries.

The new US policy was, in fact, much closer to the Pakistani advocacy of a regional approach to the non-proliferation problem in South Asia, rather than subjecting Pakistan alone to all kinds of sanctions and pressures to roll back its nuclear programme. Adoption of an equitable approach by the Americans was certainly a welcome development from Pakistan's point of view. A Carnegie Study Group report entitled: 'India and America after the Cold War' had also recommended a regional as well as a more pragmatic approach stating that:

> The US should shift from a focus on non-proliferation in South Asia to a policy designed to maintain nuclear restraint. Such a policy will seek to freeze the stockpiling of fissile material for weapons purposes, the development of military related nuclear capabilities and the development, production and deployment of nuclear weapons by both India and Pakistan.[161]

In March 1994 the Clinton administration took a new initiative, in which it indicated its willingness to seek congressional approval for release of the F-16 aircraft, held up due to the imposition of the Pressler sanctions, in return for Pakistan's agreement to 'cap' its nuclear programme and to accept 'non-intrusive' verification of that capping. It was apparent that the Clinton administration had abandoned the unrealistic goal of a 'roll back', at least for the time being, and was prepared to live with a Pakistani nuclear programme frozen in its tracks. Interestingly, the Benazir Bhutto government had made a similar offer to the Bush administration, and had even voluntarily ceased production of weapons grade uranium in 1989. However, the Americans had failed to acknowledge this step and were sceptical about it in the absence of verification. That offer had fallen through due to lack of reciprocal measures by the Indians and the unacceptable domestic political costs of allowing any kind of verification. Accepting any capping or freezing of the programme, without any corresponding limits being accepted by India, would have been political suicide on the part of any government in Pakistan. To add to the difficulties, the proposal was prematurely released by Senator Pressler to the press before it had been taken up with the Indians, Pakistanis or even sounded off with the congressional leaders. As one would have expected, the Indian Americans and their congressional backers started an active campaign against the release of F-16s. Pakistan army chief, General Abdul Waheed, who was on a visit to the US, went public with his opposition, declaring that, 'the military would not bargain away Pakistan's nuclear programme for F-16s or anything else. Were the country's political leadership willing to compromise, the army would certainly make its views known'.[162] Given the political clout enjoyed by the military in Pakistan, especially in issues related to national security, it was very clear that it would be a non-starter as far as Pakistan was concerned. Deputy Secretary of State Strobe Talbott, who carried the proposal to South Asia, received a negative response in New Delhi. While in Islamabad he was told by Benazir Bhutto that, 'If we are unilaterally pressed for the capping, it will be discriminatory and Pakistan will not agree to it'.[163]

In 1995 the Brown amendment was passed by the Congress, to ease some of the sanctions imposed under the Pressler amendment. This allowed the release of equipment worth $368 million, held up in the pipeline, and the refund of another $120 million for items that had not been produced at the time of the imposition of sanctions. However, irritants such as the alleged supply of ring magnets custom-made for use in centrifuge enrichment plants, and M-11 missiles supplied by China to Pakistan continued to raise their heads. In January 1996, National Security Advisor Samuel Berger visited Islamabad to raise the issue of US intelligence reports about Pakistan's resumption of the production of weapons grade uranium, contrary to the understanding given by Benazir Bhutto during her visit to the US in April 1995.[164] On several occasions Pakistan also became a victim of US domestic politics, related to US–China relationship, and issues such as missile transfers would inevitably come up whenever the extension of MFN status for China or peaceful nuclear cooperation with that country came up for discussion in Congress.

In September 1997 an intelligence community coordinated report submitted to Congress, to meet the legal requirement for a presidential report in connection with the implementation of the 1985 Sino–US agreement for peaceful nuclear cooperation categorically stated that:

> China declared publicly on 11 May 1996, that it will not assist un-safeguarded nuclear facilities. We have no direct evidence that China has transferred equipment or material to Pakistan's un-safeguarded nuclear programme since that time, and we have no basis for concluding that China is not honouring its pledge.[165]

The report traced the history of Chinese proliferation behaviour since the early 1980s and occasions when the US had raised its concerns with the Chinese at the highest levels. The report further elaborated that, after a close scrutiny of the available information and clarifications received from the Chinese officials with regard to past transfers, the Secretary of State arrived at the conclusion in May 1996 that there was no reason to trigger sanctions related to the Export-Import Bank Act. It also made a clear determination that:

> Since China's May 1996 commitment, we do not have a basis to conclude that China has reneged on that pledge. China, however, is continuing to provide assistance to safeguarded facilities in Pakistan. For example, under a 1991 contract, China is building the 300 MW Chashma power reactor in Pakistan. We have not asked that China end safeguarded nuclear cooperation with Pakistan as a condition for implementing the peaceful nuclear cooperation agreement, but we have on numerous occasions warned China that the risk of providing assistance to the peaceful nuclear programme of a country such as Pakistan that does not have 'full-scope safeguards' is that some of this assistance will be diverted to un-safeguarded activities.[166]

The report identified four main goals sought to be achieved by the US administration in its nuclear dialogue with China as under:

- Terminate Chinese assistance to Pakistan's un-safeguarded and nuclear explosive programme.
- Curtail Chinese nuclear cooperation with Iran's peaceful safeguarded nuclear programme.
- Establish an effective Chinese nuclear and dual use export control system.
- Get China to join multilateral export control efforts.[167]

In summarizing the report, the authors concluded that each of the above mentioned goals had been met and the Chinese had provided assurances that they neither directly nor indirectly assisted the acquisition of nuclear explosive devices or related materials by non-nuclear weapon states. It is interesting to note that while the Americans were using their clout to stifle even the peaceful nuclear programme of Pakistan, no such evidence is found that it ever took up the issue with the Chinese or the Russians, when they were providing fuel for the Tarapur nuclear plants in India. In fact, to the contrary, when the US had shown its inability to provide the fuel after the enactment of the Nuclear Non-proliferation Act in

1978, it actively encouraged the French to fill in for them. Ironically, the Americans who were warning the Chinese of the risk of diversion of technology and know how from a safeguarded to an un-safeguarded segment of the programme of a country which does not subscribe to full-scope safeguards, did not apply that same principle in the peaceful nuclear cooperation agreement with India signed in March 2006. The agreement does not have any provision to guard against such an eventuality, which once again highlights the discriminatory approach, duplicity and selective application of non-proliferation standards.

DECISION TIME FOR PAKISTAN— THE NUCLEAR TESTS IN MAY 1998

In March 1998, the National Democratic Alliance, led by the Hindu Nationalist Bhartiya Janata Party (BJP), came to power in New Delhi. During the election campaign the BJP had advocated the development and induction of nuclear weapons by India, and this was also a part of the party's manifesto. On the basis of statements by BJP leaders, and credible intelligence reports, the Pakistani government was left in no doubt about Indian intentions. As such, Prime Minister Nawaz Sharif wrote letters to major international powers including the United States, warning them of the imminent Indian nuclear tests.[168] However, based on their interactions with the leaders of the new Indian government in New Delhi, and visiting Indian officials in Washington, the Clinton administration did not give much credence to this warning and brushed it aside as another instance of Pakistan crying wolf about India. In fact, even after the Indian tests, Admiral Jeremiah, who was assigned by the CIA director to analyze the failure of American intelligence to anticipate and forewarn about the tests, in response to a question about the Pakistani warning, sarcastically remarked that they have been warning us since 1974.

It was a repeat of 1974 as far as Pakistan was concerned, except that this time around there was no hedging behind the 'PNE', and the Indian prime minister declared his country to be a nuclear weapon power. Though the Clinton administration imposed sanctions, automatically triggered by the Nuclear Proliferation Prevention Act (NPPA) of 1994, the G-8 reaction was very mild at best, while Russia and France openly announced their opposition to imposition of any sanctions on India. Clinton's attention now focused on Pakistan, to prevent it from responding in kind to the Indian tests, in just the same way as the main focus of attention of the international non-proliferation effort was directed at Pakistan in the aftermath of India's 1974 test. While the American president was using all the persuasive skills at his disposal to convince Prime Minister Sharif not to follow suit, Indian leaders such as L.K. Advani were daring Pakistan with provocative statements, and reminding the Pakistanis of the new strategic realities which had emerged in South Asia as a result of the Indian tests. India caused further provocation by conducting two more tests on 13 May 1998. As Dennis Kux points out, 'it was as if the Indians, eager to have company in the international doghouse, were egging the Pakistanis on'.[169] Clinton offered to work with Congress to remove the sanctions imposed on Pakistan and to release the F-16s, but he was not willing to give Pakistan a security guarantee against possible Indian aggression as a quid pro quo for refraining from testing.[170] While preparations were at hand for an appropriate response, Pakistan waited for the international community to act. But the spineless response of the major international players left the Pakistanis in no doubt that they had to rise to the occasion to restore the badly shaken strategic balance in South Asia, and to safeguard their national sovereignty and integrity. Dismayed by the response of the international community, the Pakistani foreign minister pronounced that, 'it is a matter of when, not if, Pakistan will test'.[171]

Given the poor state of Pakistan's economy at the time, the decision to test was not an easy one, because the costs were expected to be high. But in the absence of concrete security guarantees, which Pakistan justifiably expected, and lack of substantive economic incentives, the Pakistani leadership could not have mortgaged their national security to vague promises of political and economic benefits. This situation has been aptly described by Stephen P. Cohen, a well-known American expert on South Asia. Cohen thought that the US did not offer any 'real incentives' to Pakistan for refraining from testing, and that the price being offered to Pakistan was nowhere near the one which had been offered to Pyongyang in 1994. He explained that:

> Pyongyang got $4 billion in American assistance to cap its nuclear programme; Pakistan was given vague promises that it might finally be given the twenty-eight F-16 aircraft it bought and paid for almost a decade ago. And we and the Chinese were unwilling to offer the Pakistanis security guarantees that would have made them feel comfortable.[172]

There has also been speculation about whether the decision to test was taken by the political leadership or was it thrust upon it by the Pakistani military. But the fact of the matter is that this was a well-considered national decision, which was taken jointly by the political leadership and was fully supported by the military leadership. There were some dissenting voices within the cabinet itself, the most prominent among them being the Finance Minister, Sartaj Aziz, who was obviously concerned about the damaging repercussions of the decision for the national economy, while Foreign Minister Gohar Ayub and the foreign policy establishment were the most vocal proponents of testing. Former US deputy secretary of state, Strobe Talbott, who led a mission to Islamabad in the immediate aftermath of the Indian tests, in an attempt to dissuade the Pakistanis from following suit, gathered the clear impression from his interactions with the Pakistani foreign minister and the army chief General Jehangir Karamat, that Pakistan would eventually go for the tests. His narrative of his meetings with Prime Minister Nawaz Sharif, however, creates the impression that Sharif was confused and torn between pressures from various directions, and was at best dithering. According to Talbott, 'Nawaz Sharif seemed nearly paralyzed with exhaustion, anguish and fear...Left to his own judgment, he would not test.' He also attributed to Sharif the remarks that, 'How can I take your advice if I am out of office? If he did as we wanted, the next time I came to Islamabad, I would find myself dealing not with a clean-shaven moderate like himself but with an Islamic fundamentalist, who has a long beard'.[173] General Karamat's account of the events, however, is very different. According to him, Nawaz Sharif had called him from Almaty on the evening of 11 May and asked him to start preparations for the tests. He, however, suggested that the Prime Minister should return to Pakistan as soon as possible, and then the decision would be taken after due deliberation in the meeting of the Defence Committee of the Cabinet (DCC), the institution designed to deliberate and take such decisions.[174]

It is obvious that Sharif could not show his cards prematurely, while the preparations for the tests were underway, out of concern for a possible preventive action by an outside power. He was clearly trying to gain time while giving the impression that he had not as yet made up his mind. Talbott appears to have completely overlooked this possibility. His perception may well have been influenced by his unpleasant experience of talking to emotionally worked up and angry Pakistani diplomats in Islamabad in those eventful days. Pakistan had correctly appreciated that sanctions against India would be short lived, and in case Pakistan did not test it would be frozen into a position of perpetual strategic disadvantage. The events of the past eight years have amply proven this point, with India's political stock rising exponentially, and the US going out of its way to expand its strategic relations with India, epitomized by the 'US–India agreement on Civilian Nuclear Cooperation', while the G-8 predictably opted for a little rap on the knuckles. Any possibility of a strong reaction by the G-8 was virtually sabotaged by the Russians, who spread the rumour on the eve of the summit at Birmingham that Pakistan had conducted a nuclear test,[175] thereby deflecting the attention from India towards Pakistan.

'PAKISTAN'S FINEST HOUR'

In the afternoon of 28 May 1998, Pakistan claimed to have conducted five underground nuclear tests in the Ras-Koh mountain range in the Chaghai district of Balochistan. A beaming Sharif pronounced this as 'Pakistan's finest hour', in a televised address to the nation, adding that, 'Today we have settled a score...Our hand was forced by the present Indian leadership's reckless actions'.[176] There were scenes of public jubilation and celebrations all over the country, and according to various public opinion polls as many as 97 per cent of the Pakistan population supported the tests. Pakistan conducted another test on 30 May 1998, bringing its total number of tests to six. Experts differ on the yields claimed by Pakistan, as was the case with India. But the fact remains that Pakistan's covert nuclear capability, which had been the subject of controversy and suspicion for a long time, finally came out in the open, and through this demonstrated capability Pakistan became the seventh declared nuclear weapon power in the world. Many in India and some in Pakistan had doubts about Pakistan's nuclear capability, which might explain, to some extent, the threatening statements by Indian leaders who were probably trying to call Pakistan's bluff.

NOTES

1. For instance the title of a 1981 book by Steve Weissman and Herbert Krosney, 'The Islamic Bomb: The Nuclear Threat to Israel and the Middle East', was very provocative since it presented the Pakistani nuclear capability as a direct security threat to Israel, thereby turning the pro-Israel lobby in the US against Pakistan.
2. Amitabh Mattoo, 'India's Nuclear Policy in an Anarchic World', in Amitabh Matto (ed.), *India's Nuclear Deterrent—Pokhran-II and Beyond* (New Delhi: Har Anand Publications, 1999), p. 17.
3. Marvin Miller and Lawrence Schienman, 'Israel, India and Pakistan: Engaging the Non-NPT States in the Non-proliferation Regime', Arms Control Today, December 2003.
4. Marvin Miller and Lawrence Schienman, 'Israel, India and Pakistan: Engaging the Non-NPT States in the Non-proliferation Regime', Arms Control Today, December 2003.

5. Prime Minister Mohammad Khan Junejo in his address to UN General Assembly in 1987 declared that, 'Pakistan doesn't wish to conduct a nuclear explosion and is ready to subscribe to a comprehensive test ban in a global, regional or bilateral context'. See *Strategic Studies*, Vol. X, No. 4, Summer & Autumn 1987, Institute of Strategic Studies, Islamabad, p. 159.

6. For details of Pakistan's nuclear command and control, see Major General (retd) Mahmud Ali Durrani, 'Pakistan's Strategic Thinking and the Role of Nuclear Weapons', CMC Occasional Paper/37, Cooperative Monitoring Center, Sandia National Laboratories, Albuquerque, New Mexico, USA, July 2004; and Brig Naeem Ahmad Salik, 'Strategic Dynamics and Deterrence: South Asia', *Contemporary Security Policy*, Vol. 25, No. 1 (April 2004), pp. 179–201.

7. What I mean by hedging is that Pakistan always cited India's pursuit of a nuclear weapons programme as the main reason for its nuclear weapons programme. Whereas by independent raison d'être it was meant that Pakistan could have either asserted its right to have access to nuclear technology as a sovereign state or on the basis that it was faced with a much larger adversary with substantial superiority in conventional forces it was fully justified in seeking an equalizer in the form of a nuclear deterrent capability.

8. There is a clear difference between use of nuclear energy for peaceful purposes such as electricity generation/medicine/agriculture etc. but in case of India it conducted a nuclear explosion and termed it as a PNE (Peaceful Nuclear Explosion) which it argued would be used for peaceful purposes such as digging of canals, mining and digging harbours etc. and no country has ever attempted or successfully accomplished any of these.

9. Shirin Tahir Kheli, 'Pakistan's Nuclear Option and US Policy', *Orbis*, Vol. 22, No. 2, Summer, 1974, p. 358.

10. P.B. Sinha and R.R. Subramaniam, *Nuclear Pakistan Atomic Threat to South Asia*, Vision Books, New Delhi, 1980, p. 30.

11. Ibid.

12. Ibid., pp. 31–2.

13. Z.A. Bhutto, *If I am Assassinated*, Vikas Publishing House, New Delhi, 1979, p. 137.

14. Ashok Kapor, *Pakistan's Nuclear Development*, Groom Helm, New York, 1987, p. 53.

15. Ibid.

16. Sinha and Subramaniam, p. 31.

17. Sinha, p. 33.

18. Jozef Goldblat and Peter Lomas, 'The threshold countries and the future of the non-proliferation regime', in John Simpson (ed.), *Nuclear Non-proliferation: An Agenda for the 1990s*, Cambridge University Press, Cambridge, 1987, p. 309.

19. Sinha, pp. 34–5.

20. Ibid., pp. 34, 36.
21. Ibid., p. 35.
22. Ibid., p. 37.
23. Ibid., pp. 37–8, and Charles K. Ebinger, *Pakistan Energy Planning in a Strategic Vortex*, Indiana University Press, Bloomington, 1981, p. 84.
24. Ebinger, p. 84.
25. Ibid.
26. Ibid., p. 91.
27. Sinha and Subramaniam, p. 14.
28. United States Atomic Energy Commission, Washington, D.C., 2 October 1974, 'Prospects for Further Proliferation of Nuclear Weapons'.
29. Robert Galluci, Background Paper—'Pakistan and the Non-proliferation Issue', Department of State, Washington, D.C., 22 January 1975.
30. Ibid.
31. Bhabani Sen Gupta, *Nuclear Weapons? Policy Options for India*, Sage Publications, New Delhi, Beverley Hills, London, 1983, pp. 53–61.
32. Official-Informal, Confidential, to G Clay Nettles, American Embassy, Islamabad, from Gordon Jones, Economic Officer for Pakistan, Department of State, Washington, D.C., 1 April 1975.
33. Ibid.
34. Department of State, Washington, D.C., 30 January 1976, to Mr Hartman-Eur, from David H. Swartz, Eur/Rpe, 'Demarche to Pakistan on Nuclear Fuel Reprocessing'.
35. Department of State, Airgram No. A-253, 29 April 1964, from American Consulate Bombay, to the Department of State, 'Inauguration of Indian Plutonium Separation Plant.'
36. Ebinger, p. 91.
37. Department of State, Memorandum of Conversation, 12 May 1976, 'Proposed Cable to Tehran on Pakistani Nuclear Reprocessing'.
38. Ebinger, p. 92.
39. Ibid.
40. Ibid., p. 93. Ebinger regards the trilateral safeguards agreement concluded between the IAEA, France and Pakistan as the toughest ever negotiated. See p. 104.
41. Department of State Telegram, Dr Kissinger, 9 August 1976, Lahore Press Conference text, from Secretary of State to Washington, D.C.
42. Ibid.
43. Dennis Kux, *The United States and Pakistan, 1947–2000: Disenchanted Allies*, Woodrow Wilson Center Press, Washington, D.C., 2001, p. 222.
44. Zafar Iqbal Cheema, 'Pakistan's Nuclear Policy under Z.A. Bhutto and Zia-ul-Haq: An Assessment', *Strategic Studies*, Vol. XIV, No. 4, Summer 1992.
45. Symington Amendment to Foreign Assistance Act of 1961, was passed in 1976 and was meant to stop any assistance to any country known to be importing enrichment technology. It appeared to be targeted against

Pakistan as both India and Israel had their programmes based on plutonium technology. It was further amended in 1977 through the Glenn Amendment to include reprocessing technology as well.

46. Kux, p. 235.

47. Ibid.

48. The 1994 Glenn Amendment as it is commonly known is actually named as Non-Proliferation Prevention Act of 1994 which was meant to trigger automatic sanctions against any non-nuclear state conducting a nuclear test and were imposed on both India and Pakistan after the May 1998 tests.

49. 'Pakistan Ambassador to France Hardlines on Reprocessing Plant', Memo from American Embassy, Paris, to Secretary of State, Washington, D.C., October 1978.

50. Kux, pp. 236–39.

51. 'Pakistan Nuclear Issue: Briefing of IAEA Director General Eklund', 'Memo of Conversation' of Ambassador Gerard Smith's Discussion of Pakistan's Nuclear Issue with IAEA Director General Eklund on 25 and 27 June 1979 on Edges of IAEA Board Meeting in Vienna.

52. Department of State, General Advisory Committee on Arms Control & Disarmament, 14 September 1979, Washington, D.C.

53. 'Pakistan's Nuclear Power Programme Justification and Rationale', Address by Munir Ahmad Khan, Chairman PAEC, at Pakistan Engineering Congress, Lahore, 5 September 1979, Pakistan Publications, Islamabad, 1979, pp. 9, 10.

54. Ibid., p. 10.

55. Department of State, General Advisory Committee on Arms Control & Disarmament, 14 September 1979, Washington, D.C.

56. Ibid.

57. PR-242353 Z, October 1979, from Secretary of State, to American Embassy Islamabad, Beijing, Bonn, Kabul, London, Moscow, New Delhi, Paris, Tehran.

58. O-181055 Z, January 1980, from American Embassy Islamabad, to Secretary of State, Washington, D.C., information American Embassy Moscow, New Delhi.

59. Kux, pp. 248–52.

60. Ibid., pp. 253–4.

61. Ibid., pp. 256–7.

62. Ibid., p. 260.

63. Ibid.

64. Ibid., p. 261.

65. Ibid.

66. Author's conversation with a senior Pakistani diplomat in Islamabad in 2005.

67. Rodney W. Jones, 'Nuclear Proliferation: Islam, the Bomb, and South Asia', *The Washington Papers*, No. 82, Sage Publications, Beverly Hills, CA, 1981, p. 31.

68. Department of State, Telegram, May 1981, from American Embassy, New Delhi to Secretary of State, Washington, D.C.
69. Kux, p. 268.
70. Telegram No. 0411 from American Embassy Beijing, to Secretary of State, Washington, D.C., December 1982.
71. Ibid.
72. Telegram No. 0412, from American Embassy, Beijing, to Secretary of State, Washington, D.C., December 1982.
73. Telegram No. 0492, from, American Embassy, Beijing, to Secretary of State, Washington, D.C., December 1982.
74. State 348835, from, Secretary of State, Washington, D.C., to American Embassy, Islamabad, December 1982.
75. Telegram No. 8186, from American Embassy, London, to Secretary of State, Washington, D.C., January 1983.
76. US Department of State, 'The Pakistani Nuclear Programme', 23 June 1983.
77. Rodney W. Jones, *Nuclear Supply Policy and South Asia*, Centre for Strategic and International Studies, Washington, D.C., 1984, p. 168.
78. Department of State, 'The Pakistani Nuclear Programme'.
79. Ibid.
80. Kux, p. 271.
81. 'Secretary's Meeting with Premier Zhao—Nuclear Cooperation', to Mr Dam from Paul Wolfowitz.
82. 'Premier Zhao's Statement on Non-proliferation Published in Beijing', from American Embassy Beijing, Telegram No. 5487, January 1984, to Secretary of State, Washington, D.C.
83. American Embassy New Delhi, to Secretary of State, Washington, D.C., 'Indo-Pakistan Relations: Mistaken AP Story of Pakistani Nuclear Blast in China'.
84. Press Advisory, From Secretary of State, Washington, D.C., to American Embassy, New Delhi, March 1984.
85. Kux, pp. 272–3.
86. 'Hint of Pakistani Atom Bomb', *The Times* (London), 10 February 1984.
87. 'Zia moves to quell rumours about manufacture of bomb', *The Guardian*, 14 February 1984.
88. Kux, p. 275.
89. 'News Reports of Pakistan Nuclear Capabilities', American Embassy, New Delhi, to Secretary of State, Washington, D.C., June 1984.
90. Ibid.
91. Ibid.
92. 'Pakistan's Nuclear Programme: Press Reports of Chinese Involvement', US Embassy, Islamabad; to American Embassy, London; August 1984.
93. 'India–Pakistan: Pressure for Nuclear Proliferation', Bureau of Intelligence and Research, Department of State, 8/1/84.

94. Kux, p. 276.
95. Ibid., pp. 276–7.
96. Ibid.
97. Ibid.
98. Ibid.
99. Special Media Reaction Report No. 45, 'Pakistan's Testing of Nuclear Triggers', from American Embassy, New Delhi, to Secretary of State, Secretary of Defence, No. 7571 of July 1985.
100. Ibid.
101. 'Alleged Pakistani Nuclear Test in China', Press Advisory from Secretary of State, Washington, D.C., to American embassies, New Delhi, Islamabad, Beijing, November 1985.
102. Kux, p. 278.
103. Ibid.
104. Ibid., p. 279.
105. Ibid.
106. Pervez Musharraf, *In the Line of Fire*, Free Press, New York, 2006, p. 295.
107. Kux, pp. 282–3.
108. Pakistan Foreign Minister Visits PRC, Nuclear Cooperation and Afghanistan, Telegram from American Embassy, Beijing, to Secretary of State, Washington, D.C., September 1986.
109. Kux, pp. 283-4.
110. 'Pakistan's High Explosive Test—The View from Delhi', Telegram from US Embassy, New Delhi, to Secretary of State, Washington, D.C., November 1986.
111. Seismic signals strong enough to be detected by seismic monitors have to be in the kiloton or thousands of kilograms of TNT equivalent. The sub-kiloton explosion cannot be detected due to technological limitations. Since the nuclear trigger does not carry explosive anywhere in the kiloton range it is not technically possible to detect such an event.
112. Ibid.
113. 'Wanted…Bomb Business: Nuclear Aid for Pakistan and India', A 'WDR' Film, Egmont R. Koch, 1986.
114. Ibid.
115. Ibid.
116. Reference about Israeli agents is from the documentary by German journalist Egmont Koch.
117. Ibid.
118. Ambassador Dean Hinton, 'Reflections on Nuclear Issues in South Asia', Speech at Institute of Strategic Studies, Islamabad, 16 February 1987.
119. Ibid.
120. Ibid.
121. Kux, p. 285.
122. Ibid., pp. 284–5.

123. 'Pakistan's Nuclear Programme', Published by Directorate of Films and Publications, Ministry of Information and Broadcasting, Government of Pakistan, Islamabad, March 1987, p. 3.
124. Ibid., pp. 3–6.
125. Kux, p. 285.
126. Ibid., p. 286.
127. Background briefing by senior administration official, 20 October 1987.
128. Ibid.
129. Letter by Ambassador Jamsheed Marker, to Senator John Glenn, 20 January 1988.
130. 'President Signs Symington, Solarz Waivers', Department of State Telegram, to American Embassy, Islamabad, January 1988.
131. Ibid.
132. 'Reported Pakistani–Iranian Nuclear Cooperation', American Embassy New Delhi Telegram to Secretary of State, Washington, D.C. June 1988.
133. Sultan Shahin, 'India, the US and Nuclear Proliferation', http://www.atimes. com.
134. 'Statement of the Hanau Prosecutor on the Allegedly Illegal Exports of Nuclear Assembly Parts', American Embassy, Bonn to Secretary of State, Washington, D.C., December 1988.
135. Ibid.
136. Ibid.
137. Ibid.
138. Kux, p. 294.
139. Ibid., pp. 299–300.
140. Ibid.
141. 'Briefing Paper: President's Meeting with President Yang Shangkun', US Department of State, 8 February 1989.
142. 'Ranking MFA Official on PRC Nuclear Matters—No Proliferation or Subs for Pakistan, Zip for Pyongyang', from American Embassy, Beijing to Secretary of State, Washington, D.C., May 1989.
143. Kux, p. 302.
144. Ibid.
145. Ibid., p. 306.
146. Michael Krepon and Mishi Faruqee, Occasional Paper No. 17, 'Conflict Prevention and Confidence Building Measures in South Asia-The 1990 Crisis', The Henry L. Stimson Center, Washington, D.C., April 1994.
147. Seymour Hersh, 'On the Nuclear Edge', *The New Yorker*, 29 March 1993.
148. Kux, pp. 306–7.
149. Ibid.
150. Ibid.
151. Ibid., pp. 308–10.
152. Ibid., p. 310.
153. Ibid.

154. Ibid.
155. 'Proliferation Issues, The View from Beijing Looks Grim', from American Embassy Beijing, to Secretary of State, Washington, D.C. April 1991.
156. Ibid.
157. General Mirza Aslam Beg, 'Pakistan's Nuclear Programme: A National Security Perspective', *The Nation*, Lahore, 20–22 June 1993.
158. 'Recent Nuclear Developments in China', from American Embassy, Beijing, to Secretary of State, Washington, D.C., January 1992.
159. 'China's Nuclear Deal with Pakistan-Demarche Delivered', from American Embassy, Beijing, to Secretary of State, Washington, D.C., January 1992.
160. 'ACDA Director Lehman's Beijing Consultations; Non-CWC Topics', American Embassy, Beijing, to Secretary of State, Washington, D.C., August 1992.
161. *The Nation*, Lahore, 24 May 1993.
162. General K.M. Arif, 'Facing the Nuclear Reality', *Pakistan Observer*, Islamabad, April 1993.
163. Kux, pp. 326–7.
164. Ibid.
165. Ibid., pp. 332–3.
166. Classified Report to Congress on the Non-proliferation Policies and Practices of the People's Republic of China, September 1997.
167. Ibid.
168. Ibid.
169. *The Nation*, Lahore, 24 May 1998.
170. Kux, pp. 345–6.
171. Ibid.
172. Ibid.
173. Hasan Askari Rizvi, 'Pakistan's Nuclear Testing', *Asian Survey*, 41, 6, 2001, pp. 943–955.
174. Strobe Talbott, *Engaging India—Diplomacy, Democracy and the Bomb*, Brookings Institution Press, Washington, DC, 2004, p. 65.
175. Author's personal interview with General Jehangir Karamat, Washington, D.C., June 2006.
176. Talbott, op. cit., p. 67.
177. Kux, pp. 345–6.

4

Indian and Pakistani Policies towards the Non-proliferation Regime

The last decade of the twentieth century saw arms control and disarmament issues occupy centre stage in the international arena. The end of the Cold War and the demise of the former Soviet Union helped shift the focus of the global powers from East–West confrontation to efforts aimed at containing the proliferation of weapons of mass destruction (WMDs). The progress made in this regard in the early and mid-1990s was unprecedented. The chemical weapons convention (CWC), aimed at the total elimination of a whole category of weapons, originally signed in 1993, entered into force in April 1997. From the point of view of the nuclear weapon states (NWS), however, the biggest diplomatic break-through was the indefinite extension of the Nuclear Non-Proliferation Treaty (NPT) in 1995, although the attempt to bring on board the three threshold states: India, Pakistan and Israel, failed.

The successful extension of the NPT was followed by a series of hectic negotiations aimed at the completion of the Comprehensive Test Ban Treaty (CTBT) at the UN conference on Disarmament (CD) in Geneva. These discussions were initiated as a follow up to the resolution jointly sponsored by the US and India, and passed by the UN General Assembly in 1994. The CTBT was finalized in September 1996. India, however, cast a negative vote when its demands with regard to a time-limited programme for nuclear disarmament and a change to the entry into force provision of the treaty were not met. The draft treaty was then moved to the UN General Assembly in the form of a resolution, which was passed by a large majority with only India, Libya and Bhutan casting negative votes. The treaty was signed by the five NWS and Israel among others. Pakistan voted in favour of the treaty, but refused to sign it in view of India's refusal to do so. However, even after the passage of more than a decade since the opening for signatures, the treaty is still awaiting implementation, due to non-ratification by many of the forty-four countries whose accession is obligatory for its entry into force (EIF). Although the CTBT had not entered into force, it had established an international norm against nuclear testing, and all nuclear weapon states had put unilateral moratoriums on nuclear testing in place. France and China, who were still testing in 1996, also wound up their testing programmes before the finalization of the treaty. The prospects of the CTBT suffered a very serious setback in October 1999, when the US Senate refused to authorize its ratification by the US administration.

The next major item on the non-proliferation agenda, the proposed Fissile Materials Cut-off Treaty (FMCT) has become mired in a deadlock between the major powers on other strategic issues, and the CD has not even been able to agree on its scope.

In more recent times a shift in the anti-proliferation policies, from non-proliferation to counter proliferation, has been clearly discernible. The common perception is that this change has come about as a consequence of the events of 9/11 and the concerns of the international community about the perceived efforts on the part of international terrorist organizations to gain access to WMDs. However, this is only partially true, as 'counter proliferation' has been part of the US policy since the early 1990s, though kept at a low key for years.[1] The past few years have been very eventful, and in a way fateful, for the future of non-proliferation, both from the point of view of substantive changes in the priorities of US anti-proliferation policy as well as efforts to move away from multilateral to unilateral policies, or those based on restrictive multilateralism built around 'coalitions of the like minded'.[2] The Geneva-based Conference on Disarmament, the primary UN negotiating body on arms control and disarmament related issues, has been rendered ineffective for years by differences amongst some of the major powers. However, instead of making efforts to break this logjam at CD, the non-proliferation agenda has been moved to the Security Council. The UNSC Resolution 1540, passed in April 2004, was the first manifestation of this approach. The problem with this approach lies in the structure of the Security Council itself, which does not allow a level playing field to all member states, is dominated by the P-5 and is not a truly representative body.[3]

Indian and Pakistani non-proliferation policies have been largely driven by their respective security imperatives and threat perceptions. With the exception of late 1950s and early 1960s, when it was one of the leading proponents of nuclear disarmament and an active participant in the formulation of the NPT, Pakistan has shown a preference for a bilateral or regional approach to nuclear non-proliferation, which is a natural corollary to the direct linkage of its policies with those of India. Pakistan's policy has largely been security driven, unlike the high ideals and utopian goals such as universal disarmament advocated by India. In India's case, pretensions to a major regional and international power status, a claim to a permanent seat in the UN Security Council, and its rivalry with China, especially after the bitter experience of its 1962 border war with that country, have played a major role.

From the early 1970s onwards a clear linkage began to emerge between the Indian and Pakistani nuclear programmes and policies. Given the fact that Pakistan was lagging far behind India in terms of nuclear development, its non-proliferation efforts were primarily aimed at retarding India's march towards becoming a fully-fledged nuclear weapon power. The proposal for a South Asian Nuclear Weapon Free Zone, presented before the United Nations General Assembly in the aftermath of India's first nuclear test in 1974 was, besides other considerations, based on the expectation that it would bring to bear greater international pressure on India, thereby providing an opportunity for Pakistan to do some catching up. Subsequently, Pakistan's policies were even more tightly coupled with those of India.

Pakistan's often repeated pronouncements of its willingness to sign the NPT simultaneously with India, and making its signatures to the CTBT contingent upon India's signatures, are cases in point. Such a policy was easier to devise and implement, since it did not require any ingenuity and provided a convenient shelter for Pakistan to hide behind when subjected to international pressure. But the downside of such an approach has been that Pakistan's policy has remained a virtual hostage to Indian policy and has been defensive to the extent of being apologetic. India, on the other hand has been assertive in claiming its sovereign right to have access to nuclear technology. India was also able to make a convincing case with regard to the Chinese nuclear threat to its security, thereby evoking a greater degree of understanding of, and sympathy for, its nuclear ambitions. Pakistan, on the other hand, has been unable to articulate an independent and convincing rationale for its nuclear capability. The direct linkage with India's nuclear programme and policies has created a situation in which Pakistani policies are bound to be affected by the actions and policy positions taken by India, with the undesirable possibility of being wittingly or unwittingly sucked into a nuclear and missiles arms race with India.

CURRENT CHALLENGES TO THE NON-PROLIFERATION REGIME

The existing non-proliferation regime is built around a complex web of freely negotiated multilateral arms control and disarmament treaties, such as the NPT, the CWC, the BWC, the CTBT and export control arrangements such as the NSG, the Zangger Committee, the Wassenaar arrangement, the MTCR and the Australia Group. While CWC and BWC have helped eliminate whole categories of WMDs, the NPT with its associated verification and safeguard arrangements anchored in the IAEA has played the most significant role in curtailing the proliferation of nuclear weapons. This treaty, which came into force in 1970 for a period of twenty-five years and was subsequently extended indefinitely in

1995, has near-universal membership, but the three de-facto nuclear states India, Pakistan and Israel still remain outside its purview, while efforts are in hand to bring North Korea, which had opted out of the NPT, back into its fold.

The non-proliferation regime, with NPT as its centrepiece, has had a mixed record of successes and failures. On the positive side it has succeeded in restricting the number of nuclear weapon states to nine, contrary to some predictions of around thirty nuclear-armed states by the end of the twentieth century.[4] On the negative side, not only has it failed to resolve the dilemma with regard to the status of the outliers, it has also faced problems of non-compliance or deliberate violations of its obligations by the regime insiders.

Currently there is a widespread perception that the non-proliferation regime is under serious threat, both from within and without, with all kinds of pessimistic scenarios emerging with regard to its future. For instance, there are serious concerns and doubts about Iran's nuclear ambitions, and it is generally feared that Iran will break out of the treaty once it has developed enough confidence in its uranium enrichment capabilities. The cascading effect of such a development in the Middle East cannot be ruled out, as is evident from the December 2006 decision by the six member Gulf Cooperation Council (GCC) to initiate a joint nuclear energy development project.[5] Similarly, DPRK's overt demonstration of its nuclear capability[6] created serious pressure for countries like Japan and South Korea, who already possess the technological wherewithal to follow suit. This negative perception has been further cemented by the acrimonious and fruitless NPT Review Conference, held in New York in May 2005, which highlighted the deep fissures among the ranks of states party to the NPT. This view was also influenced by the US decision to get into civilian nuclear cooperation, by changing its domestic laws and asking the NSG to make an exception to its rules for India. Many non-proliferation experts feared that this would set off a chain reaction, and break the consensus in NSG and other such forums, with disastrous consequences. Basically the regime is faced with two types of challenge, i.e. political and technical. The political challenges are related to the determination of the status of the regime outsiders, without unravelling the regime itself, as well as to the present impasse with regard to DPRK. The technical challenges pertain to the insiders failing to comply with, or deliberately trying to circumvent, their treaty obligations.

The general view is that the May 1998 nuclear tests by India and Pakistan constituted the most serious challenge to the regime thus far. However, many analysts ignore the fact that India's first nuclear explosion of 18 May 1974 carried equally serious ramifications. According to Marvin Miller and Lawrence Scheinman:

> India acquired a nuclear weapon capability under the cover of an ambitious nuclear power programme that received considerable support from the major nuclear suppliers, particularly Canada and the United States, until India detonated a so-called peaceful nuclear explosive (PNE) in 1974.[7]

In fact that particular event served as a wake-up call to the international community, and led to the initiation of a variety of measures to strengthen the non-proliferation regime. This, in turn led to the tightening of export controls through the establishment of arrangements such as the NSG.[8] Equally significant are the implications of Israel's undeclared nuclear arsenal, in fuelling the nuclear ambitions of some of its neighbouring countries. Similarly, Iraqi efforts to clandestinely develop a nuclear weapons capability in violation of its obligations as a state party to the NPT, Iran's failure to fully comply with its safeguards agreement with the IAEA, and Libya's ill-conceived attempt to acquire a military nuclear capability, have posed very serious challenges to the regime from within.

Should that lead to the conclusion that the non-proliferation regime is indeed in danger of an imminent breakdown or is about to collapse? So far the regime has successfully weathered many serious challenges. For instance, Iraq's nuclear ambitions were successfully laid to rest by the systematic and sustained effort by

UNSCOM and UNMOVIC inspectors in the aftermath of the 1991 Gulf War. The IAEA has successfully unearthed the previously undeclared aspects of the Iranian nuclear programme, by gradually expanding the scope and sweep of its safeguards and inspections regime in that country. Libya has been successfully persuaded, through diplomatic efforts by the US and the UK, to finally abandon its WMD related programme, leaving the IAEA to complete the task. This is indeed an impressive list of successes, and has effectively reigned in the nuclear ambitions of the states which have long been regarded as those of most serious proliferation concern to the international community. North Korea has been a hard nut to crack, but it is no longer a technical problem but a political one. The current situation on the Korean peninsula has been brought about as much by the North Korean paranoia and intransigence, as the unimaginative diplomacy of the US. However, the growing unease amongst the non-nuclear weapon states resulting from the failure of the P-5 to make serious progress towards nuclear disarmament, and the US tendency to make exceptions and bend the rules based on its own characterization of countries as friends and foes, as is evident from its nuclear deal with India, do not bode well for the future of the non-proliferation regime.

The problem of proliferation with regard to regime insiders such as Iraq, Iran and Libya has two distinct dimensions. Firstly, there is an anomaly in the NPT itself, which, according to the provisions of Article-IV allows member states access to nuclear technology for peaceful purposes. This provision allows the acquisition/ development of reprocessing, as well as enrichment technologies so long as the IAEA is aware of it and it remains subject to verification/ inspection mechanisms. However, a determined proliferator can continue to legitimately develop all the elements of the nuclear fuel cycle until it has developed enough confidence in its expertise and then, using the escape clause, it can quit the treaty.[9] The second dimension is the existence of an international black market in nuclear equipment and technology, which has recently come to light but has existed for many decades. This problem is a manifestation of the loopholes and weaknesses in the export control mechanisms, and has led to the recent unfolding of aggressive interdiction policies, such as the US led Proliferation Security Initiative (PSI).[10] At the moment neither India nor Pakistan has joined the PSI. One of the clauses of the Indo–US Defence Agreement, signed on 28 June 2005 during Indian Defence Minister's visit to Washington, stipulated the enhancement of capabilities 'to combat WMD proliferation'. This effectively means cooperation in America's counter-proliferation policies, but it was not specifically stated as to whether or not this would entail Indian participation in PSI as such.[11] However, the Bill passed by the US Congress in 2006 to amend the Atomic Energy Act-1954, and signed into Law by President Bush, to allow nuclear commerce with India, called for India's participation in the PSI.[12] Pakistan on its part has chosen to stay out of the PSI due to concerns about its possible infringement with existing international laws, such as the 'Law of the Sea Treaty' and the 'International Civil Aviation Protocols'. The US has made a commitment to work with its allies to ease the NSG strictures against India.[13] This could create a situation in which India may find it easier to join the PSI in the future.

Pakistan has generally tried to make positive contributions towards the cause of non-proliferation by actively participating in multilateral negotiations towards this end. It has supported all universally applicable and non-discriminatory treaties and agreements. It is a party to the Biological, as well as Chemical Weapons Conventions, made useful contributions in the formulation of the CTBT, has expressed its willingness to participate in the negotiations leading to the finalization of the Fissile Materials Cut Off Treaty and, despite certain reservations, played its due role in developing a consensus on the UNSC Resolution 1540.[14] However, its policies have been conditioned by its complex security environment, which has been mainly impacted upon by India's ambitious nuclear, missile and now defunct chemical weapons programme. Describing Pakistan's arms control policy, Rodney Jones wrote that:

...Over the years, Pakistan has developed sophisticated arms control positions and activities, despite sceptical receptions among some in the West. Pakistan has been specifically rebuffed by India, however, on a series of specific proposals for a South Asian nuclear free zone, simultaneous accession to the 1968 Treaty on the Non-proliferation of Nuclear Weapons (NPT), and even bilateral nuclear non-proliferation guarantees.[15]

Speaking at the National Defence College in May 2000, Foreign Minister Abdul Sattar summarised Pakistan's policy as follows:

For the past decade or so, nuclear capability has been the bedrock of our defence and security policy...its sole purpose is to deter and prevent war. Unlike some other countries, Pakistan neither aspires to great power status nor permanent membership of the Security Council, nor nourishes any design for regional dominance...We support a global, non-discriminatory international regime of nuclear and missile restraints, voted for the CTBT, will participate in negotiations for FMCT, and are prepared to strengthen our existing stringent controls against export of strategic weapons technology...[16]

INDIA, PAKISTAN AND THE NPT

It was in 1958, that Ireland moved a resolution in the UN General Assembly, asking the assembly to establish an ad hoc committee to study the dangers inherent in the further spread of nuclear weapons. This resolution was passed by 37 votes to none, but 44 countries including the nuclear weapon states abstained. The large number of abstentions prompted the Irish delegate to withdraw the resolution. In the subsequent sessions of the General Assembly between 1959–61, various resolutions on the subject sponsored by Ireland and Sweden were adopted. Pakistan and India voted positively for these proposals enshrined in the General Assembly Resolutions 1380 (xiv), 1576 (xv), 1664 (xvi) and 1665 (xvi). The focal issue in these deliberations was the nth country problem.[17] It may appear ironic that India and Pakistan, who had been at the forefront of international efforts to prevent the proliferation of nuclear weapons, should turn out to be two of the most intransigent outliers of the NPT. Both countries, however, had their own rationales and justifications to refrain from joining the NPT, based on their respective perceptions of the evolving nuclear environment in and around South Asia.

INDIA AND THE NPT

India was amongst those countries at the forefront of international efforts to formulate an international treaty to prevent the proliferation of nuclear weapons, in the 1950a and early 1960s. However, when the treaty was opened for signatures in 1968 it refused to accede to it for various reasons. It was unhappy at the way the issue of security guarantees by NWS to the NNWS was treated by the major powers, and also considered the NPT discriminatory. Some analysts argue that a change in India's policy was brought about by the Chinese nuclear explosion of 16 October 1964, and the fact that China had opted to stay out of NPT at that time. What is generally overlooked is the fact that India had by then achieved the distinction of being the only Asian country to have an operational 'Plutonium Reprocessing' facility. Dr Homi Bhabha, the architect of India's nuclear programme, had also claimed, in the immediate aftermath of the Chinese nuclear test, that given the political decision to go ahead, India could explode its own nuclear device within eighteen months.[18] This clearly indicates that India's efforts to achieve a nuclear weapons capability were in an advanced stage even before the Chinese nuclear explosion.

The issue as to whether it was the Chinese nuclear test, or the growing confidence in its own technological ability, which caused this change of heart on part of India is indeed a contentious one. It is clear, however, that the Chinese nuclear test provided India with a convenient smoke screen behind which to hide its own nuclear ambitions. While justifying this change in India's stance, Indian analyst, B.M. Kaushik, has criticized Pakistan for changing its policy in turn,[19] arguing that a nuclear China did not pose any threat to Pakistan. He shows great naivety in ignoring the fact that, if not a nuclear China, a nuclear India did indeed pose a threat to Pakistan's security.

India's criticism of the NPT was built around the following arguments:

- India was convinced that by legitimizing the five NWS and closing the doors for the other aspiring members of the nuclear club, the treaty had perpetuated the division of the world into nuclear 'haves' and 'have nots'.
- Secondly, India objected that, although, the treaty was aimed at preventing horizontal proliferation, it did nothing to check vertical proliferation.
- India was also concerned about the inequality in the rights and obligations of various signatories, since the non-nuclear weapon states would have to abdicate their right to produce nuclear weapons and accept the comprehensive safeguards regime for their nuclear facilities, while the NWS were not obliged to accept any such restrictions.
- India also cited its security concerns vis-à-vis China, which after an initial reluctance decided to accede to the treaty only in 1992.
- Lastly, India asserted its right, as a sovereign state, to have access to advanced technologies including nuclear technology.

In essence, India tried to play down the problem of horizontal proliferation because it was itself a potential proliferator, while it tried to focus attention on the dangers of the ever-growing nuclear stockpiles of the nuclear weapon states. It was logical, therefore, that once the non-proliferation treaty was finalized in 1968, both India and Pakistan refused to sign it. India's opposition was mainly based on what it termed as the 'discriminatory' nature of the treaty, and also because China chose to stay out of the NPT's fold.

India started expressing greater concern about *vertical proliferation* rather than *horizontal proliferation*, particularly after the Chinese entry into the nuclear club. The Indian point of view was forcefully represented by K. Subrahmanyam:

What is the problem of proliferation? The United States, the first country to become nuclear, made a decision to explore the possibility of developing nuclear weapons in 1940, found it feasible at the end of 1942 and successfully developed them in 1945....The Soviet Union became a nuclear power in 1949...and Britain in 1952...This was a period of very rapid proliferation. After that, France took its decision sometimes in 1956 and became a nuclear power in 1960. China took its decision in 1957 and became a nuclear power in 1964. India conducted its nuclear test ten years after China. It is, therefore, reasonable to conclude that the pace of proliferation of weapon countries is slowing down...But the pace of nuclear weapon proliferation within the five nuclear weapon countries has accelerated.[20]

India's nuclear explosion in 1974 brought about some important changes in the NPT related policies of both the countries. Pakistan, for instance moved a resolution in the General Assembly in December 1974, calling for the establishment of a nuclear weapons free zone in South Asia. This Pakistani resolution was adopted by the General Assembly with a large majority, but the Indians vehemently opposed the proposal. India objected to the idea of a South Asian nuclear weapons free zone (NWFZ) for two main reasons. First, it did not agree with the Pakistani definition of South Asia, and insisted on the inclusion of China in the South Asian region. Secondly, it believed that a South Asian NWFZ would be meaningless as long as the superpowers' naval task forces, equipped with nuclear weapons, were stationed in the Indian Ocean in close proximity to South Asia. In contrast to Pakistan's preference for a regional and bilateral approach towards non-proliferation, India insisted on a global solution to the problem as illustrated by the statement of the Indian delegate to an international conference on non-proliferation held under the auspices of Institute of Strategic Studies, Islamabad in 1987.

M. Rasgotra, a former foreign secretary, at the Indian ministry of external affairs, represented India's views regarding the non-proliferation issues in a global context in general, and the South Asian context in particular. He criticized non-proliferation as a myth, created by the nuclear weapons powers to perpetuate their monopoly over nuclear technology. In his view, the interest of nuclear monopolists in the NPT was understandable, but what baffled him was the unquestioned acceptance of the NPT by a large number of non-nuclear states. Criticizing the rationale behind the non-proliferation measures, he argued:

> I cannot bring myself around to accepting the argument advanced by some nuclear weapon powers, especially the United States of America, that other countries must not develop nuclear weapons because these would constitute threats to their security and to global stability or complicate their strategic planning. It would be a different matter if the world as a whole, including the present nuclear weapon powers, were to abjure nuclear weapons.[21]

The Indian view of the problem was that, regardless of the fact that the South Asian countries possessed nuclear weapons or not, the security of the region was threatened by the nuclear weapons of China, the Soviet Union and the USA, deployed in the vicinity of the region. As pointed out by Rasgotra:

> In today's world, non-proliferation cannot be rationally considered country by country or on a sub-regional basis. The only practical way to proceed with it is in the global context. Non-proliferation to be meaningful must be vertical and it must begin with those who have done the most proliferating.[22]

India has always maintained that, by demonstrating its technological ability to go nuclear in 1974, it had enhanced its leverage vis-à-vis the nuclear weapon powers, and that its demands for rectification of the imbalances in the NPT now carried more weight. These views were also aired by the former Indian foreign secretary stating that:

> ...Perhaps, only wider horizontal proliferation may persuade the present nuclear weapon powers to move forward towards an agreed programme of substantial and meaningful reductions in nuclear arms and to place their own facilities under international inspection and safeguards.[23]

The Indians were also very critical of Western perceptions that acquisition of nuclear weapons by India and Pakistan would inevitably lead to a nuclear war in the subcontinent. They argued that it was unfair to rate the chances of a nuclear exchange between India and Pakistan any higher than the chances of a nuclear war between the Soviet Union and the USA during the Cold War years. In support of these arguments, they cited the examples of the India–Pakistan wars, in which both sides refrained from bombing each other's population centres, in stark contrast to the strategic bombing campaigns of the Second World War in Europe and the fire bombings of the Japanese cities in the Pacific theatre.[24]

Since the entry into force of the NPT in 1970, India's multiple nuclear tests in May 98 posed the most serious challenge to the treaty, as this event triggered a Pakistani reaction. The earlier Indian test in May 1974 did not face the NPT head on, since it was projected as a PNE, although it acted as a catalyst for a Pakistani nuclear weapons effort. After the 1998 explosions, Indian Prime Minister Vajpayee claimed that India was now a fully fledged nuclear weapons power. India also reiterated that it would only consider signing the NPT if its newly acquired nuclear status was accepted by the global powers, by rewriting the NPT. A senior Indian external affairs ministry official stated that:

> The NPT divided the world into nuclear haves and have nots. It is unacceptable to us. Today, we have a different reality and the international community should see this reality and accept us as a nuclear weapon state......The international community has to find ways and means to see this reality.[25]

PAKISTAN AND THE NPT

Pakistan, along with India and Israel, poses a dilemma for the non-proliferation regime, with regard to determination of its status in relation to the NPT.[26] Pakistan, which had been an active participant in the international non-proliferation efforts culminating in the formulation of the NPT, decided not to join the treaty because of India's refusal to do so. Pakistan, like India, continued to express anxiety over the dangers posed by nuclear proliferation. Pakistan's concerns were voiced by President Ayub Khan in his address to the 17th session of the General Assembly, saying that:

> An aspect of disarmament which is of deep concern to Pakistan is the clear and present danger of the spread of nuclear weapons and the knowledge of their technology to states which do not now possess them...This imminent peril demands that the General Assembly give urgent consideration to conclusion of a treaty to outlaw the further spread of nuclear weapons and the knowledge of their manufacture.[27]

Pakistan continued to express its apprehensions about the possible spread of nuclear weapons, and even showed concern about the proliferation of the technological know how which could enable the recipients to produce nuclear weapons. India's growing nuclear potential, including the acquisition of a French supplied reprocessing plant by the mid-1960s, was a major cause of concern for Pakistan. After the conclusion of the PTBT in 1963, both India and Pakistan pressed for an early conclusion of a CTBT, and continued to take more or less similar positions at various fora including the UN and the Eighteen Nation Disarmament Committee (ENDC), the precursor of the conference on disarmament in Geneva. By 1965 Indian and Pakistani views about the nature of the proliferation problem had become widely divergent. Pakistan now seemed to be more perturbed by the possibility of India joining the nuclear club, rather than by the global spread of nuclear weapons. In his address to the 20th session of the General Assembly, Pakistan's representative, Agha Shahi, termed India's opposition to the NPT, on the basis of its demand for an acceptable balance of mutual responsibilities and obligations of the nuclear and non-nuclear powers, as a ploy to gain time for the fulfilment of its nuclear ambitions.[28] Mr Shahi pointed out that India represented the *nth country* problem by refusing to open its nuclear establishment to international inspections and safeguards.

By 1968, when the NPT was finalized, Pakistan had moved away from idealistic goals of global non-proliferation to the more pragmatic, focusing on issues likely to impinge directly on its own security. Pakistan now seemed to be more perturbed by the possibility of India joining the nuclear club, rather than the global spread of nuclear weapons. Pakistan's security concerns were forcefully articulated by Zulfikar Ali Bhutto, a former foreign minister and the future prime minister of Pakistan, in a book published in 1969 as follows:

> All wars of our age have become total wars;...it would be dangerous to plan for less and our plans should, therefore, include the nuclear deterrent....it is vital for Pakistan to give the greatest possible attention to nuclear technology, rather than allow herself to be deceived by an international treaty limiting this deterrent to the present nuclear powers. India is unlikely to concede nuclear monopoly to others and judging from her own nuclear programme and her diplomatic activities,...it appears that she is determined to proceed with her plans to detonate a nuclear bomb. If Pakistan restricts or suspends her nuclear programme, it would not only enable India to blackmail Pakistan with her nuclear advantage but would impose a crippling limitation on the development of Pakistan's science and technology.[29]

Consequently, as with India, Pakistan refused to sign the treaty. While India's opposition to the treaty was more assertive, and based on its opposition to the discriminatory nature of the treaty, as well as the Chinese decision not to sign, Pakistan hedged behind India's decision. India's refusal to sign the NPT therefore, made it politically suicidal for Pakistan to accede to the treaty. Up till its nuclear explosions in May 1998, in response to India's nuclear tests, Pakistan continued to express its willingness to accede to the NPT simultaneously with India. It is however, very difficult to establish whether Pakistan was sincere in this offer, or was making it in the knowledge that India was unlikely to take the bait, in view of its seemingly uncompromising stand on the issue.

By contrast to India, Pakistan has shown a preference for a bilateral and regional approach towards non-proliferation. Pakistan's viewpoint was articulated by Foreign Minister Sahabzada Yaqub Khan during his address to an international conference in Islamabad. While explaining the reasons for the failure of the NPT to attract the threshold countries, he argued that:

Although over 100 non-nuclear states have since acceded to the NPT, the majority of those countries which it was designed to attract have maintained their distance from the treaty. For these states, the inequalities of the treaty's obligations have become accentuated....Some of them see nuclear weapons as a status symbol that will enable them to establish domination over other regional states. Some are fearful of the threat to their security posed by one or more nuclear weapon states. Others are concerned about the threat to their security arising from the nuclear capabilities or intentions of neighbouring states, or from their overwhelming superiority in conventional weapons.[30]

While making these observations he clearly had India and Pakistan at the back of his mind. Reiterating Pakistan's concern about a possible nuclear arms race in South Asia, he argued that if one of the South Asian states acquired nuclear weapons capability it would undermine the prospects of non-proliferation in the region as a whole. The situation could only be stabilized by a solemn denunciation of nuclear weapons by all concerned, in order to alleviate the dangers of a nuclear arms race. The Pakistani Foreign Minister stressed Pakistan's abhorrence regarding the spread of nuclear weapons in South Asia, and repeated Pakistan's commitment not to develop nuclear weapons. While announcing Pakistan's continued adherence to the provisions of the Partial Test Ban Treaty (PTBT), Sahabzada Yaqub expressed Pakistan's readiness to conclude a comprehensive test ban in South Asia.[31]

Pakistan's proposal for a regional non-proliferation arrangement was also dealt with by Yaqub Khan when he explained the general framework for a regional agreement as follows:

The obligations to be assumed by the regional states could be given legally binding effect in one of several ways. A regional treaty, similar to those establishing nuclear free zones in Latin America and the South Pacific, is perhaps the most attractive option. Alternately, those South Asian states which are outside the NPT could accede to it simultaneously. Or, unilateral declarations made by each of the South Asian states could be recognized and endorsed by the UN Security Council in a legally binding resolution.[32]

'A Third View' was presented by an American expert Rodney Jones. While commenting on Pakistan's policy he said that:

> Pakistan's policy expressed readiness to accept any of a list of specified bilateral or multilateral non-proliferation arrangements, or to consider any new proposals, provided only that India would join on equal terms, is a formally flexible position that deserves to be tested. The pre-requisite is India's response in kind...India seems loath to accept a bilateral non-proliferation agreement with Pakistan. This is usually declaimed as implying, invidiously, some sort of 'equation' of India with much smaller and weaker Pakistan. If this argument is taken at face value, it would signify that India's aspirations for power and status overwhelm its willingness to pay any significant price to check proliferation by Pakistan.[33]

Jones also criticized a proposal circulating in unofficial Indian circles for a 'mutual nuclear non-use pledge'. His basic objection to this proposal was that it implicitly accepted the possession of nuclear weapons by the regional states, while asking the concerned parties to denounce their use or threat of use against other regional states. He argued the case for both India and Pakistan to renounce the production, testing or deployment of nuclear weapons against each other for a specified period, and their renewal of this pledge after specified intervals. Jones believed that such an arrangement would bind the two countries in a bilateral agreement without impinging on their declared policies, which, in any case were based on the renunciation of nuclear weapons.[34]

He did not see any possibility of a breakthrough in the future with regard to the acceptance of the NPT by India or Pakistan or both, when he said that:

> The grand design or global solutions of the NPT and the formal non-proliferation regime face practical impediments in the context of India and Pakistan, at least for the foreseeable future, though they have taken root in most other non-nuclear states in South Asia and its neighbouring regions, and remain the preferred outcomes as far as the major powers are concerned.......Hence, the practical point of departure in the subcontinent for a non-proliferation outcome must

be a political solution between the two near nuclear states that arrests
the pressures to become committed to nuclear weapons programmes
and deployments.........But the critical choices lie in India and
Pakistan. The first steps are necessarily bilateral.[35]

PAKISTANI PROPOSAL FOR A FIVE-NATION NON-PROLIFERATION CONFERENCE

During his address to the National Defence College on 6 June
1991, Prime Minister Nawaz Sharif presented a fresh proposal to
address the issue of nuclear proliferation in the South Asian region.
It may be appropriate to quote the relevant extracts from his
speech, as reported in the national media. The Prime Minister
said:

> I would like to propose specifically that the United States, the Soviet
> Union and China consult and meet with India and Pakistan to discuss
> and resolve the issue of nuclear proliferation in South Asia. The aim
> of the meeting should be to arrive at an agreement for keeping this
> region free of nuclear weapons on the basis of proposals already made
> or new ideas that may emerge. The nuclear non-proliferation regime
> to be negotiated during the proposed multilateral consultations should
> be equitable and non-discriminatory. We hope that the proposals
> would receive an early response from the countries concerned so that
> the arrangement can be finalized and the conference held as quickly as
> possible.[36]

This proposal by Nawaz Sharif was in line with the policy
Pakistan had been advocating since 1974, for a bilateral or a
regional solution to create a nuclear weapons-free zone in South
Asia. However, the new elements which were introduced into the
proposal were designed to counter the Indian objections, i.e. that
it was not the nuclear threat from Pakistan which concerned them
but the one posed by China, and unless the Chinese were also
bound by such an agreement, it would not be acceptable to them.
Secondly, India had stressed that a nuclear weapons free zone in
South Asia would be meaningless, till a time when American and

Russian nuclear weapons were deployed within striking range of the South Asian region. By involving the two major powers, as well as China, an effort was being made to effectively address the Indian objections.

The proposal was welcomed by China, the Soviet Union and the United States. The Indian government, however, dismissed the proposal out of hand, dubbing it another political ploy by Pakistan to divert the attention from its nuclear activities. The follow-on 5+2 proposals, to include Britain and France, and 5+2+2 to additionally include Germany and Japan, were also summarily dismissed by India.

India–Pakistan and the CTBT

The CTBT was basically conceived as a means to check any 'Vertical Proliferation'. The major powers' interest in implementing a comprehensive test ban can be attributed to a lack of any incentive for further accumulation, or qualitative improvement, in their nuclear stockpiles at the end of the Cold War. At the same time, having failed to secure the consent of the threshold states to join the NPT, they saw the CTBT as a means to curb any qualitative development of their rudimentary first generation nuclear warheads. Another potential benefit would be that the Chinese plans to modernize their relatively unsophisticated nuclear warheads and delivery systems would also be halted in their tracks. Ironically India, despite being the co-sponsor of the UN Resolution for the commencement of negotiations for a CTBT, assumed the role of a spoiler. India's objections to the CTBT were mainly on the following grounds:

- Firstly, it objected to the scope of the treaty, which prohibited all kinds of nuclear explosive tests but did not put a ban on sub-critical, laboratory and hydro-nuclear testing and computer simulations. These would allow the major powers to continue qualitative improvements in their arsenals.

- Secondly, India objected to the treaty because it did not include a time-tabled commitment from the established nuclear weapon powers towards complete nuclear disarmament.

- Thirdly, India criticized the 'Entry Into Force' (EIF) provision of the treaty, in which ratification of the treaty by 44 named states, including India, was to be a pre-requisite for its EIF. India considered it an infringement of its sovereign right to decide whether or not to join an international treaty.

By conducting nuclear explosive tests in May 1998, India openly flouted the norm against nuclear testing established by the CTBT, and the informal moratorium being observed by the P-5. Many Indian analysts believe that with the finalization of the CTBT, despite India's reservations, the window of opportunity for India to establish its credentials as a nuclear weapons power was rapidly closing, and thus forced India to conduct its Shakti series of tests in May of 1998. After the tests, India announced a unilateral moratorium on further nuclear tests and expressed its readiness to discuss all issues related to non-proliferation.[37] It also announced that it was prepared to abide by some provisions of the CTBT. A noted Indian analyst, Kanti Bajpai, has criticized India's statement regarding its willingness to abide by some provisions of the treaty, since the CTBT basically has two main obligations, i.e. not to conduct nuclear test explosions and not to encourage others in doing so. It is far from clear as to what is really meant by adherence to parts of the treaty.[38]

The Indian prime minister, during his address to UNGA in September 1998, expressed his country's willingness to sign the treaty in due course. However, following the collapse of his coalition government, he expressed his inability to take a decision in this regard until after the new elections. With the return to power of the BJP in October 1999, the Indian Foreign Minister, Jaswant Singh, declared that the government was trying to obtain a national consensus on the issue before taking a final decision on CTBT. It was widely expected that India would announce its accession to the CTBT during President Clinton's visit to India in early 2000. By then, as a result of the refusal of the Republican dominated US Senate to ratify the treaty, the US President had lost the moral authority needed to press India for its signature on the treaty. With the advent of the Bush administration, its known distaste for multilateral arms control agreements, and its antipathy towards the CTBT, it was no longer an issue on the international non-proliferation agenda. There was, therefore, no pressure or compulsion for India to sign the treaty. Neither has there been any domestic debate on the issue with a view to achieve a national consensus. Although India has stuck to its unilateral moratorium on testing since May 1998, it is not willing to accept any binding commitments in this regard. This is evident from the fact that during the course of the ongoing composite dialogue between India and Pakistan, India turned down a Pakistani proposal to convert their respective unilateral moratoria into a bilateral moratorium on nuclear testing, and instead insisted on the reiteration of unilateral moratoria.[39] Strong opposition has also been expressed by various shades of political opinion, as well as retired scientists, against attempts by some US congressmen to seek an Indian commitment not to conduct any further nuclear tests as a quid pro quo for the Peaceful Nuclear Cooperation agreement.

Pakistan, despite its support for the objectives of the CTBT, and having played a constructive role in the formulation of the treaty, expressed its inability to sign until India also signed. This linkage with India has been the main plank of Pakistan's policy towards both NPT and CTBT. However, after having conducted its own nuclear tests, for a time there appeared to be a visible change in Pakistan's stance, at least with regard to the CTBT. This took the form of the apparent de-linking of its policy from that of India. Pakistan indicated that its decision whether or not to accede to the CTBT would be based on its own supreme national interest, irrespective of the Indian decision. Foreign Secretary Shamshad Ahmad alluded to the possibility of Pakistan finally deciding to put its signatures on the CTBT. He is reported to have said: 'Pakistan has no problem with acceding to the CTBT as the treaty was finalized with Pakistan's support. We will decide the time when we are absolutely sure that our vital security concerns have been safeguarded'.[40] This was followed by the commitment by the Prime Minister of Pakistan on the floor of UN General Assembly in September 1998, that Pakistan would accede to the treaty by September 1999, provided a 'coercion free' atmosphere was created by way of the lifting of all sanctions applied against Pakistan. Unfortunately, the sanctions, including the infamous Pressler Amendment, were not lifted by the US, thereby, making it difficult for Pakistan to take the final decision.

PAKISTAN'S DOMESTIC DEBATE ON CTBT

Pakistan had taken policy decisions on whether or not to join an international arms control/disarmament treaty without any domestic public debate whatsoever in the past. CTBT is, however, unique in the way it evokes an animated and wide-ranging domestic debate and the kind of public interest it arouses. For instance, though it gained public acceptability, the decision to stay out of NPT was taken by the government of Pakistan without any public discourse on the issue. Similarly, not many people in Pakistan knew of Pakistan's accession to the Biological Weapons Convention, or even the signing of the Chemical Weapons Convention (CWC). The CWC, with its intrusive verification regime, only became a subject of debate at the time of its ratification, but even then the debate remained confined to statements by some scientists and retired military officers, who were concerned about the possible misuse of its verification provisions. This lack of informed debate on issues having serious national security implications can be attributed to many factors, among them low literacy levels, weak and under-developed national institutions, and the non-existence of a culture of public debate on security issues until the late 1980s.

Pakistan had been emphasizing the need for a CTBT since its signature of the PTBT in 1963. However, in view of the ongoing nuclear arms race between the super powers, and the frequent testing of newer weapon designs at the time, the idea was not granted the importance it should have been due. Later on, more concerned with India's growing nuclear potential, Pakistan even proposed a bilateral test ban agreement with India. Prime Minister Mohammad Khan Junejo, in his address to the UN General Assembly in 1987, declared that:

> ...Pakistan does not wish to conduct a nuclear explosion...is prepared to go further and subscribe to comprehensive test ban in a global, regional or bilateral context. In June this year, I proposed to Prime Minister Rajiv Gandhi that Pakistan and India should conclude a bilateral nuclear test ban treaty. I look forward to a positive response. The conclusion of such a bilateral test ban agreement between Pakistan and India would serve to assure each other and the world that neither country has any intention of pursuing the nuclear weapons option.[41]

When the negotiations for a CTBT commenced in the CD in Geneva around the mid-1990s, Pakistan actively participated in the deliberations and made positive contributions towards its finalization. When the Treaty was moved to the General Assembly in the form of a resolution Pakistan voted in its favour. However, Pakistan could not sign the treaty in view of India's refusal to do so. Pakistan's fears were vindicated when India conducted multiple nuclear tests on 11 and 13 May 1998, forcing Pakistan to respond by demonstrating its own nuclear prowess, in order to restore the strategic balance in the region. After the May 1998 tests Pakistan announced a unilateral moratorium on nuclear testing. In a statement, Foreign Secretary Shamshad Ahmad suggested that, 'Pakistan and India could formalize their unilateral moratoriums into a binding bilateral agreement'.[42]

A botched attempt was made by the Sharif government to develop a consensus on the divisive issue of signing the CTBT, by placing it for debate before a joint session of both houses of the Pakistan parliament in September 1998.[43] The purpose behind this move was ostensibly to strengthen the prime minister's hand by gaining the backing of parliament before his address at the UN General Assembly session. During the three-day debate prominent scientists such as Dr A.Q. Khan and Dr Samar Mubarakmand were invited to brief the legislators on the technical issues involved, and the implications of signing the treaty on the future of Pakistan's nuclear weapons programme.[44] The purpose behind inviting the scientists was not really to educate the parliament members on the technicalities of the treaty, but to alleviate their concerns with regard to government intentions, and to convince them that it would not impinge upon Pakistan's nuclear capability. However, the debate remained directionless, confused and acrimonious. The opposition members staged a walkout even before the 'winding-up' speech by the foreign minister, and two prominent parties, the PPP and the Pakhtun nationalist Awami National Party, did not take part in the deliberations. Many members of the ruling party, while eulogizing the prime minister for initiating a debate on this key issue, nevertheless opposed accession to the treaty. Some members even demanded of the government that it should link the signing of the CTBT with the resolution of the Kashmir dispute. The fact that the government, which had made known its decision to lay before the House a draft resolution seeking authorization to take an appropriate decision on the issue in the best national interest, finally decided to drop this idea, is a clear indication of the lack of consensus in parliament.[45] In fact, no substantive discussion took place on the subject matter of the treaty and it turned so unsavoury and embarrassing for the government that the debate was suddenly terminated after four days, without reaching any conclusion.[46] Minister of State for Foreign Affairs, Mumtaz Kanju, responding to opposition members' accusations of a sell-out by the government on CTBT, reminded them that in 1996, when CTBT was put to a vote in UN General Assembly, the Benazir Bhutto government had taken a decision to vote for it, without taking Parliament into confidence.[47]

Despite his failure to gain parliamentary support Prime Minister Nawaz Sharif, in his address to UN General Assembly in September 1998, hinted at Pakistan's readiness to sign the CTBT by the next General Assembly session, pending the lifting of all sanctions imposed on Pakistan.[48] Unfortunately, the sanctions remained in force, and Pakistan subsequently backed off from its earlier position. Foreign Secretary Shamshad Ahmad, while briefing the newsmen at the conclusion of his two day talks with US Deputy Secretary of State Strobe Talbott in November 1998, said that, 'Pakistan has told the US it will not sign the CTBT under duress or in a coercive atmosphere of sanctions'.[49] Interestingly, at that time voices in support of signing the CTBT were emanating from unexpected quarters. General Aslam Beg, who was generally known for his hawkish views on national security issues, stated at a public meeting that the signing of the CTBT would not harm Pakistan's nuclear capability, and went on to add that even if the FMCT was concluded, Pakistan's nuclear capability would not be affected.[50]

Another interesting aspect of the debate was that many of the most vocal opponents based their arguments on hypothetical scenarios, such as hordes of international inspectors barging into any and every Pakistani nuclear facility they wished, under the guise of CTBT verification mechanism, thereby, raising public concerns about the negative consequences of signing the treaty. Many of them had not even bothered to read the text of the treaty, much less understood it. At the same time, some scientists and technical experts expressed strong reservations about the negative ramifications of accession to CTBT. Sultan Bashiruddin Mahmood, then a senior serving nuclear scientist who is credited with the design and construction of the Khushab Reactor and is known for his strong religious leanings, was among the most ardent critics of the CTBT. He believed that the signing of the CTBT would be the first step towards the eventual denuclearization of Pakistan, unless its nuclear status was recognized beforehand. Failing this pre-cognition, 'Pakistan would have to pay a very heavy price'. He went on to argue that after the CTBT, Pakistan would be asked to sign the FMCT, followed by the NPT and finally asked to roll back its nuclear programme.[51] His public outburst cost him his job in the Atomic Energy Commission,[52] but this so called 'slippery slope' argument was taken up by many others as the most potent weapon against the proponents of the CTBT. Not that he was alone among the scientific community in his scepticism. A long serving former chairman of the Pakistan Atomic Energy Commission and a well respected scientist, Munir Ahmad Khan, also expressed his opposition, but on technical grounds. According to Munir Khan, 'Any claim that the CTBT will not adversely affect the further development of Pakistan's nuclear capability is, therefore wrong. If it were so, the US and others would not insist on India and Pakistan signing the CTBT....CTBT is aimed at keeping the level of Indian and Pakistani arsenals to that of the mid-1960s'.[53] Professor Khurshid Ahmad, a prominent leader of the Jamaat-i-Islami, accusing the government of trying to de-link the nuclear deterrence from India and the Kashmir issue, termed the CTBT as the only 'gateway to total de-nuclearization' and characterized the de-linkage as 'nothing short of a betrayal'.[54]

In the early part of 1999, a new external factor appeared to have an impact on the CTBT debate, besides the internal issues and the politico-diplomatic pressure being exerted by the US. The Japanese Economic Affairs Minister, on a visit to Pakistan, announced that, 'Japan wants Pakistan should sign CTBT as it is necessary for overall peace in the region. It is only after it signs the CTBT that new loans and grants could be given for various welfare projects'.[55] This statement by a minister, from a country which had been the largest source of economic assistance to Pakistan for many decades, was very significant at a time when Pakistan was in dire economic straits, owing to the sanctions imposed in the aftermath of its May 1998 nuclear tests. The anti-CTBT lobbies projected it as an attempt at economic pressure of Pakistan by Japan at the behest of United States. They argued that Pakistan could not compromise on its vital security interests for the sake of an annual dole of $500 million.

In the wake of the Brownback Amendment entitled: 'India–Pakistan Relief Act of 1998' easing some sanctions on India and Pakistan related to agriculture, rural development, food and drug administration and related agencies, Foreign Minister Sartaj Aziz, speaking on the floor of the National Assembly, hinted at the possibility of Pakistan signing the CTBT even before September 1999. The foreign minister said that, 'there is already some good progress towards creating a conducive environment. It is worth mentioning that since last September, when Pakistan faced unjustified sanctions, the coercive atmosphere has eased'.[56] By May 1999 two new and critical developments had taken place. Firstly, the Vajpayee led coalition government in India had fallen, making it uncertain that India would sign the treaty until after the new government was firmly in the saddle, probably towards the end of the 1999, and secondly the Kargil conflict had erupted across the Line of Control in the disputed Kashmir region. Against this backdrop Prime Minister Nawaz Sharif, speaking at the National Defence College, reiterated Pakistan's readiness to sign CTBT, in a pressure free atmosphere and said that at the same time it could not remain unmindful of the changes in the region affecting its security.[57]

The ungainly manner in which the Nawaz government extricated itself from the Kargil crisis, and the consequent flak it drew from the political opposition and general public alike, made its political position very precarious. It found itself in a situation in which it just could not afford to take yet another unpopular decision. The signs of change became visible when, briefing newsmen at the Pakistan High Commission in London after his meeting with British Foreign Secretary Robin Cook, Foreign Minister Sartaj Aziz reverted to the old theme by stating that Pakistan could not sign the CTBT unless sanctions were lifted.[58] On 17 August 1999 India announced what it termed as its 'Draft Nuclear Doctrine', which was seen as very ambitious and provocative by Pakistan. Speaking at the Institute of Strategic Studies in Islamabad on the subject of 'India's Nuclear Doctrine: Implications for Regional and Global Peace and Security', Foreign Secretary Shamshad Ahmad said: '… The very possibility that India may conduct further nuclear tests creates doubts in Pakistan regarding the advisability of our early adherence to the CTBT. If India does conduct further nuclear tests, this will once again oblige Pakistan to respond'. However, he added that: '…Pakistan and India could formalize their unilateral moratorium into binding bilateral arrangement'.[59]

This statement by the most senior Pakistani diplomat was very significant from many points of view. The timing, on the eve of the forthcoming UN General Assembly meeting where Prime Minister Sharif was expected to announce Pakistan's accession to the Treaty, virtually ruled out that possibility. The statement also made clear that the de-linking of Pakistan's policy on CTBT from that of India, which had been effected after the May 1998 tests, had been abandoned. At the same time reports appeared in the national press suggesting that, besides security considerations, domestic politics was now emerging as the most important reason for Sharif's dithering on the issue of signing the CTBT.[60] Shamshad Ahmad's statement also pre-empted any decision by the Defence Committee of the Cabinet (DCC) due to meet on 10 September 1999 to deliberate upon the pros and cons of Nawaz Sharif's imminent visit to the UN, and the issue of whether or not to sign the CTBT.[61] During the DCC meeting, the prime minister announced his decision to cancel his visit to New York, which was a clear signal that Pakistan had decided not to sign the CTBT in the near future.[62] This view was widely held, despite the foreign secretary's clarification that the cancellation of prime minister's visit to the United Nations had no direct bearing on Pakistan's decision on whether or not to sign the treaty before 30 September 1999.[63]

A few days later the secretary general of the Jamaat-i-Islami, Syed Munawwar Hassan, alleged that Nawaz Sharif had made a commitment to roll back the nuclear programme in his July 1999 meeting with President Clinton.[64] Other Islamist parties joined in the chorus.[65] Responding to queries by journalists, CJCS and army chief, General Musharraf expressed the hope that the government would take a decision concerned with signing the CTBT in the best national interest. Denying that there was pressure from the Pakistan army on the government not to sign the CTBT, he said that the armed forces strongly believed that any government decision in this regard would be in keeping with the best national interest.[66] While denying that Pakistan was adding new qualifications to its position, Foreign Minister Sartaj Aziz, in an address at the Woodrow Wilson Center, said that Pakistan would not sign the CTBT until there was further easing of the US sanctions.[67] However, despite India's decision not to attend the meeting, Pakistan decided to attend the CTBT Review Conference, held in Vienna in October 1999, as an observer in order to signal its continued interest in the treaty.[68]

THE SECOND CTBT DEBATE

The US Senate rejected the ratification of CTBT on 14 October 1999, thereby adding a new element into the discourse on the issue. This decision by the Senate was frequently referred to by the opponents of the treaty. An unnamed senior official of the Pakistan government commented that, 'for all practical purposes the treaty is dead as there is no chance for the US administration to get a two-thirds majority vote'.[69] Nevertheless President Clinton warned Pakistan and India not to see the rejection of the CTBT by the US Senate as a sign of lack of interest on part of Washington, saying that, 'Do not take yesterday's vote as a sign that America doesn't care whether you resume nuclear testing and build up your nuclear arsenal. We do care. You should not do it.'[70] On 12 October 1999, the military took over the reins of government in Pakistan. In his address to the nation on 17 October 1999, Chief Executive General Musharraf gave a glimpse of his prospective policy stating that: 'Pakistan has always been alive to international non-proliferation concerns. I wish to assure the world community that while preserving its vital security interests Pakistan will continue to pursue a policy of nuclear and missile restraint and sensitivity to global non-proliferation and disarmament objectives'.[71] However, in his maiden press conference, General Musharraf said that he had more pressing issues than CTBT on his agenda.[72] A subtle shift in Pakistan's stance, bringing in regional stability as a new factor, was also discernible from the statement by Ambassador Munir Akram in the First Committee of UNGA, in which, while reiterating Pakistan's positive approach towards CTBT, he said, 'its disarmament policies are inevitably interlinked with its priority objective of promoting regional peace, security and stability'.[73]

Foreign Minister Abdul Sattar, who took on the responsibility of steering Pakistan's policy on CTBT, in his first Press Conference reaffirmed Pakistan's moratorium on further testing, amplifying that, 'in essence Islamabad would observe the spirit of the treaty as it had no plans to take provocative steps on nuclear issues in general and on CTBT in particular'.[74] In a keynote address at the Institute of Strategic Studies in Islamabad, he outlined Pakistan's policy parameters in great detail, stating that:

> We did not sign the CTBT only because India's opposition to the treaty raised suspicions about its intentions. Our apprehensions proved to be correct. On 11 and 13 May 1998, India conducted multiple nuclear explosions. Immediately, warmongers in New Delhi hurled threats against our country. It became necessary to demonstrate that, Pakistan too, possessed nuclear capability. However, having made that point Pakistan declared a moratorium on further testing.[75]

Commenting on the impact of the refusal of the US Senate to ratify the treaty, and its repercussions on the future prospects of CTBT, Sattar said that, 'The prospects of the treaty entering into force have dimmed because the US has rejected ratification. The world must hope that the Senate will reverse itself. But never before has it done so after having rejected a treaty'.[76]

Referring to Pakistan's positive vote for CTBT in the UNGA in September 1996, and in a bid to convince the sceptics that the signing of the CTBT would not curtail Pakistan's options to respond to any future Indian nuclear tests, he argued that, if the earlier vote in favour of CTBT did not prevent Pakistan from responding to Indian nuclear tests in May 1998, the signing of the treaty would also not in any way restrict Pakistan's options to react to any more Indian tests. He also assured the audience that the government had no intentions of taking a hasty decision in favour or against signing the treaty, in view of the importance of the issue, adding that for any decision domestic consensus would be a pre-requisite.[77]

Sattar's speech shifted the emphasis from demanding a coercion free atmosphere before Pakistan could sign the treaty, to the need to evolve a domestic consensus, and thus triggered a renewed debate on the issue. At this moment, a new factor entered the reckoning of the policy makers, by way of India's signing of the treaty in the near future, probably during President Clinton's proposed visit to India at the beginning of 2000. The foremost question then was whether Pakistan should follow India's lead, or take the initiative and sign the treaty before India in order to gain some political mileage and probably some economic reprieve. Apparently, the government mapped out a strategy to take key political parties into its confidence, while debating the issue at various assemblies such as the Foreign Policy Advisory Group (FPAG),[78] a disparate group of former diplomats, retired military officers, journalists and academics. However, when the issue was placed before the FPAG, two of its members, Pervez Hoodbhoy, an academic and an anti nuclear lobbyist, and Nasim Zehra, a journalist and security analyst, brought their differences into the public domain through newspaper articles, thereby triggering a premature public debate before the necessary spadework had been done.[79] Dispelling rumours about Pakistan's signing the CTBT, on 15 January 2000 General Musharraf said that, 'it was a sensitive issue and technical, domestic political and international diplomatic aspects had to be examined thoroughly'. He urged the journalists to generate a debate on the issue, so that the government could be informed by a useful public input. He also explained that any decision with regard to the CTBT would be taken in Pakistan's own national interest emphasising that there had been no re-linking of the decision with India's actions.[80]

The wisdom of the government's decision to initiate a public debate on an issue whose technicalities could not be comprehended by many analysts and so-called experts, in a society with low literacy rates, and as politically and socially polarized as Pakistan, is difficult to fathom. Dr Rasul Baksh Rais very aptly summed up the situation saying that:

> Like the nuclear programme, the subject of signing the CTBT has become unnecessarily politicized, which shows primacy of politics over all other issues that may concern our collective well being...the traditional attitude of our political rank and file in rejecting whatever is proposed by the government, without looking at the merits of each

case, creates policy gridlock, disabling us from pursuing a rational agenda of national interest.[81]

The debate raged on, with both sides sticking to their guns and hurling accusations at each other. In a seminar held by Institute of Policy Studies in Islamabad, Foreign Minister Abdul Sattar said that, 'not signing the CTBT has identifiable costs but no benefits, whereas signing has no identifiable costs even though the benefits, too, are more intangible than concrete.' However, General (retired) Hameed Gul rejected the idea saying, 'there is a consensus against the treaty and the people will not tolerate signing it'.[82] Chief of Jamaat-i-Islami, Qazi Hussain Ahmad, warned the military government of the dangerous consequences of the decision to sign the CTBT, terming it an attempt to sabotage Pakistan's nuclear programme. After this the debate continued for a while, but remained inconclusive, and gradually tapered off through the following months, especially in view of the fact that India's expected signatures during Clinton's visit failed to materialize, and with the advent of the Bush administration it became a dead issue. Pakistan's current policy on CTBT can be summed up in three sentences as follows:

- Pakistan was not the first to start testing.
- It will not be the first to resume testing.
- It will not stand in the way of the implementation of this treaty.[83]

POLICIES ON FMCT

During negotiations with the US interlocutors in CD at Geneva, and in the wake of their nuclear explosions in May 1998, both India and Pakistan agreed that they would allow the negotiations for a Fissile Materials Cut Off Treaty to proceed. Both countries have been participating in the negotiations held on this subject at Geneva since that time. Due to conflicting interests, the demands of the major powers and the developing countries represented by the G-21, negotiations for an FMCT have made no progress since 1999. To begin with, it was the Chinese and Russian concerns over US plans to deploy National and Theatre Missile Defence Systems which held back the negotiations. The Russian opposition softened slightly after their agreement with the US to scrap the 1972 ABM Treaty, however the Chinese remained firm in their insistence on the inclusion of 'Prevention of Arms Race in Outer Space' (PAROS) in CD's agenda and commencement of parallel negotiations on this issue alongside the FMCT. The G-21, representing the Third World countries, has also been insisting on the inclusion of issues such as security guarantees and nuclear disarmament in the negotiating agenda side by side with the FMCT. Recently, when the Chinese agreed to the 'Amorim proposals' for resumption of dialogue in the CD, the US started insisting on a non-verifiable fissile materials treaty, which amounted to crippling the prospective treaty, and this created new fissures among the members of the CD. It would only be possible to take up the technical issues such as the scope of the treaty, and the negotiating mandate for its conclusion, once the procedural and political issues were out of the way. The US inclination against freely negotiated multilateral treaties is a major hurdle, and unless there is a fundamental change in the current policy, the chances of an FMCT coming to fruition seem to be very bleak.

As part of the recent India–US nuclear deal, both sides have agreed to work towards the finalization of an FMCT. However, there are major differences of approach between the two countries, especially on the issue of verification. Pakistan has continued to declare its intention to go along with the consensus at the CD on the issue of FMCT. However, as pointed out by many experts, a serious consequence of the US–India nuclear agreement would be a substantial increase in Indian fissile material production capability. The mere fact that India insisted, and has succeeded, in keeping eight of its existing nuclear power plants out of IAEA safeguards, besides its dedicated military nuclear facilities, is a pointer in that direction. Currently India has CIRUS, a 40 MW reactor, and Dhruva, with a capacity of 100 MW, as its main sources of fissile material production. Assuming that these reactors run at 70 per cent capacity, their total annual output is approximately 36 kg of plutonium. By contrast each of the eight power reactors kept out of safeguards is of 220 MW capacity, and running at the same efficiency as that of CIRUS and Dhruva, can produce 56 kg of plutonium per annum. If all of these eight reactors are used for fissile material production, their combined annual yield would amount to a staggering 448 kg annually, worth about 75–90 additional weapons per year. This would be more than twelve times the current annual production of fissile material in India.

The proponents of the US–India nuclear agreement, such as Ashley Tellis, argue that these plants were currently not under safeguards, and if India had wanted to use these for fissile material production it could have done so. But what they omit to mention is the fact that, though theoretically possible, this was practically unattainable due to the acute shortage of uranium in India. When the Indians start receiving American supplied nuclear fuel for their safeguarded plants, however, they would be able to use their domestic uranium resources for the production of plutonium in these reactors. Unless the FMCT is implemented within next few years, which at this moment appears highly unlikely, the Indians would have an overwhelming advantage in terms of fissile material stocks vis-à-vis Pakistan. This would seriously erode the credibility of Pakistan's nuclear deterrence. In that eventuality, Pakistan may be forced to reconsider its current stance on FMCT and distance itself from the treaty, until it has ensured that it could adequately meet the requirements of its credible minimum deterrence, despite a substantial increase in India's fissile materials production.

PORTENTS OF THE FUTURE

In the post-1998 environment, Pakistan is obviously not in a position to revert to its traditional stance on NPT, and it is not possible any more for it to join the NPT as a non-nuclear weapon state. Neither will India do so. The NPT structure, rooted in the realities of another era, is not flexible enough to accommodate the reality of nuclearization of India and Pakistan as well as Israel's current nuclear status. The six-party talks have succeeded in convincing the North Koreans to dismantle their nuclear capability, averting the possibility of the further deterioration of the regional security environment. Given the very complex amendment procedure for the NPT, and the fear that the pandora's box, once opened, would be difficult to close again, the challenge for the international community now is to find some innovative ways to ensure some kind of an associate membership of the NPT for India and Pakistan and possibly Israel as well. As far back as 1993, before the NPT Review and Extension Conference, and well before overt nuclearization by India and Pakistan, analysts such as Paul Doty and Steven Flank had suggested that:

> The 1995 Conference might consider a one time admission of new nuclear weapon states (Pakistan, India and Israel) to the Treaty, in return for a strengthened prohibition against the transfer of weapons or technology to non-weapons states and for increased transparency for all nuclear programmes.[84]

Such ideas have also been explored by analysts, including Avner Cohen and Thomas Graham Jr., suggesting the formulation of an additional protocol to the NPT. This would recognize the nuclear status of India, Pakistan and Israel by granting some sort of an associate membership to these countries in return for the assumption of some of the obligations of the states party to the NPT.[85] In a similar vein John Simpson, highlighting the problem of the status of Israel, India, and Pakistan has raised two questions:

> Firstly, whether they [India and Pakistan] can be persuaded to act in the non-proliferation policy area as though they were recognized nuclear weapon states, and secondly, whether the NPT and the regime can operate indefinitely on the basis of a legal agreement that is patently at odds with the situation on the ground i.e. that there are no additional nuclear weapons states beyond the NPT five and those outside can only enter the treaty as non-nuclear weapon states.[86]

The 2005 NPT Review Conference was expected to provide an opportunity for exploring such initiatives. However, the review conference got entangled into competing interests and serious differences in approach between the NWS and the NNWS parties to the NPT and unfortunately in ended in acrimony without achieving any positive results.

The US–India agreement for cooperation in civil nuclear technology, which has been passed by Congress as a law to incorporate necessary amendments into the Atomic Energy Act of 1954, to enable its implementation, is being touted by the Bush administration as a means of bringing India into the fold of the non-proliferation regime. It is yet to be seen whether it will only facilitate India's access to civil nuclear technology or would go beyond it, to create a niche for India in the NPT itself by granting some kind of recognition of its nuclear status. The question then would arise as to whether it is possible or indeed advisable to accommodate India alone and leave Pakistan out in the cold. Such a short-sighted policy will neither be good for the health of the non-proliferation regime nor for the regional stability in South Asia.

Within the ambit of the ongoing composite dialogue, India and Pakistan have discussed the nuclear and missiles related issues, and have agreed on some CBMs as well. The question now is that, with the preferential treatment being given to India by the US and the efforts being made by some elements, both within as well as outside the US administration, to build India up as a strategic counter-weight to China, would India have any incentives to negotiate nuclear stabilization measures with Pakistan, or would it further harden its attitude and policies? Either way the outcome is going to have far-reaching consequences for the future of South Asia.

NOTES

1. Robert G. Joseph, 'WMD: A Proliferation Overview', in Stuart E. Johnson and William H. Lewis (eds.), *Weapons of Mass Destruction: New Perspectives on Counter Proliferation*, National Defence University Press, Washington

D.C., 1995. Also see Woodrow Wilson Center for Scholars, Working Paper No. 99, Mitchell Reiss and Harald Muller (eds.), Washington D.C., January 1995.

2. See a highly critical article by two Democratic Senators, Carl Levin and Jack Reed, 'Toward a More Responsible Nuclear Strategy', *Arms Control Today*, January/February 2004.

3. Statement by Pakistan's Permanent Representative to the UNSC, Ambassador Munir Akram, *The News*, Islamabad, 24 April 2004.

4. George Bunn, 'The Non-proliferation Treaty: History and Current Problems', *Arms Control Today*, December 2003.

5. Simon Tisdall, 'Gulf States intention is warning to Bush', *Dawn*, Karachi, 13 December 2006. http://Dawn.com.

6. Sanger & Broad, ibid.

7. Marvin Miller and Lawrence Scheinman, 'Israel, India and Pakistan: Engaging the Non-NPT States in the Non-proliferation Regime,' *Arms Control Today*, December 2003.

8. Ibid.

9. 'Curbing Nuclear Proliferation', an interview with Mohammad El Baradei, *Arms Control Today*, November 2003. Also see article by ELBaradei in the 16 October 2003 issue of *The Economist*.

10. See a critique of PSI by Brahma Chellaney, 'Bush's PSI-Counter-proliferation versus non-proliferation', *The Daily Times*, Lahore, 24 April 2004.

11. 'India, US sign framework for defence cooperation', *The Hindu*, New Delhi, 30 June 2005. http://www.thehindu.com. hindu.com/2005/06/30/stories/2005063004261200.htm

12. Daniela Deane, 'Bush Signs Nuclear Deal with India', *The Washington Post*, 18 December 2006.

13. 'India, US sign framework for defence cooperation', op. cit.

14. See Statement by Pakistan's Foreign Office Spokesman Masood Khan on 28 April 2004.

15. Rodney W. Jones, 'Pakistan's Nuclear Posture: Quest for Assured Nuclear Deterrence—A Conjecture', *Regional Studies*, Vol. XVIII, No. 2, Spring 2000, Institute of Regional Studies, Islamabad, p. 26.

16. Abdul Sattar, address at the National Defence College, Islamabad, 24 May 2000.

17. B.M. Kaushik and D.N. Mehrotra, *Pakistan's Nuclear Bomb*, Sopan Publishing House, New Delhi, 1989, p. 48.

18. Ibid., p. 49.

19. Ibid., pp. 49–50.

20. K. Subrahmanyam, in Marwah & Schulz eds., p. 127.

21. M. Rasgotra, 'Non-Proliferation Issues: The South Asian Context', *Strategic Studies*, Summer & Autumn 1987, ISS, Islamabad, pp. 82–3.

22. Ibid., p. 83.

23. Ibid., p. 85.

24. Ibid., pp. 84, 86.
25. *The Asian Age*, New Delhi, 21 May 1998.
26. Miller and Scheinman, op. cit. Also see John Simpson, 'The Nuclear non-proliferation regime; back to the future?', Disarmament Forum-One 2004, UNIDIR, Geneva.
27. Kaushik & Mehrotra, op. cit., p. 49.
28. Ibid., p. 50.
29. Zulfikar Ali Bhutto, *The Myth of Independence*, Oxford University Press, Karachi, 1969, p. 153.
30. Sahabzada Yaqub Khan, in 'Strategic Studies', Summer and Autumn, 1987, Institute of Strategic Studies, Islamabad, p. 16.
31. Ibid., p. 17.
32. Ibid., p. 19.
33. Rodney, W. Jones, 'Non-proliferation Issues: The South Asian Context', *Strategic Studies,* ISS, Islamabad, p. 72.
34. Ibid., p. 73.
35. Ibid., p. 74.
36. *The News,* Islamabad, 7 June 1991.
37. *The Pioneer,* New Delhi, 21 May 1998.
38. *Daily Telegraph*, Calcutta, 16 May 1998.
39. 'Joint Statement, India–Pakistan Expert-Level Talks on Nuclear CBMs', Ministry of External Affairs, New Delhi, 20 June 2004.
40. *The Nation,* Islamabad, 24 July 1998.
41. *Strategic Studies*, Vol. X, No. 4, Summer & Autumn, 1987, ISS, Islamabad, p. 159.
42. Statement by Mr Shamshad Ahmad, Foreign Secretary of Pakistan on 'Indian Nuclear Doctrine: Implications for Regional and Global Peace and Security', at the ISS, Islamabad on 7 September 1999.
43. Arms Control Association, *Arms Control Today*, News Briefs, August/September 1998. [http://www.armscontrol.org/act/1998_08-09/bras98.asp?print] Also see Pakistan Television Corporation Limited, National News Bureau, English News Headlines, 1800 hrs dated 11 September 1998. file://H:\The per cent20Government per cent20of per cent20PakistanENGLISH 19ENG26-1998.htm
44. 'No Harm in Signing the CTBT: Qadeer,' *Pakistan Link*, 25 September 1998, http://www.pakistanlink.com; quoted in Gaurav Kampani, 'CTBT Endgame in South Asia?', Center for Non-proliferation Studies, January 2000.
45. *The Hindustan Times*, 17 September 1998. [defenselink.mil/pubs/prolif 97/so_asia.html]. Pakistan Television Corporation Limited, National News Bureau, English News Headlines, 1800 hrs dated 16 September 1998. file://H:\Eng 16.htm
46. Umer Farooq, 'To sign or not to sign CTBT a million-dollar question', *The News,* Islamabad, 24 December 1999.

47. Associated Press of Pakistan, News Summary, 16 September 1998. file://H:\ The per cent20Government per cent200f per cent20Pakistan3.htm
48. Address by Prime Minister Nawaz Sharif to the 53rd Session of the UN General Assembly on 23 September 1998.
49. 'No CTBT signing under Duress—Shamshad', *The Nation*, Lahore, 7 November 1998.
50. 'CTBT signing not to harm nuke capability: Beg', *Frontier Post*, 8 February 1999.
51. 'Scientist Warns against signing CTBT', *Dawn*, Karachi, 23 September 1998.
52. Gaurav Kampani, op. cit.
53. Munir Ahmad Khan, 'Let us face realities on CTBT,' *The News*, 29 November 1998.
54. 'CTBT only gateway to total denuclearisation: JI Leader', *The News*, Islamabad, 1 May 1999.
55. 'Loans only after Pakistan signs CTBT, says Japan', *The News*, Islamabad, 12 February 1999.
56. 'Sartaj Hints at CTBT signing by September', *The Dawn*, Karachi, 19 March 1999.
57. 'Pakistan ready to sign CTBT, says PM', *The Dawn*, Karachi, 20 May 1999.
58. *The News*, Islamabad, 30 July 1999.
59. *The Nation*, Lahore, 8 September 1999.
60. 'Politics and Defence Worries Nawaz', *The Nation*, Lahore, 10 September 1999.
61. 'DCC discusses CTBT, defence matters today', *The Nation*, Lahore, 10 September 1999.
62. 'CTBT signing unlikely as PM calls off US visit', *The Frontier Post*, Peshawar, 15 September 1999.
63. 'PM's not visiting UN has no bearing on CTBT: Shamshad', *The News*, Islamabad, 10 September 1999.
64. 'Jamaat warns government against signing CTBT', *The News*, Islamabad, 21 September 1999.
65. 'Nawaz warned against signing of CTBT', *The Frontier Post*, Peshawar, 22 September 1999.
66. 'COAS hopes decision in national interest', *The News*, Islamabad, 1 October 1999.
67. 'Pakistan links CTBT signing to lifting of sanctions', *The Dawn*, Karachi, 2 October 1999.
68. 'Islamabad to attend UN's CTBT moot', *The Dawn*, Karachi, 6 October 1999.
69. Quoted in *The News*, Islamabad, 25 November 1999.
70. 'US Warning', *The Dawn*, Karachi, 15 October 1999.

71. General Musharraf's address to the nation as reported in the national newspapers of 18 October 1999.
72. Syed Talat Hussain, 'Pakistan's new CTBT stand', *The Nation*, Lahore, 10 November 1999.
73. 'Pakistan links disarmament to regional stability', *The Nation*, Lahore, 22 October 1999.
74. 'Pakistan to adhere to no first N-testing', *The News*, Islamabad, 9 November 1999.
75. Text of Foreign Minister's Address at Institute of Strategic Studies' Seminar on Pakistan's response to Indian Nuclear Doctrine', *The News*, Islamabad, 26 November 1999.
76. Ibid.
77. Ibid.
78. 'Advisory Group Discusses CTBT signing today', *The News*, Islamabad, 20 December 1999.
79. Nasim Zehra, 'Flawed Policy Moves', *The News*, Islamabad, 24 December 1999. Also see Pervez Hoodbhoy, 'Seven good reasons to sign the CTBT now', *The News*, 23 December, 1999.
80. 'No CTBT signing without consensus, says Musharraf', *The Nation*, Lahore, 25 December 1999.
81. Rasul Baksh Rais, 'One vote for CTBT', *The News*, 25 December 1999.
82. 'Sattar makes strong pitch for CTBT signing', *The News*, Islamabad, 5 January 2000.
83. Keynote Address by Foreign Minister Abdul Sattar at the Carnegie International Non-proliferation Conference: 'New Leaders, New Directions', 18 June 2001, Washington, D.C.
84. Paul Doty and Steven Flank, 'Arms Control for New Nuclear Nations', in Robert D. Blackwill and Albert Carnesale (eds.), *New Nuclear Nations—Consequences for US Policy*, Council on Foreign Relations, New York, 1993, p. 55.
85. Avner Cohen and Thomas Graham Jr., 'An NPT for non-members', *Bulletin of the Atomic Scientists*, May/June 2004, Volume 60, No. 3, pp. 40–44.
86. John Simpson, op. cit., p. 10.

5

Nuclear Delivery Systems

The classic nuclear deterrence structure is based on a triad comprising air delivered weapons, surface to surface missiles and submarine launched ballistic missiles, and it is quite natural for any new entrant into the nuclear club to endeavour to acquire a triad or at least a dyad of nuclear delivery systems to enhance the credibility of its deterrent, and to have flexibility in targeting options. While aircraft, with their greater payload capacity, can deliver even unwieldy first generation nuclear bombs, any missile with a payload capability of 500 kg or over is considered to be nuclear capable. Missiles with much less carrying capacity can also be used for nuclear delivery, but that would require miniaturization of warheads based on more sophisticated designs developed after a series of tests. Once launched, the ballistic missiles cannot be recalled as can aircraft, but with their high speed and trajectory profile, they have a much greater ability to penetrate through enemy air defences as compared to the aircraft. Foolproof defensive systems against longer-range ballistic missiles are extremely costly and complex to devise. As General Thomas Powers, former commander-in-chief of the US Strategic Air Command commented in 1960, 'because of their tremendous speed...ballistic missiles offer a unique advantage to an aggressor who plans a surprise attack'.[1] Other experts also agree that, 'ballistic missiles add to the credibility of classical nuclear deterrence by their near-certainty of arrival'.[2] Their high costs and limited payload capability also makes them more suitable for delivering non-conventional munitions. As an analyst very aptly remarked, '...Using them merely to dump a little high explosive somewhere near their targets is like buying a Ferrari to collect groceries'.[3]

In 1988, during the closing stages of the Iran–Iraq War, ballistic missiles were used on a large scale in the so-called 'war of the cities'. Employment of missiles in the role of weapons of terror was not an entirely new phenomenon in view of the use of V-1 and V-2 rockets by the Germans against London and other British targets during the Second World War. However, due to the fact that Iraq enjoyed an advantage both in terms of numbers as well as reach of missiles, Iran was compelled to accept cessation of hostilities, which it had so stubbornly resisted for many years. India had already taken the lead in introducing ballistic missiles into the South Asia region in February 1988, by test firing its short-range ballistic missile 'Prithvi'. With a range of 150 km and a payload of 1000 kg, Prithvi was powerful enough to carry a nuclear warhead.

Writing in 1991, Janne E. Nolan argued that the development of missiles through adaptation of available technological resources is already taking place in over a dozen third world countries. This development, in her view, had the potential to radically alter the security landscape, which the US and its allies were going to be confronted by at the turn of the twentieth century. Amongst the countries known to have actual or potential ballistic missile development programmes, India and Israel are rated as the most advanced in the fields of space and missile technologies. Pakistan has, in the last decade or so, made considerable advances in this field, and has acquired a proven missile capability with the successful testing and induction of a variety of ballistic missiles and more recently a cruise missile. However, India still retains its edge in space technology.

INDIA'S MISSILE PROGRAMME

After the 1974 nuclear test India did not declare itself a nuclear weapons power. Aside from the politico-economic reasons, this was mainly due to the fact that it seriously lacked the requisite nuclear delivery system. The only possible nuclear delivery platforms available to India at that time were some Second World War vintage Canberra bombers.[4] There were also serious deficiencies in terms of the systems needed to exercise nuclear command and control. Strategic surveillance, target acquisition and early warning systems were also non-existent. A premature pronouncement of nuclear status would not only have lacked credibility, it would have run the risk of inviting a pre-emptive strike from its main rival China, although there is nothing on record to indicate that the Chinese ever considered a preventive or pre-emptive strike against India's nuclear facilities. At that time the Chinese, who were just emerging from the throes of the 'Cultural Revolution', lacked the reach and capability to accomplish such a mission, and after the opening up of relations with the US in the early 1970s, they would not have risked this fledgling relationship by plunging into such precipitate action. Against this backdrop, it was prudent on the part of India to hold back its claim of nuclear status, and focus greater attention towards the development of appropriate delivery means alongside the development of its nuclear weapons potential.

Recognizing the critical importance of space and missile capabilities, the Indians had already initiated a space programme in 1967, and by 1972–73 the first indigenously developed two-stage rocket, 'Rohini-560', was test fired. The space programme was sharply upgraded in the early 1970s, and was closely integrated with the nuclear programme in the famous 'Sarabhai profile', the ten year programme for development of nuclear and space technology announced in 1970 and adopted by the government a year later.[5] In the first half of the 1970s, the space research establishment in India developed and tested various components including the inertial guidance systems, on board computers, rate gyroscopes, heat shields, nose cones and different types of solid and liquid propellants for use in the space rockets. In July 1974, the director of the Indian Space Commission claimed that the country already possessed the ability to produce medium range missiles with locally developed solid fuels and guidance systems.[6] This proved to be a premature and exaggerated claim, as India was only able to test fire its first short range ballistic missile in 1988 and its medium range missile in 1989. In early 1975, a scientific research satellite was also launched from a Soviet Cosmodrome.[7]

In view of the importance of a sophisticated electronics base, for both nuclear as well as the space programmes, important policy decisions were also taken in this field. In 1972 the newly created 'Electronics Commission' and the 'Department of Electronics' were assigned objectives and schedules similar to those fixed for the nuclear and space activities. In the electronics field India already possessed a broad civilian base, and the decision makers were mainly concerned with integrating the activities of the public and private enterprises in this field.[8]

During the 1960s and 1970s India's Defence Research and Development Organization (DRDO) experimented with liquid fuelled missile technologies. Work was carried out on two parallel programmes called 'Devil' and 'Valiant' respectively. While Devil was aimed at producing short-range missiles through reverse engineering and adaptation of Soviet supplied SA-2 surface-to-air missile, Valiant was meant to produce inter-continental range missiles using satellite launch rocket technology.[9] These programmes were later abandoned, but valuable experience was gained through the projects. In 1983 India initiated an ambitious Integrated Guided Missiles Development Programme (IGMDP), with the declared objective of developing five missile systems, namely the anti-tank guided missile—'Nag', a short range surface-to-air missile—'Trishul', a medium range surface-to-air missile—'Akash', the short range battlefield support missile—'Prithvi', and the intermediate range—'Agni'.[10] The Devil technology, based on components of SA-2 system, was employed in the development of the 'Prithvi'[11] while ISRO's solid fuelled space launch rockets based on the American supplied 'Scout' rockets[12] were used as the first stage of Agni. Agni's second stage was based on the liquid fuel rocket used in Prithvi. This mismatch between solid and liquid stages caused some problems, resulting in the failure of two of its first three tests, until the testing programme was suspended in the mid 1990s only to be revived by the BJP government in April 1999.

As mentioned earlier, India had tested its 150 km range/1000 kg payload liquid fuelled missile 'Prithvi' for the first time in February 1988. The missile underwent another 14 tests before its induction in the Indian Army's 333 Missile Group. The Indian army placed an order for 75 such missiles and had started receiving the first deliveries in 1994.[13] The experiments then shifted to the testing of other variants of Prithvi tailored to the requirements of the Indian Air Force and Navy. The Indian Air Force had placed an order for twenty-five Prithvis with a range/payload combination of 250 km and 500 kg.[14] The enhanced range for the air force version was simply achieved by reducing its payload. This missile causes considerable confusion in the minds of many people, as to its role and configuration. With the term 'air force version' many people tend to assume that it may well be an air-launched missile, which is not true. It is a surface-to-surface missile which has been inducted by the Indian Air Force for missions such as interdiction of Pakistani airfields, instead of risking costly aircraft, in view of the growing lethal nature and effectiveness of air defence weapons.

In April 2001, India commenced testing the naval version of the Prithvi. This missile has a range of 350 km and a payload of 250–500 kg and is also known as 'Dhanush'. The first Dhanush test, carried out from the reinforced deck of a surface vessel, was a dismal failure[15] and the missile fell into the sea after travelling only a few hundred metres from its launch pad. Later trials were relatively more successful, but Dhanush is still undergoing development tests and has not matured as an operational system as yet. The naval ships usually carry cruise missiles and their top decks have to be reinforced to sustain the powerful thrust generated by the launch of a ballistic missile. Arrangements have also to be made to provide a stable launch platform because of the ships' continuous movement in both axes. In the case of Dhanush, the additional problem is that of its liquid fuel. Liquid fuel is very corrosive and, therefore, cannot be filled into the missile until just before its launch, necessitating its storage in barrels on board the ship. With the ship continuously pitching and yawing the chances of the fuel oozing out of the drums or producing toxic vapours cannot be ruled out, thereby, creating a hazardous situation for the sailors. If India persists with the installation of the Dhanush on its naval platforms, it is likely to be converted into a solid fuelled system. In fact some Indian sources claim that Dhanush is a solid fuelled missile.[16] There have also been indications that India is in the process of converting all the Prithvi versions into solid fuelled missiles. That should explain the resumption of Prithvi-I test flights in 2003. The video clips of these tests shown on various TV networks also showed a clear white smoke plume, characteristic of solid propellants, as opposed to the orange plume of liquid fuel propellants.[17]

The Prithvi SS-150 is generally underrated as a tactical missile due to its short range, and designation as a short-range battlefield-support missile, but when it is related to Pakistan's geography it assumes strategic proportions. Given Pakistan's lack of strategic depth Prithvi can reach most of the vital strategic targets in Pakistan including the capital Islamabad. Repeated tests of this missile, while causing considerable consternation in Pakistan, did not ruffle any feathers around the world. In June 1997, the movement of some of the Prithvis to Jallandhar[18] in the Indian Punjab, close to the Pakistani border, caused a serious controversy. Pakistan considered this a forward deployment, while the Indians and Americans explained it away as forward storage of the missiles. In view of the fact that the terms deployment and storage are subject to more than one interpretation, such a move would always be viewed as provocative, especially because these road-mobile missiles can be moved up and readied for launching within hours. During the 2002 military stand off Prithvis were moved closer to the Pakistani border, and the launch authority was delegated to the Indian Army chief. However, the Indian Chiefs of Staff Committee realizing the destabilizing potential of these missiles, made a recommendation to their government to talk to Pakistan about the issue of short-range missiles once the crisis was over.[19]

Indian efforts in the field of missile development received a major boost on the 22 May 1989, with the successful test firing of its first intermediate range ballistic missile Agni from a launch site on the Bay of Bengal. The 60 feet long Agni, with a range of 1500 km and a payload of 1000 kg, is capable of carrying a nuclear warhead.[20] However, the Indians preferred to call it a *technology demonstrator*' rather than a weapon delivery system. This is despite the fact that some Indian commentators acknowledged that Agni was undoubtedly intended to be a nuclear delivery system. For instance, Bharat Warianwala, an analyst at the Institute for Defence Studies and Analysis (IDSA) in New Delhi, said: 'Like good Hindus and pacifists, we say the programme is only for peaceful uses, but the "Agni" is, in every sense, a system for nuclear weapons'.[21]

The test firing of Agni caused ripples around the world, and many amazed and startled Western commentators acknowledged that India, one of the poorest nations in the world, had gate-crashed into an elite club of nations capable of producing and launching ballistic missiles of this category. This select club had until May 1989, comprised the United States, the Soviet Union, France, Britain, Israel and China. The American officials denounced it as a 'highly destabilizing development in the region'.[22] During a hearing in the US Senate sub-Committee on Defence Industry and Technology, the sub-committee's chairman, Jeff Bingaman commented:

> Although India has promised not to arm its missiles with nuclear payloads, the possibility that it could arm the 'Agni' missile with nuclear warheads is profoundly disturbing to all countries of the region and indeed, to the world community. This is especially true because India has not signed the treaty on non-proliferation of nuclear weapons.[23]

In an article published in the British daily newspaper *The Independent* on 23 May 1989, on the proliferation of ballistic missiles in the Third World countries, Martin Navias, a defence analyst, expressed the view that Agni could enable the Indians to attack targets in both China and Pakistan. He also pointed out that, with some modifications to the satellite launcher (SLV-3), India could probably produce an intercontinental ballistic missile by the turn of the century, which could hit targets not only throughout China but also in the Soviet Union and Europe'.[24] However, the two subsequent tests of the missile were not successful and further testing was suspended by the Narasimha Rao government, ostensibly under US pressure. The BJP, which had declared in its manifesto that, on coming to power it would not only induct nuclear weapons but would also resume the testing of Agni missile, made good its promises by conducting nuclear tests in May 1998 and testing an improved version of Agni, the two stage solid fuelled Agni-II with a range of 2500 km, in April 1999.[25]

In addition to the five missile systems, identified for development in the IGMDP starting in 1983, India has initiated the development of several other missile systems. One such system is 'Sagarika' which as its name suggests would be a naval system—*Sagar* in Hindi means Sea/Ocean. However, beyond this, not much is precisely known about the characteristics of this missile. There is also considerable confusion surrounding its type, as it has variously been described as a Submarine Launched Cruise Missile (SLCM) or a Submarine Launched Ballistic Missile (SLBM). Nor have there been any reported tests of this missile. If it is intended to be an SLBM with long-range strategic missions, then its development would take a much longer time. In the case in which it was meant to be an SLCM, the question arises as to whether there would be any need or justification for a new system once 'Brahmos' has been successfully developed. Russian supplied 'Klub' class cruise missiles have already been fitted onto India's kilo class submarines and some surface vessels. Some analysts even believe that Sagarika may well be a modified naval version of the Prithvi missile, which is a ballistic and not a cruise missile. In that case, it is already being tested under the name of Dhanush. Neither the Indian political leadership nor the DRDO has attempted to clear the mystery surrounding Sagarika's status. However, an Indian source claims that Sagarika is, in fact, the name for the naval version of Prithvi and states that 'Dhanush' which means 'bow' in Sanskrit is the name for the special launch platform developed for firing the missile from the deck of a ship.[26]

According to some reports, India has been trying to develop its 'Akash' medium range surface-to-air missile into an ATBM system, and has claimed that it is comparable in capabilities to the US Patriot system.[27] Contrasted with the development of ballistic missiles, the progress in the development of surface-to-air missiles Trishul and Akash has not been satisfactory, forcing India to purchase Israeli made Barak missiles for its navy as defence against aerial threats. This lack of success can be gauged from the fact that, after an effort spanning twenty-three years and an expenditure of hundreds of millions of dollars, none of these systems is ready for induction into the Indian military. There have been rumours in the past that India has decided to abandon the Trishul missile, but it has been resuscitated, ostensibly with some technical help from the Israelis. India has been negotiating a deal with Russia since the 1990s, for the purchase of an S-300V theatre missile defence system, but it appears that this interest was of an exploratory nature because they have not followed it through. India has also sought the acquisition of 'Arrow' anti-missile systems from Israel. However, since US technology and funding went into the development of the Arrow missiles, the Israelis have to seek the clearance for any export of this technology. The US has not granted that clearance so far, due to the requirements of its own export control laws as well as needing to avoid the possible infringement of MTCR rules. The US itself has offered to sell its Patriot anti-missile systems to India, and US experts have briefed Indian officials on the technical/ performance parameters of the system. Apparently, not much progress has been made and the Manmohan Singh government seems to be much less enthusiastic about the acquisition of these systems than the BJP government. This may be due to the fact that the US has offered to sell India the Patriot-II version, while the Indians are interested in the Patriot-III system in case they finally decide to induct these ABMs.

On 26 November 2006, India claimed to have carried out a successful missile interception test. M.K. Nataranjan, scientific adviser to the defence minister in a telephone conversation with the Hindu newspaper declared that India had acquired missile defence capability, describing it as a 'significant milestone' in India's missile defence.[28] The press coverage of the event, which was named the 'Prithvi Missile Defence Exercise', has been highly confused and self-contradictory, and so have the claims by various government officials. For instance, *The Indian Express,* a prestigious newspaper, reported it as 'the coordinated launch of two surface-to-surface Prithvi-II missiles from two different ranges on the Orissa coast'.[29] This statement does not make any sense because you do not intercept a ballistic missile with another ballistic missile. The *Outlook* reported that the interceptor missile, which was not identified by officials, was in anti-missile mode and had inertial, mid-course and active seeker guidance in the terminal phase.[30] The *Outlook* also seemed to repeat the *Indian Express* story by saying that various versions of Prithvi have a range of between 150 to 350 km, and quoted DRDO officials as saying that it was important to validate the capability of interception.[31] Interestingly, it also quoted defence ministry officials as saying that, 'Notwithstanding the success of today's interception, we will continue to observe development of the US Patriot-III as well as other competing systems'.[32] This statement itself indicates a lack of confidence in the indigenous development of missile defence systems and continued interest in importing the technology from foreign sources.

To further confuse the picture, the *Outlook* referred to the fact that, faced with the failure of the Trishul project, India had been negotiating with the US, Israel and Russia with the intention of procuring an alternative anti-missile defence system.[33] Trishul is supposed to be a short-range surface-to-air missile probably with a 5–10 km range, intended to provide point defence especially for the Indian navy ships, and is neither intended nor capable of a ballistic missile defence role. Another report by A.K. Dhar in the *Outlook* said that India had unveiled an indigenous supersonic anti-missile system which according to Indian scientists had the capability to intercept the incoming ballistic missiles 'thousands of miles away'[34]—again an erratic statement without any technical basis. Dhar also stated that the new missile, which has been named as the AXO, intercepted the target missile at an altitude of 40–50 km. Based on the statements of DRDO officials, he also mentioned that the missile was not part of the IGMDP, which means that it could not have been a Prithvi as reported by some newspapers. The missile, according to unnamed DRDO officials is 'completely indigenous', is 10–12 meters long, has divert thrusters for generating lateral acceleration and can also be used for air defence missions.[35] Interestingly, just one day earlier, Dhar had reported in *Outlook* that, hit by 'time over runs and technical hitches' in the production of a surveillance system aimed at providing early warning of incoming missiles, India had sought Israeli assistance. According to *Outlook*, 'Elbit systems' of Israel had joined hands with the Defence Research and Development Laboratory, Electronics Corporation of India and Tata Power Company Limited to develop this advanced system.[36]

Given DRDO's record of failures to meet deadlines and targets, huge wastage of resources and exaggerated claims, it is quite possible that this missile interception test had been blown out of proportion as a public relations exercise. Given widespread public criticism of its failure to meet the goals set for the IGMDP, and especially the dismal failure of the Agni-III test,[37] which the DRDO had been publicizing for the previous three years, it is understandable that such laurels were being claimed. The Indian Defence Minister A.K. Antony was quick to congratulate the DRDO scientists on yet another achievement.[38]

There are other technical issues of concern. For instance, the target missile, a modified Prithvi-II, was fired from Chandipur Test Range on the coast of Orissa, while the interceptor missile was fired from Wheeler Island, which is 70 km away. Going by the claims of the Indian press and officials, it intercepted the target at 40–50 km altitude.[39] The press reports also assert that the interceptor was fired 60 seconds after the target missile and interception time was 110–117 seconds.[40] None of this makes much sense. It is not possible that the incoming missile, moving at supersonic speed, had just travelled 50 km in 110 seconds. But if it was intercepted at a distance of 50 km from its launch it means that the missile was intercepted while it was still in its boost phase. This also means that it had not yet shed its rocket motor and was in one piece, thereby presenting a much bigger target than at the time of re-entry in the terminal phase. In an actual operational environment, it would not be possible to deploy the interceptor so close to the hostile missile launch position, and the incoming missile would only be detected by radar when it had risen above the horizon. Given the bare minimum response time, it is impossible to intercept a missile in the boost phase, which usually lasts around 60 seconds or so in the case of a medium range missile, unless the interceptor travelled at the speed of light. That is why the US is experimenting with the development of airborne laser systems for boost phase interception. If an incoming missile cannot be caught in the boost phase, then it is engaged in the terminal phase, which raises problems of its own. Firstly, the size of the target and its radar cross-section is greatly reduced, i.e. from a launch size of 10–15 meters it comes down to around one to two meters, and secondly, it is travelling at a very high velocity, providing a time window of only 30–45 seconds.

INDIGENOUS DEVELOPMENT OF INDIA'S MISSILE PROGRAMME—MYTH OR REALITY

There is a pervasive myth that India's missile development has been largely indigenous, while Pakistan has mainly relied on the import of key components or even complete missile systems. Like its nuclear programme, which was initially designed to exploit the peaceful uses of nuclear technology, the Indian missile programme was also initiated as a civilian space development programme. As a result, it received generous technological assistance from advanced industrialized nations, before it unfolded its ambitious missile development plan in 1983, and thus avoided the strictures imposed on missile related technologies by the US led western industrialized nations through the institution of the MTCR. This aspect has been alluded to by Rodney Jones, when he commented that, 'By the terms of the art in proliferation assessments, India's development of space and missile technologies is said to have accrued more 'indigenous content' and India, therefore, has more easily escaped the sanctions of the major supplier countries'.[41] This argument has also been corroborated by others analysts such as Janne Nolan when she says:

> Unlike the growth of its Defence industry, the steady expansion of India's military space potential has occurred until recently without much active scrutiny from more advanced nations. Under the peaceful cast of civilian research, the nation had considerable latitude to acquire needed technologies and expertise through routine and unpublicized channels.[42]

The Agni IRBM programme owes its genesis to the adaptation of civilian space technology and generous technical assistance provided by the Soviet Union, the United States, France and Germany since the inception of India's Space Research Programme in 1962.[43] Despite the Agni test in May 1989, the Bush administration did not cancel a meeting, scheduled a week later, to discuss issuance of a licence to export technology related to missile testing to India, and the US government also dismissed suggestions that it should reconsider growing American involvement in India's efforts to modernize its space technology.[44]

By contrast the Russians, who have been a major catalyst for India's achievements in missile technology, have been seeking commercial and political advantages in return for their assistance in India's space programme.[45] India's Prithvi missile is, in fact, a direct derivative of Russia's SA-2 SAM system. In the early 1990s, Russia entered into a deal to transfer technology to India for the production of 'Cryogenic Rocket Engines' in India itself. This technology was intended for use in India's Geo-Synchronous Satellite Launch Vehicles (GSLVs). These engines also have possible applications for India's ICBM programme. The Russians backed out of the deal under intense US pressure. However, they did provide some manufactured cryogenic engines, which would have possibly helped India develop its own cryogenic technology.

Reportedly, France has also offered to sell advanced technology related to cryogenic rocket engines to India. [46]

India started launching sounding rockets from its 'Thumba' test range, which had been built with US assistance, and the first batch of Indian engineers were trained in rocketry in the US. These included A.P.J. Abdul Kalam, the pioneer of India's missile programme and the architect of the Agni programme. Kalam underwent four months training in the US in 1963–64, and during the course of his training visited NASA's research facility at Langley in Virginia, where the Scout rocket was developed, as well as the Wallops Island Flight Center, where Scout flight tests were being carried out. In 1965 Homi Bhabha, the Chairman of the Indian Atomic Energy Commission, made enquiries of NASA regarding the cost of developing a Scout type rocket. In response NASA sent technical reports on Scout's design. Kalam had also collected the necessary information which enabled him to design and build India's Space Launch Vehicle (SLV-3). [47] The same SLV, based on Scout technology, constituted the first stage of the Agni missile, and has now been adapted to constitute both of its solid stages.

The French initially assisted India in building 'Centaure' sounding rockets, and then helped India in the field of liquid propulsion technology. Indian engineers were associated with the development of the 'Viking' liquid propelled rocket. India was then allowed to build its own version of Viking under licence. [48] Expertise in liquid propulsion obviously helped in the development of the Prithvi missile. The most wide-ranging assistance, however, came from Germany, which helped India in the fields of guidance, rocket testing and the use of composite materials. This assistance was ostensibly for peaceful uses of space technology, but had clear applications in military missile technology. The onboard computers installed on Indian rockets and satellite launchers were based on German supplied Motorola processors and related software. The same processors, which constitute the brain of a missile, were later used for missile guidance in the Prithvi and Agni series missiles. Interestingly, German cooperation continued, despite Germany's joining the Missile Technology Control Regime in 1987. [49]

India has not been the only beneficiary of foreign technical assistance in its missile programme. In the short history of missile development, spanning little over half a century, there have been numerous such instances. To begin with, in the immediate post Second World War era, it was the German scientists and technicians, whisked away by both the Americans and the Soviets, who worked on their respective missile programmes. Since the early 1960s, when Britain abandoned its 'Skybolt' programme, its submarine based nuclear deterrent has been dependent on initially the import of 'Polaris', and currently the 'Trident' SLBMs from the US. On the other hand, Israel received short range Lance missile from the US, while French assistance helped Israel in producing Jericho-I missile in the 1960s.[50] More recently, Israel received not only funding, but technology transfers, for its Arrow ABM programme. Similarly, America sold Nike-Hercules surface-to-air missiles to Taiwan and South Korea. South Korea was able to convert this system into a surface-to-surface missile system.[51]

PAKISTAN'S MISSILE PROGRAMME

Pakistan's missile programme, like its nuclear programme, is driven by its security imperatives and threat perception. As with the nuclear programme, which serves not only to deter the threat or use of India's nuclear weapons, but also aims at neutralizing India's numerical advantage in conventional forces, the missile capability is also dual purpose. Firstly, it provides a reliable means of nuclear delivery, and secondly it has helped Pakistan to bridge the widening gap between Pakistani and Indian air forces, particularly after the imposition of sanctions in 1990. Though Pakistan had initiated its space research programme a few years ahead of India in the early 1960s, through experiments with sounding rockets, progress remained painfully slow due to lack of commitment and resultant inadequate funding. This programme was initiated with the assistance of the US and France, who had also extended a similar kind of assistance to other countries including India, Argentina, and Brazil. However, when Pakistan embarked on its missile development programme in the late 1980s, Missile Technology Control Regime (MTCR) was already in place. It therefore, faced obstacles in the procurement of the necessary technologies and components critical for the programme. Pakistan's dilemma has been aptly summed up by Rodney Jones as follows:

> As with nuclear weapons capabilities, India has set the pace in the acquisition of missile delivery capabilities on the subcontinent. Pakistan invariably has come from behind, usually facing tougher procurement obstacles and the consequences of greater planning uncertainty. Key export controls and other barriers to nuclear and missile proliferation have usually been instituted after key Indian acquisitions from abroad, but before Pakistan's...Pakistan's later development efforts have been caught in ever-tightening intelligence scrutiny and export controls.[52]

Much like its nuclear programme, Pakistan followed India's lead in embarking on a missile development programme. To begin with in the early 1990s, while it was trying to bridge the technological gap with India, it tried to restrain India's efforts by proposing a 'Zero Missile Regime' for South Asia,[53] mirroring its earlier efforts to bring diplomatic pressure to bear on India to retard the progress of its nuclear programme, through proposals such as the nuclear weapons free zone in South Asia. As expected the Zero Missile Regime proposal did not evoke a positive response from India, since India had already invested heavily in its space and IGMDP. Pakistan has also reiterated, on a number of occasions, that it does not intend matching India missile for missile, and that it has no intention of entering a nuclear/missile arms race with India. After a modest beginning in the late 1980s, with the first test-firing of short range Hatf-I and Hatf-II missiles, Pakistan slowly moved to consolidate and develop its indigenous technological base. However, it was not a smooth progression, since Pakistan had embarked on its missile programme after the coming into force of the MTCR in 1987. It therefore faced many obstacles, and has been repeatedly subjected to various kinds of sanctions and export control restrictions under the technology denial regimes.[54] Despite these difficulties it has come a long way in its missile development efforts, and has acquired the capability to produce short and medium range ballistic missiles of both liquid and solid fuelled varieties.

As a late starter Pakistan had to do a lot of catching up and had to develop its missile programme on a fast track. Consequently, different entities were assigned independent tasks, which resulted in creating a highly competitive environment. This not only produced quick results but also created a diversity of delivery systems. Pakistan started its missile development programme by acquiring a few short-range missiles in the late 1980s, and through reverse engineering and retooling was able to produce what were essentially unguided free flight rockets. After the initial experiments Hatf-II, with a range of 70–80 km and a payload of 500 kg, was introduced into the army. Hatf-I range was later increased to 100 km. This missile was last tested in February 2000. Nevertheless, it remains an unguided missile, and with its short range has a very limited utility for strategic missions. Hatf-II, which was publicized as having a range/payload combination of 300 km/500 kg, was abandoned along the way and nothing was heard of it, until a new missile called 'Abdali' with a range of 200 km was designated as Hatf-II. Abdali, which is basically an extended range version of Hatf-I, was first tested in May 2002 and is still in the testing phase. Both Hatf-I and Hatf-II are produced by the Space and Upper Atmosphere Research Organization (SUPARCO). However SUPARCO's role in missile development became secondary, as other organizations were tasked in early 1993 by then army chief General Abdul Waheed Kakar to start research and development work on their own missile systems.

A.Q. Khan was determined not to be left behind. He was able to convince Prime Minister Benazir Bhutto to procure missile technology from DPRK. An agreement to this effect was signed between the two governments during the Pakistani prime minister's visit to North Korea in December 1993. Contrary to speculations that some kind of a barter deal was done, Pakistan paid in hard cash to DPRK for some complete missile systems as well as transfer of technology. Pakistan was to find out, to its consternation, that it was not a good investment because of a plethora of serious problems in the North Korean technology. Consequently, KRL scientists have incorporated major modifications and technical improvements in the design of the missile through collaboration with the NDC scientists, and the 'Ghauri' in its current configuration does not even remotely resemble the original Nodong system.

There has been a considerable amount of speculation about a possible 'missiles for nuclear technology' barter deal between Pakistan and North Korea, especially after the revelation of the activities of the A.Q. Khan network. Such speculation has, however, been debunked by both President Musharraf as well as former Prime Minister Benazir Bhutto.[55] The main argument employed by various analysts to support their contention of a barter deal is based on their perception that, at the time the putative missile deal was struck, Pakistan's economy was not in good shape and therefore Pakistan could not possibly pay for the cost of the missiles. After a detailed and systematic analysis of this claim, Christopher Clary has concluded that this assumption is unfounded. According to Clary the estimated price tag for the missile deal ranges between $48 and $100 million. Given the fact that in 1995–96 Pakistan's arms imports were estimated by SIPRI to be $819 million, while the annual defence budget in the mid-1990s was around $3 billion, accommodating a missiles purchase valued at $100 million dollars does not appear to be beyond Pakistan's financial capability.[56]

In July 1997 several Pakistani newspapers reported the test firing of what they called the 'Hatf-III' missile, ostensibly in response to India's deployment of Prithvi missiles close to the Pakistani border. The news item was picked up by the foreign media and continues to be quoted in many serious academic publications. In fact no such test was carried out at the time and it is difficult to ascertain the motives behind this highly speculative news. It is quite possible that the misinformation may have been provided to the media by someone from within the strategic organizations concerned with the missile development. In April 1998, Pakistan tested its liquid fuelled MRBM Ghauri for the first time. The Ghauri test was significant for many reasons. Firstly, for the first time it provided Pakistan with a capability to reach high value targets in India's heartland, thereby enhancing Pakistan's deterrent capability, and constituted a counterpoise to India's Agni missile, tested almost a decade earlier. Secondly, Ghauri also had a symbolic psychological value, since it was named after Shahabuddin Ghauri, a Muslim invader who had, for the first time, laid the foundations of a permanent Muslim Empire in India after defeating a powerful Hindu warrior Prithviraj Chauhan. The timing of the Ghauri test was also significant, and was seen as a response to, not only India's deployment of Prithvi missiles in July 1997 at Jallandhar, close to the Pakistani border, but also as a reply to the declared intention of the BJP in its election manifesto to weaponize India's nuclear capability.

This was followed by the test firing of an improved version of Ghauri and the first test firing of the solid fuelled Shaheen-I missile in April 1999, in response to India's testing of its advanced version of the Agni missile designated as Agni-II, with a range of 2500 km.[57] Since then Pakistan has, as a result of a conscious decision, broken out of the 'Action-Reaction Syndrome', which has characterized the relations between the two South Asian neighbours. Pakistan has refused to be provoked into responding in kind to frequent Indian tests conducted since then. Improved versions of the Ghauri missile have since been tested on three more occasions and it has been introduced into the Pakistan Army's Strategic Forces. Following its maiden test flight in April 1999, Shaheen-I, has undergone four more tests and has been handed over to the Army Strategic Forces Command. Alongside Shaheen, yet another solid fuelled missile called 'Ghaznavi' was also under development. This missile, with a range of 290 km, was first tested in May 2002 and, after two subsequent tests, it has also been inducted into the Strategic Forces. Pakistan tested its longest-range missile thus far for the first time in March 2004. This missile, called Shaheen-II/Hatf-VI, was first unveiled on 23 March 2000 but at that time had not been tested. The successful testing of this two stage solid fuelled missile, with a range of 2000–2500 km, demonstrated Pakistan's capability to produce and fire a multi-staged missile, which will subsequently enable Pakistan to achieve a space launch capability. The missile was tested again in 2005, 2006 and 2007 but has, to date, not yet been formally inducted in the Army Strategic Forces. In August 2004 Pakistan achieved another breakthrough, when it announced the first test firing of its cruise missile 'Babur'. This missile, with a range of 500 km and a payload of 300 kg has since been tested twice, and is still in the testing and development stage. A press release issued after the most recent test of Babur in March 2007 claimed the range of the missile to be 700 km.[58] It is apparent that Babur's range has been enhanced following the incorporation of changes based on the results of its earlier tests, and it can be assumed that its range may see further improvement after more tests.

The second test of Ghauri in April 1999 was erroneously reported by the Pakistani media as a test of Ghauri-II, whereas it was actually the second test firing of the same Ghauri, which had been tested a year earlier. This perception was fuelled by A.Q. Khan's statements, in which he had announced his plans for developing a missile with over 3000 km range that was supposed to be named 'Ghaznavi'. This non-existent missile is sometimes referred to in some publications as 'Ghauri-III'. The designation of Pakistani missiles appears confusing to many analysts, since there is a dual nomenclature system. All missiles have the generic name of 'Hatf' and then also have their individual brand names. For instance, Hatf-II is called 'Abdali', while Hatf-III is also known as 'Ghaznavi'. 'Shaheen-I' and 'Ghauri' are also called 'Hatf-IV' and 'Hatf-V' respectively. The two-staged solid fuelled Shaheen-II is similarly designated as 'Hatf-VI' and the cruise missile 'Babur' as Hatf-VII. Of all the Pakistani missile systems, Ghauri is the only liquid fuelled missile, whereas all other missiles are of the solid fuel type.

Pakistan's missile programme is aimed at achieving a credible, reliable and survivable deterrence capability, and is not aimed at achieving a power projection capability beyond its immediate security arena. As a result, the goals and objectives of the programme have been confined to achieving the reach commensurate with the requirements of credible minimum deterrence. The testing programme is limited to meet the requirements of the technical validation of systems, though the tests carried out in May 2002, at the height of the military stand-off with India, were seen by many as an effort to send signals of its resolve to enhance the credibility of its deterrent. At the moment Pakistan is simultaneously pursuing both liquid propellant and solid propellant systems, and apparently this is going to be the likely pattern in the near to mid term. It is obvious that a variety of delivery systems always has its advantages. Moreover, it will be imprudent for any country, and the more so for a country with limited resources, to abandon a programme which has yielded encouraging results, and thereby waste the funds already expended towards research and development.

MYTH AND REALITY OF PAK–CHINA COLLABORATION

Despite repeated denials by both China and Pakistan, the myth of technological collaboration between them in the field of ballistic missile development has been pervasive. Both countries have declared, on numerous occasions, that they have not engaged in any technology exchange/transfer in violation of the MTCR guidelines, but newspaper reports based on alleged intelligence leaks keep appearing with monotonous regularity in the western media. As a result Pakistan has repeatedly been at the receiving end of MTCR related sanctions. In November 2000, as its parting gift to the Indian government, the Clinton administration decided to enforce MTCR Category-I sanctions against Pakistan's ministry of defence and Space and Upper Atmosphere Research Commission (SUPARCO). In this particular case Pakistan was punished for 'sins' committed in the past, whilst at the same time the alleged supplier, China, was exonerated because it was found to be inconvenient to impose sanctions on Chinese entities, due to US economic and commercial interests. One of the sentences in the press statement announcing the sanctions told it all, saying that the Indians should be pleased that China has declared that it will not indulge in any more missile related transactions with Pakistan. Another ironic aspect of these sanctions was the imposition of sanctions against the Pakistan ministry of defence, which is not an entity involved in the production of missiles or any other strategic systems. A press release issued in Islamabad on 22 November 2000, stated that:

> ...China had categorically stated that it had not supplied to Pakistan any missile technology or missiles which violated the MTCR guidelines accepted by China voluntarily, even though it was not a party to the regime. Pakistan had also stated that it had not received any transfers of technology from China inconsistent with MTCR guidelines.... Accordingly, the US decision announced yesterday to impose sanctions on Pakistani Ministry of Defence and SUPARCO on the basis of the alleged transfers of technology is unwarranted and unjustified...... Pakistan has an indigenous missile development programme which is part of our nuclear deterrent and indispensable to our security. This programme will be maintained and will not be affected by any discriminatory regimes such as MTCR.[59]

A closer look at the above statement, and earlier denials by both China and Pakistan, reveals that the two countries did not appear to be denying any kind of missile cooperation at all. However, what they seemed to insist was that these transfers were not in violation of the MTCR. In 1996, China had made a commitment to the Clinton administration that it would not transfer any missile technology to Pakistan in contravention of the MTCR guidelines. The US, however, did not accept this interpretation and considered it a violation of its export control laws. The fact of the matter is that neither Pakistan nor China were members of the MTCR, and were not bound by any of its obligations, and secondly the sale of missiles by one country to another is not deemed illegal according to any international law. This was made obvious when the US Navy intercepted a consignment of North Korean Scud missiles destined for Yemen, but found that it had no legal grounds to stop this shipment.

At the beginning of September 2001, MTCR Category-2 sanctions were imposed against the National Development

Complex. The allegations of selling missile technology to Pakistan was once again denied by China.[60] Unfortunately, while Pakistan was being singled out for the imposing of MTCR sanctions, activities in clear contravention of MTCR guidelines happening next door were totally ignored. The announced range of the joint Russian-Indian missile Brahmos-PJ-10 is 290 km, just to keep it out of the MTCR Category-1 restrictions. This range limit of 300 km in the case of cruise missiles is in any case meaningless because of their stand-off capability, as these weapons can be carried over hundreds of miles by naval or aerial platforms, and then launched against the intended targets. The Indians have publicly acknowledged that the propulsion system for the 'Brahmos' was provided by the Russians, which is in clear violation of MTCR Category-2 prohibitions. However, neither India nor Russia was subjected to any kinds of sanctions. Similarly, some of the other programmes, such as the 'Arrow' programme, were moving ahead unhindered, and in fact receiving active technological and financial assistance from the US. The MTCR-related sanctions were again imposed against KRL and a North Korean firm in February 2003. These sanctions, which are effective for a period of two years, have since expired.

According to an NIE estimate, 'Since the 1980s Pakistan has pursued the development of an indigenous ballistic missile capability in an attempt to avoid reliance on any foreign entity for this key capability. Islamabad will continue with its present ballistic missile production goals until it has achieved a survivable, flexible force capable of striking a large number of targets throughout most of India.' However, Pakistan does not see the need to match India missile for missile.

AIR DELIVERY SYSTEMS

Both India and Pakistan have aircraft, capable of delivering nuclear weapons. Theoretically, any aircraft with a payload capacity of 1000 kg or above can deliver nuclear bombs. Other relevant characteristics are the range or operating radius of the aircraft, and its ability to penetrate the enemy's air defences. India's preferred air delivery platforms against Pakistani targets are likely to be its Mirage-2000s, Jaguars and SU-30s, though it can also use its MIG-27s. According to some reports the Indian air force pilots had practiced 'toss bombing' technique with Jaguars, Mirages and MIG-27s in the late 1980s. All of these aircraft have a sufficient range to cover the whole of the territory of Pakistan. However, they can hardly reach any meaningful target in China, unless they resort to air-to-air refuelling, which is a dangerous proposition in hostile air space, or they could send the aircraft on one-way missions. The Indian navy has four Russian supplied TU-22 M Backfire bombers, however, and these have a fairly long operating radius of 4400 km. Another 12 of these aircrafts are planned for introduction. The Indian navy also has eight TU-142 Bears with an operating radius of 6200 km. These aircrafts can be modified for use as nuclear delivery platforms.[61] Citing a 2001 internal memorandum of the Indian air force, the authors of the 'Deadly Arsenal' claim that fighter-bomber aircraft will remain the only feasible nuclear delivery system until the end of the decade.[62] This claim does not appear to be logical, because of the fact that by 2001 India had already inducted Prithvi missiles into the Indian army and had also successfully tested its IRBM Agni-I and Agni-II. If indeed the Indian air force did circulate this memorandum, it could well be reflective of service bias, and something to do with the intense rivalry and competing claims of the Indian armed services to stake their claims to control over the strategic assets.

In Pakistan's case, it also has several aircrafts suitable for nuclear missions, such as F-16s and Mirage-Vs. Some analysts have even listed the Chinese origin A-5 aircraft[63] as a possible nuclear delivery platform, which does not make much sense. Firstly, this aircraft is specially designed for providing close support to ground troops and has a very limited range and endurance, which makes it unsuitable for strategic missions and secondly, it is an old vintage aircraft which is becoming obsolete, and is likely to be replaced in the near future. Because the Pakistan air force has a much smaller inventory of aircrafts when compared with India, the aircraft designated for strategic missions will probably be assigned other tasks as well. This would mean that in Pakistan's case surface-to-surface missiles are likely to remain the primary means of delivery, at least for the foreseeable future.

NOTES

1. Janne E. Nolan, *Trappings of Power—Ballistic Missiles in the Third World*, The Brookings Institution, Washington, D.C.,1991 p. 16.
2. Rodney W. Jones, 'Pakistan's Nuclear Posture: Quest for Assured Nuclear Deterrence—A Conjecture', Institute of Regional Studies, Islamabad, *Spotlight on Regional Affairs* Vol. XIX No. 1, January 2000, p. 9.
3. Nolan, op. cit., p. 10.
4. K. Subrahmanyam, 'India's Nuclear Policy', in Onkar Marwah & Ann Schulz (eds.), *Nuclear Proliferation and Near Nuclear Countries*, Ballinger Publishing Company, Cambridge, Mass., 1975, pp. 138–9.
5. Bhabhani Sen Gupta, *Nuclear Weapons? Policy Options for India*, Sage Publications, New Delhi, Beverly Hills, London, 1983, p. 4.
6. Onkar Marwah and Ann Schulz (eds.), *Nuclear Proliferation and Near Nuclear Countries*, Ballinger Publishing Company, Cambridge Massachusetts, 1975, p. 103.
7. Ibid.
8. Ibid., p. 104.
9. Dinshaw Mistry, 'Military Technology, National Power and Regional Security: The Strategic Significance of India's Nuclear, Missile, Space and Missile Defence Forces', in Lowell Dittmer (ed.), *South Asia's Nuclear Security Dilemma*, New Delhi, Pentagon Press, 2005, p. 54.
10. *Indian Defence Review Digest*, Vol. IV, New Delhi, Lancer Publications, 1992.
11. Ibid.
12. Gary Milhollin, 'India's Missiles—With a Little Help from Our Friends', *Bulletin of the Atomic Scientists*, November 1989, pp. 31–35.
13. Ibid.
14. Ibid.
15. Ibid., p. 55.
16. http://www.bharat-rakshak.com/MISSILES/Prithvi.html.
17. Based on author's personal observations and discussions with missile experts.
18. Ibid., p. 54.
19. Fernandez, India's Missiles in Position, *The Times of India*, 26 December 2001 and 'Brahmastra as last resort', Army Chief to Clear Prithvi deployment, *The*

Pioneer, 31 January 2002, http://www.bharat-rakshak.com/MISSILES/ News/2002/02-Jan

20. 'Indian Missile Launch Prompts Nuclear Fears', *The Independent*, London, 23 May 1989. Also see Nolan, op. cit., p. 45.
21. Sheila Tteft, 'India's Homemade Missile Heats Up Arms Race', *The Christian Science Monitor*, 4–10 May 1989.
22. Nolan, op. cit., p. 1.
23. *The Independent*, London, 23 May 1989.
24. Ibid.
25. Rodney W. Jones, Mark G. Mcdonough, et al. (eds.), *Tracking Nuclear Proliferation—A Guide in Maps and Charts*, Carnegie Endowment for International Peace, Washington, D.C., 1998, p. 117.
26. http://www.bharat-rakshak.com/MISSILES/Prithvi.html.
27. Indranil Banerjie, *Indian Defence Review Digest*, Lancer Publications, Pvt. Ltd., New Delhi, 1992, p. 71. Also see Jones et al. (eds.), *Tracking Nuclear Proliferation*, p. 117 and Gregory Koblenz, 'Theatre Missile Defence and South Asia: A Volatile Mix', *The Non-proliferation Review*, Vol. 4, No. 3, Spring/Summer 1997, p. 54.
28. 'Prithvi Interceptor Missile tested successfully', *The Hindu*, 28 November 2006.
29. 'India conducts missile vs. missile test', *The Indian Express*, 27 November 2006.
30. 'India acquires anti-missile capability', http://www.outlookindia.com/pti_ print.asp?id=432674.
31. Ibid.
32. Ibid.
33. Ibid.
34. A K Dhar, 'India develops new anti-missile system', http://www.outlookindia. com/pti_print.asp?id=432771.
35. Ibid.
36. A.K. Dhar, 'DRDO seeks Israeli expertise in key surveillance system', http:// www.outlookindia.com/pti_print.asp?id=432403.
37. Gavin Rabinowitz, 'India's new missile falls short in test', Associated Press/ boston.com, 10 July 2006.
38. http://www.outlookindia.com/pti_print.asp?id=432674.
39. Ibid, http:outlookindia.com/pti_print.asp?id=432771.
40. Ibid.
41. Jones, *Pakistan's Nuclear Posture*, p. 10.
42. Nolan, op. cit., p. 46.
43. Ibid., p. 2.
44. Ibid.
45. Ibid., p. 22. Also see Dr Maleeha Lodhi, 'Testing Times in the Subcontinent', *The News*, Islamabad, 12 April 1998.
46. Nolan, op. cit., p. 43.

47. Milhollin, op. cit.
48. Ibid.
49. Ibid.
50. Nolan, pp. 27–8.
51. Ibid.
52. Rodney W. Jones, 'Pakistan's Nuclear Posture: Quest for Assured Nuclear Deterrence—A Conjecture', Institute of Regional Studies, Islamabad, *Spotlight on Regional Affairs* Vol. XIX No. 1, January 2000, p. 9.
53. Address by Mr Shahbaz Hussain, Director General Disarmament, Ministry of Foreign Affairs, reported in *The News*, Islamabad, 24 February 2001.
54. Rodney W. Jones, 'Pakistan's Nuclear Posture: Quest for Assured Nuclear Deterrence-A Conjecture', Institute of Regional Studies, Islamabad, *Spotlight on Regional Affairs* Vol. XIX, No. 1, January 2000, p. 9.
55. Pervez Musharraf, *In the Line of Fire*, Free Press, New York, 2006, p. 286. Also see Christopher Clary, 'The A.Q. Khan Network: Causes and Implications', Master's thesis submitted to Naval Postgraduate School, Monterey, California, December 2005, p. 62.
56. Clary, pp. 62–68.
57. Nasim Zehra, 'Pakistan has no choice but to bolster its security', *Gulf News*, 16 April 1999, *The News*, Islamabad, 16 April 1999. Also see Jones, op. cit., pp. 13–14.
58. 'Nuclear Capable Cruise Missile Test Fired', *The Dawn*, 23 March 2007.
59. Press Release No. 170/2000, Ministry of Foreign Affairs, Islamabad.
60. Afzal Khan, 'China exporting missiles to Pakistan, says US—Beijing denies selling weapons', *The Nation*, Islamabad, 28 July 2001.
61. Mistry, op. cit., p. 53, also see Joseph Cirincionne et al. (eds.), *Deadly Arsenals*, Carnegie Endowment for International Peace, Washington, D.C., 2005, p. 221.
62. Cirincionne, ibid.
63. Ibid., p. 239.

6

Nuclear Doctrines, Command and Control

A doctrine is the principle of belief or bedrock on which organizational and force structures are built. It provides the guidelines for force configuration and the nature, type and number of weapons and delivery systems that would be needed to implement the doctrine. However, before embarking upon a review of Indian and Pakistani nuclear doctrines, command and control systems it may be pertinent here to summarize the main characteristics of the prevailing nuclear environment in South Asia, which has provided the background, and has influenced the nature and direction of these evolving doctrines, command and control systems.

CHARACTERISTICS OF SOUTH ASIAN NUCLEAR ENVIRONMENT

Some of the key features of the existing South Asian nuclear environment are as follows:

- Indian and Pakistani nuclear forces are still evolving, and these relatively vulnerable assets are likely to provide tempting targets for a pre-emptive strike, at least in the short term, irrespective of the probability of success of such a strike.
- India has a fairly advanced space programme, and Pakistan has started to move down the same road and is likely to have some sort of a space surveillance capability in the near to medium term. However, at the moment both countries lack real time

surveillance, early warning and target acquisition means, which will not only limit deployment options but will also enhance crisis instabilities.

- While the command, control, communications and intelligence infrastructure are developing they will remain susceptible to the threat of a decapitating strike, thus encouraging pre-emptive tendencies during crises and periods of heightened tension.

- The incentive for development of an assured 'second strike' capability is likely to be fairly strong on both sides. However, deterrence instability will prevail in the short term.

- India's planned introduction of Anti-ballistic missile systems, and the likely expansion of its fissile material production capacity as a consequence of the implementation of the US–India nuclear cooperation agreement, is likely to disturb the evolving strategic balance and could lead to an undesirable nuclear/missile arms race.

- Contiguity of the two countries and short flight times of ballistic missiles are likely to result in hair trigger postures, and may lead to the adoption of Launch-on-Warning strategies. Due to technical deficiencies in the surveillance and early warning systems, this increases the chance of launching of weapons in response to inaccurate or misinterpreted information. Hence, the need for the adoption of confidence building and restraint measures.

- Peculiar value systems, emotive tendencies and a proclivity for risk taking, coupled with politically weak governments, will create uncertainties of responses in crises, highlighting the need for mutually agreed and institutional risk reduction mechanisms. The absence of institutional crisis management mechanisms is likely to result in impulsive decision-making.

- There is a general lack of awareness of the devastating effects of a nuclear conflict amongst the masses on both sides. This ignorance of the gravity of the situation will generate undesirable public pressure on decision makers during crises.

- In Pakistan the military is fully integrated into nuclear command and control, and decision making mechanisms, while in India the armed forces are still kept out of the loop. This may create problems when they are asked to take over the operational responsibility in a crisis.

INDIAN NUCLEAR DOCTRINE/POLICY

On 17 August 1999, India's National Security Advisor, Brajesh Mishra, announced what he termed as 'India's Draft Nuclear Doctrine'.[1] This ambitious doctrine was announced in a peculiar set of circumstances, coming close on the heels of the Kargil conflict in Kashmir and in the midst of an election campaign forced by the fall of the Vajpayee government in April 1999. The doctrine was prepared by a group of twenty-seven individuals with diverse backgrounds and experience. They were nominated by the Indian government as members of the National Security Advisory Board (NSAB), led by the veteran Indian strategic analyst K. Subramaniam. It was announced that this document would have to be approved by the Indian government before it became official policy. There were many anomalies in the way the document was made public. For instance, it was not presented for scrutiny before the two higher tiers of India's national security establishment, i.e. the Strategic Advisory Group, which includes the three services chiefs, and the National Security Council, which comprises more or less the same individuals who constitute the Cabinet Committee on Security. The members of the NSAB were private individuals, handpicked by the government. As could be expected from such a disparate group of individuals, the final document is full of contradictions, and represents the lowest common denominator in an effort to accommodate varying points of views.

The draft itself was announced by the National Security Advisor, a senior government functionary. Interestingly, though, the status of the document remained that of a 'draft' until January 2003, at which time another policy document was issued. The characterization of the August 1999 document allowed the Indian leaders to embrace or disown it to suit the expediency of the situation. Some of the salient aspects of the 'Draft Doctrine' are as follows:

- India shall pursue a doctrine of credible minimum nuclear deterrence. [Actual size of the force has, however, not been quantified.]
- India will have a 'no first use' policy, but will respond with punitive retaliation should deterrence fail.
- India will maintain sufficient, survivable and operationally prepared nuclear forces, capable of shifting from peacetime deployment to fully employable force in the shortest possible time.
- A robust command and control system with effective intelligence and early warning capabilities would be established, for which space- based and other assets shall be created. Authority for the release of nuclear weapons will vest in the person of Prime Minister of India, or his designated successor(s).
- Comprehensive planning and training for operations will be carried out in line with the strategy.
- India will demonstrate the political will to employ nuclear forces.
- Highly effective conventional military capabilities will be maintained to raise the threshold of outbreak of both conventional as well as nuclear war.
- India will have effective, diverse, flexible and responsive nuclear forces based on a triad of land based missiles, aircraft and sea based assets.
- Survivability will be ensured through redundancy, mobility, dispersion and deception.
- India shall not accept any restraints on its R&D capability and will continue to conduct sub-critical nuclear tests even if it decides to sign the CTBT at a future date.
- India will not use nuclear weapons against non-nuclear weapon states (NNWS), other than those which are aligned to any nuclear power.

On 4 January 2003, more than four and a half years after the Pokhran-II tests, India finally announced the broad contours of its nuclear command and control structure, and reiterated some key elements from its draft doctrine while modifying some others. Whether these can now be taken as the official policy parameters of India's nuclear doctrine is not clear, as is also the case with the status of the 'Draft Nuclear Doctrine'. It has not been clarified as to whether the Draft Doctrine is still valid or has been superseded by the new document. In the latter case the question would arise regarding the Indian position on those elements of the August 1999 document that have not been recapitulated in the new policy document, which is only a one page document as opposed to the original six page document. Some of the salient features of the new document issued by the Cabinet Committee on Security on 4 January 2003 are:

- Building and maintaining a credible minimum deterrent.
- A posture of 'no first use'.
- Retaliatory attacks can only be authorized by the civilian political leadership through the NCA.
- No use of weapons against non-nuclear weapon states.
- In the event of a major attack against India or Indian forces anywhere, by biological or chemical weapons, India will retain the option of retaliating with nuclear weapons.
- A continuance of controls on export of nuclear and missile related materials and technologies, participation in the Fissile Material Cut-Off Treaty negotiations and observance of the moratorium on nuclear tests.

ANALYSIS

In the new document while reiterating the essence of the Draft Nuclear Doctrine, some new elements have been introduced as follows:

- Declaration of the option to use nuclear weapons against any use of 'Nuclear', 'Chemical' or 'Biological' weapons against Indian territory, or Indian Armed Forces anywhere in the world, thereby, not only extending the threshold of nuclear use but also expanding its geographical scope. It has virtually nullified the 'no first use' commitment.

- Strict control over the export of sensitive technologies and materials. This was ostensibly designed to allay prevailing international concerns over the surreptitious transfers of sensitive materials and technological knowledge from the secondary proliferation sources, and thus project India in a positive light. This ploy has worked in the form of receiving US acknowledgement of India as a 'responsible' nuclear power and leading to the signing of the US–India civilian nuclear cooperation agreement.

- A clear commitment to participate in FMCT negotiations. This fact has also been reflected in the India–US agreement, where it has been stated that the two countries will jointly work towards the formulation of a fissile materials cut off treaty.

- Continued observance of the 'moratorium' on nuclear testing. However, this will remain a unilateral commitment and India is not willing to accept any binding obligations in this regard. When Pakistan proposed that the two countries should convert their respective unilateral test moratoriums into a bilateral moratorium during the early rounds of the ongoing dialogue in 2004, the Indians declined the offer, and instead insisted on the reiteration of a unilateral moratorium. Similarly, it has been a contentious issue in the bilateral agreement with the US.

- A reaffirmation that India 'would not use nuclear weapons against non-nuclear weapon states', however, the caveat in the original doctrine 'other than those aligned with nuclear weapon states' has been removed. The authors of the original document probably did not think through the implications of this statement, which actually meant that countries such as Japan, South Korea and Australia as well as Canada and all the European members of NATO were 'eligible' for an Indian nuclear strike. Apparently, they meant to dissuade countries in the immediate neighbourhood from getting close to either China or Pakistan, but obviously this formulation attracted lot of criticism and was duly modified in the subsequent document.

The doctrine was viewed in Pakistan with scepticism and concern because of its provocative nature. From a Pakistani perspective, the doctrine will not only have far reaching implications in determining the trajectory of India's nuclear development, but will consequently impact upon Pakistan's decisions related to its nuclear force posture. Pakistan felt that:

- India has effectively scuttled any possibility for the establishment of a Strategic Restraint Regime in South Asia.
- India's declaration of a 'no first use policy' is aimed at gaining high moral ground and has no credence, as India had itself refused to give any credence to China's 'no first use' policy.
- India's declared intention to upgrade its conventional forces ostensibly to 'raise the threshold' of both nuclear as well as conventional conflict, will in effect accentuate the existing conventional imbalance and thereby lower Pakistan's nuclear threshold.
- By not specifying the source of nuclear threat to its security, India has kept the size of its 'minimum' deterrent open ended.
- The timing of the announcement of the doctrine suggested that the BJP government wanted to convince the domestic public that it had the requisite resolve to take the process initiated in May 1998 to its logical conclusion.
- It exposed the hypocrisy in the stance of the interim government, that it was not in a position to take any decision on CTBT, while it did not feel constrained in announcing a nuclear doctrine with far reaching consequences.
- India wants to drag Pakistan into a nuclear, as well as conventional arms race, to exploit Pakistan's relative economic weakness and engineer an economic collapse (US–USSR Syndrome!).

PERCEIVED GOALS AND OBJECTIVES

There are differing perspectives and views with regard to the ultimate goals and objectives of India's nuclear policy. It will be instructive to review some of these, to provide an insight into the parameters of the Indian Nuclear Discourse. In his book entitled *India's Emerging Nuclear Posture*, Ashley Tellis has tried to rationalize India's nuclear policy and has even attempted to fill the gaps and clarify the ambiguities in the Indian Nuclear Doctrine. Tellis, in his seminal study, has explored five possible options, ranging from 'Renunciation of Nuclear Option' to a 'Ready Arsenal', with 'Regional Nuclear Free Zone', 'Maintenance of Nuclear Option' and 'Recessed Deterrent' lying in the middle. He has concluded that India is most likely to choose a 'Force-in-being' option falling in between the recessed deterrence and ready arsenal. The implication of this posture would be that Indian nuclear capabilities will be 'strategically active', but remain 'operationally dormant'. Translated into practical terms, this would afford India the ability to undertake a retaliatory strike within hours to weeks. This kind of posture will be demonstrative of Indian restraint, while providing it with deterrence capability vis-à-vis both China and Pakistan. The other advantages would be avoidance of the costs of maintaining a ready arsenal, while ensuring the retention of civilian politico-bureaucratic control over the nuclear assets, which in the case of a ready arsenal would automatically be passed over to the military.[2] How realistic this appraisal is may be difficult to say, but in view of the noises coming out of Indian strategic circles this appears to be an effort to present a rather benign view of India's nuclear ambitions.

On the domestic front a survey of the public opinion polls, conducted in the aftermath of the 1998 tests, showed that 'self esteem' and 'pride' emerged as predominant themes. In a poll conducted by the Indian Market Research Bureau (IMRB), 91 per cent of the respondents felt a sense of pride at India's pronouncement of its nuclear status. The same argument was echoed by Prime Minister Vajpayee, when he declared on the floor of the Indian Parliament that, 'It is India's due, the right of one-sixth of humanity'. In a 1994 poll, 49 per cent of those favouring weaponization of the nuclear option advocated the development of nuclear weapons by India to 'improve its bargaining position in international affairs', while another 38 per cent favoured the acquisition of nuclear weapons to enhance India's 'international status'. In two other opinion polls, conducted in June 1974 and May 1998, the results were identical. Around 90 per cent of people felt proud of this achievement and thought that it had raised India's stature in the comity of nations.[3]

Statements by various Indian leaders also demonstrate this self-consciousness of India's greatness. For instance, Foreign Minister Jaswant Singh, in an interview with National Public Radio in the United States, said that, 'All that we have done is to give ourselves a degree of strategic autonomy by acquiring those symbols of power…which have universal currency'.[4]

The issue of viewing nuclear weapons as a means of power and prestige is a recurring theme elsewhere as is evident from the statement by former prime minister I.K. Gujral quoted earlier.

Bharat Karnad, one of the better-known Indian strategic analysts representing hawkish views and a former member of the Nuclear Security Advisory Board (NSAB), and responsible for formulating the 'Draft Nuclear Doctrine', argues that India needs to rationalize its nuclear testing and weaponization programmes, rather than pursuing the abstract goal of disarmament, stating that:

> Collateral security objectives of dampening Pakistani ardour for mindless confrontation but, more importantly, for containing a wily and wilful China and of deterring an over-reaching and a punitive minded United States leading the Western combine of nations, will be realized provided the deterrence solution is right.[5]

Karnad is critical of any decision by India to sign either the CTBT or FMCT, because in his view these will limit India's weapons yield to below the megaton range, and cap the number of nuclear weapons respectively, thereby endangering national security. He goes on to add that, 'for a self proclaimed nuclear weapon state, disarmament is a manifestly counter-productive policy.' Karnad asserts that India should bargain hard to obtain as many concessions as possible in return for its signatures to the CTBT and FMCT. To him the minimum acceptable results should be provision for India to conduct additional thermonuclear tests and to accumulate enough fissile material stocks for 1000 plus nuclear warheads. He implicitly threatens that failing to strike an attractive enough bargain, India could, as an alternative, export its nuclear technology and materials. Characterizing the 'No first use doctrine' as merely a hoax, he comments that, 'it is one of those restrictions which countries are willing to abide by, except in war.' He supplements his argument by quoting from Herman Kahn, who stated that, ''No first use' stops just where war begins,' and Michael Quinlan, who calls it, 'political posturing that cannot alter strategic reality.' In the same breath he also dismisses the notion of a 'minimum nuclear deterrence' relying once again on Kahn's statement that, 'it is a new kind of Maginot mentality'.[6]

However, Karnad contradicts his earlier argument himself later in his same chapter by saying that:

The Indian offer of no first use was timely, will go a long way in making the Pakistanis rethink their demonology and should be unilaterally subscribed to. More convincing proof that India is not gearing up for a nuclear war could be provided by Indian force design. Not nuclearizing the short range Prithvi and, in fact, withdrawing it from present near-border deployment, should constitute the core concept.'[7]

The contradictions inherent in India's nuclear stance are exposed by one of the more objective Indian analysts, Kanti Bajpai, who says that, 'New Delhi's pronouncements suggest that China is the more important threat. But the rhetoric from South Block and India's day-to-day diplomatic and strategic moves indicates that Pakistan is a co-equal if not greater threat....' According to Bajpai, the Indian strategic community also keeps giving vent to its concerns vis-à-vis the US mainly in the context of the potential threat to India posed by America's counter-proliferation policy, and its hostility against rising powers like India, on account of geo-political factors. At the moment this criticism is muted, but more open references to the American threat should be expected when the ICBM and SLBM capabilities come on line, and it will become technically feasible to strike against continental United States.[8]

Bajpai holds India responsible for Pakistani nuclear weaponization, and believes that Islamabad would not have gone all the way if New Delhi had unambiguously closed off the nuclear option in the 1960s. He goes on to argue that:

A second opportunity to avoid a nuclear arms race was lost in the 1970s and 1980s when Pakistan stated publicly, on several occasions, that it would sign any de-nuclearizing agreement India was prepared to accept. Islamabad's various offers were seen as tactical manoeuvres, designed to embarrass India diplomatically. But if India had called Islamabad's bluff it is difficult to see how, given the weight of world opinion, as well as influential sectors of its domestic opinion, Islamabad could have reneged on its own commitments.'[9]

Rebutting the argument with regard to the inevitability of Pakistani nuclearization, he expresses his belief that, 'talks on Kashmir plus a conventional force agreement would have stood a very good chance of reassuring Pakistan and stopping the advance of its nuclear weapons programme'.[10]

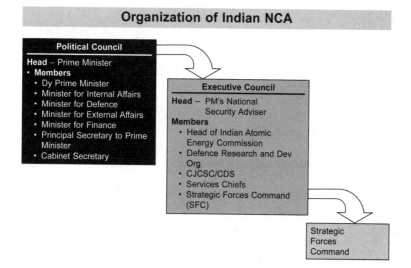

Organization of Indian NCA

Political Council
Head – Prime Minister
• Members
 • Dy Prime Minister
 • Minister for Internal Affairs
 • Minister for Defence
 • Minister for External Affairs
 • Minister for Finance
 • Principal Secretary to Prime Minister
 • Cabinet Secretary

Executive Council
Head – PM's National Security Adviser
Members
 • Head of Indian Atomic Energy Commission
 • Defence Research and Dev Org
 • CJCSC/CDS
 • Services Chiefs
 • Strategic Forces Command (SFC)

Strategic Forces Command

PAKISTAN'S NUCLEAR DOCTRINE/POLICY

Unlike India, Pakistan's nuclear policy is driven entirely by the threat to its security emanating from India and is, therefore, India-centric. The discourse on the direction, aims and objectives of the nuclear policy is mainly confined to officialdom. Public debate on such issues is not very broad based and the published literature on the subject is very limited, compared to the volume of published material emanating from India's academic circles and think tanks. It would, therefore, be appropriate to quote from some key government officials to gain an insight into Pakistani thinking concerning doctrinal and policy issues related to nuclear deterrence. Three former Pakistani officials Abdul Sattar, Agha Shahi, and Zulfiqar Ali Khan, in a widely quoted jointly written article, claimed that:

> Deterrence was the sole aim and a small arsenal was considered adequate. At no time did Pakistan contemplate use of nuclear weapons for war fighting or seek to develop capability for a pre-emptive attack. Apart from the obvious constraint of resources, it was not so unrealistic as to entertain such thoughts. India is too large and too well armed to be vulnerable to a disabling strike. Besides, any such attempt would provoke retaliation with disastrous consequences.[11]

This line of argument clearly indicates a rational and realistic approach to deterrence, discarding any notions of a futile arms race with India or the temptation to build up an arsenal in excess of Pakistan's legitimate security needs. However, these analysts appear to be reluctant to suggest any figures to quantify the size of Pakistan's nuclear forces. In fact, they believe that 'minimum deterrence' is not an abstract number, which remains static for all time, but something which is subject to change with changing circumstances. They believe that the efficacy of Pakistan's deterrent can only be maintained by keeping the size of the force flexible, explaining that:

> Minimum deterrence has been and should continue to be the guiding principle of Pakistan's nuclear pursuit. Of course minimum cannot be

defined in static numbers. In the absence of mutual restraints, the size of Pakistan's arsenal and its deployment pattern have to be adjusted to ward off dangers of pre-emption and interception. Only then can deterrence remain efficacious.[12]

Later, speaking at a seminar at Islamabad in November 1999, Abdul Sattar appointed Foreign Minister by the Musharraf government, elaborated that Pakistan was compelled to go nuclear to deter aggression and prevent war, and to safeguard its peace and security. Its decision was in no way motivated by any pretension to great power status or desire for regional domination. He emphasized Pakistan's determination not to get embroiled in a nuclear arms race with India, repeating his earlier statement that:

> Minimum nuclear deterrence will remain the guiding principle of our nuclear strategy. The minimum cannot be quantified in static numbers. The Indian build-up would necessitate review and reassessment…But we shall not engage in any nuclear competition or arms race.[13]

At an international seminar on Command and Control of Nuclear Weapons in Islamabad in February 2000, Agha Shahi, a former foreign minister and senior retired diplomat, invoked the traditional 'action-reaction syndrome' that has dominated India–Pakistan relations for more than half a century, arguing that since India wants to keep the size of its minimum deterrent flexible and subject to change with changing circumstances, Pakistan will perforce have to keep its deterrent dynamic in the same way.[14]

Speaking at the National Defence College in May 2000, Foreign Minister Abdul Sattar stated that:

> For the past decade or so, nuclear capability has been the bedrock of our defence and security policy…its sole purpose is to deter and prevent war. Unlike some other countries, Pakistan neither aspires to great power status or permanent membership of the Security Council nor nourishes any design for regional dominance…We support a global, non-discriminatory international regime of nuclear and missile restraints, voted for the CTBT, will participate in negotiations for FMCT, and are prepared to strengthen our existing stringent controls

against export of strategic weapons technology. Our policy of Minimum Credible Deterrence will obviate any strategic arms race... the idea of no-first-use of nuclear weapons needs to be expanded into a no-first-use of force, lest the former should be interpreted to sanction first use of conventional weapons.[15]

In his keynote address at the Carnegie International Non-Proliferation Conference on 18 June 2001 in Washington D.C., Abdul Sattar declared that, 'Pakistan was not the first to conduct nuclear tests, similarly, we will not be the first to resume tests. In effect, Pakistan is observing the CTBT in anticipation of its coming into force.'

On the issue of nuclear safety and security, and export controls, he elaborated that, 'We have also taken measures to further tighten administrative and legal mechanisms to prohibit and prevent export of fissile materials and leakage of sensitive technology...the Government has also established the Pakistan Nuclear Regulatory Authority, another monitoring body for safety and checks'.[16]

Though Pakistan has not formally announced a nuclear doctrine, the two statements by Abdul Sattar clearly highlight the salient aspects of Pakistan's nuclear policy and can be summarized as follows:

- Pakistan's policy will be based on a minimum credible deterrence.
- It will eschew a strategic arms race with India.
- It will continue to support international arms control regimes, which are non-discriminatory in nature.
- It will participate in the FMCT negotiations.
- It will refrain from further nuclear testing.
- Pakistan will strengthen existing controls on the export of nuclear technology through administrative and legal mechanisms.

On other occasions, responsible officials and those at highest levels of leadership have also alluded to some key points of Pakistan's nuclear policy. Former President Musharraf recently also used the term 'Minimum Defensive Deterrence', which apparently is meant to convey the same meaning as 'Minimum Credible Deterrence', but with an emphasis on the defensive nature of Pakistan's nuclear deterrence.

Pakistani officials have repeatedly stated that Pakistan's nuclear policy is built around the twin principles of 'restraint' and 'responsibility', and driven by its security concerns in contrast to India's pretensions to a global power status. Inamul Haq, former minister of state for foreign affairs, further magnified this contrast in the goals and ambitions of the two countries when he declared that: 'Instead of a triad of nuclear forces Pakistan seeks a triad of peace, security and progress'.[17] He went on to suggest a Strategic Restraint Regime involving measures for nuclear and missile restraints, as well as conventional balance. He expressed Pakistan's readiness to enter into reciprocal arrangements with India to agree on:

- Non-deployment of ballistic missiles.
- No operational weaponization of nuclear capable missiles.
- Formalization of the existing understanding on pre-notification of missile flight tests.
- Declaration of a moratorium on the development, acquisition or deployment of ABM systems.

In Inamul Haq's view the three pillars of South Asian peace, security and progress, namely, 'a high level dialogue to resolve Jammu and Kashmir, mechanism to promote trade and economic cooperation, and a strategic restraint regime' would complement, sustain, support and reinforce each other.[18] Outlining Pakistan's Command and Control mechanisms, he stated that:

> We have over the last two years upgraded command and control mechanisms. A National Command Authority, chaired by the head of the government and including three federal ministers and chiefs of armed services, provides policy direction, oversees development and employment of assets, and approves measures to ensure custodial safety and complete institutional control over fissile materials and sensitive

technology. Procedures have been implemented to minimize the chances of accidental or unauthorized launch. We are studying the US Personnel Reliability and Nuclear Emergency Support Teams concepts for adaptation.[19]

PAKISTAN'S NUCLEAR COMMAND AND CONTROL

During its formative phase, from mid-1970s to May 1998, Pakistan's nuclear weapons programme remained covert and, because of the official policy of denial of the pursuit of nuclear weapons to deflect international pressure, it was obvious that no public debate on issues such as nuclear doctrine, command and control, or safety and security could take place. However, more inexplicable is the fact that even an in-house debate did not take place within the military or the foreign policy establishment, nor was there any discourse on these aspects within the few think tanks and academia. How, then, did Pakistan proceed so quickly to set up its Nuclear Command and Control in the aftermath of the May 1998 nuclear tests?

In late 1996, General Jehangir Karamat had established a small think tank in GHQ, working directly for the Army Chief's Secretariat, and providing analyses and conducting studies on various strategic issues. It was by coincidence that in February 1998, during a brainstorming session, the issue of Pakistan's nuclear command and control structure came up. At the time no such structure existed. Former Army Chief General Aslam Beg had been talking about a nuclear command arrangement, which was nothing more than a decision-making council comprising the president, the army chief and the senior scientists. He envisaged that they would take decisions regarding developmental aspects of the nuclear capability. This arrangement was certainly not designed to handle the operational aspects or employment of the nuclear assets. It was, therefore, decided to write a concept paper on Strategic Command and Control Organization. This was the first attempt at dealing with the issue, and fortunately happened at an opportune moment, shortly before the Indian and Pakistani nuclear tests in May 1998.

In the immediate aftermath of the tests, a team of officers was put together in GHQ to start working on the formulation of a nuclear doctrine, and to suggest an appropriate command and control organization. The original paper prepared by the research cell came in handy. In the meantime, a two star army general was appointed to head the prospective secretariat of the National Command Authority. He further refined the original concept and prepared a detailed organization, specifying the roles and charters of duties of its various components. In February 1999, a presentation was made to General Musharraf, who had taken over as the army chief from General Karamat. After the initial approval by the army chief, a presentation was made to Prime Minister Nawaz Sharif in GHQ in April 1999. The prime minister, while agreeing with the concept, held back his formal approval and wanted some of his cabinet ministers to deliberate on it further. However, pending formal government approval, a core group of officers had already started functioning in GHQ from March 1999. The prime minister, for some inexplicable reasons, continued to vacillate and did not give his formal approval until the military take-over in October 1999. The Musharraf government was quick to bring the subject before the cabinet and a formal approval of the structure of the National Command Authority and its various tiers was granted at a joint meeting of the federal cabinet and the National Security Council in February 2000.

Pakistan's Nuclear Command and Control comprises a three-tiered structure. The first tier is the National Command Authority (NCA), which is chaired by the president with the prime minister as its vice chairman. It has two main committees, i.e. the Employment Control Committee and the Developmental Control Committee. The Employment Control Committee, which by its composition is a politico-military committee has the foreign minister as its deputy chairman and includes ministers of defence, interior and finance as its members, besides the chairman joint chiefs of staff and the three services chiefs. The director general of the strategic plans division (SPD) acts as the secretary. This committee is the main policy making and decision making committee. The developmental control committee is in essence a military-scientific committee with the chairman of joint chiefs of staff as its deputy chairman and the three services chiefs and heads of various strategic organizations as its members. This committee translates the decisions of the employment control committee into developmental goals and oversees their implementation. The second tier of command is the SPD, which acts as the permanent secretariat of the NCA. SPD formulates policy options for approval by the NCA and, once the decisions have been taken, oversees their implementation. SPD is organized in a manner so that it can take care of all aspects related to the management of the nuclear capability, and takes care of the administrative, budgetary, safety and security aspects of the nuclear entities. The third tier is the services strategic force commands, which are the custodians of the delivery systems and are responsible for training, maintenance and administration of these systems. The operational control, however, is retained by the NCA. The organizational structure of the NCA and the SPD is as follows:

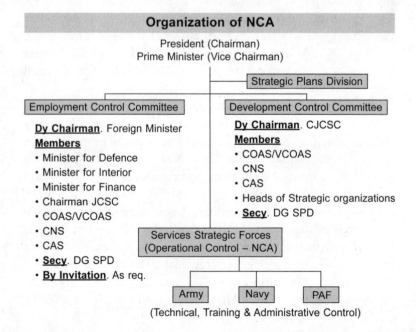

Organization of NCA

President (Chairman)
Prime Minister (Vice Chairman)

Strategic Plans Division

Employment Control Committee

Dy Chairman. Foreign Minister
Members
- Minister for Defence
- Minister for Interior
- Minister for Finance
- Chairman JCSC
- COAS/VCOAS
- CNS
- CAS
- **Secy**. DG SPD
- **By Invitation**. As req.

Development Control Committee

Dy Chairman. CJCSC
Members
- COAS/VCOAS
- CNS
- CAS
- Heads of Strategic organizations
- **Secy**. DG SPD

Services Strategic Forces
(Operational Control – NCA)

Army   Navy   PAF

(Technical, Training & Administrative Control)

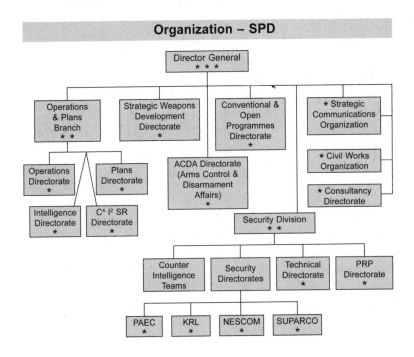

Organization – SPD

NATIONAL COMMAND AUTHORITY ORDINANCE

Organization of the SPD, as originally conceived, has withstood the test of time over the years. However, some changes have been made to enable it to effectively perform its assigned responsibilities, and some of its components have seen substantial growth. A case in point is the security division of the NCA, which is not only responsible for the physical security of assets and installations, but also personnel security. It now has 9000–10000 personnel, is headed by a two star general and a dedicated Personnel Reliability Programme (PRP) Directorate.

The NCA was formally instituted in February 2000 through an executive decision taken in a joint meeting of the federal cabinet and the NSC. In order to provide it with legal cover and to equip its various officials with the necessary powers, not only to perform their duties, but to effectively deal with any infringements of security and violation of laid down procedures by any employee working in any of the component organizations, a need was felt for appropriate legislation. The president of Pakistan, therefore, promulgated an ordinance entitled National Command Authority Ordinance, 2007 on 13 December 2007.[20] The ordinance has not brought about any changes in the existing command and control structure, which would continue to function as it has been doing since February 2000. The Ordinance defines powers and responsibilities to investigate and punish, lays down the jurisdiction of relevant courts, and specifies the offences and penalties. The maximum punishment that can be awarded to any offender could be up to twenty-five years imprisonment. This is also a declaration of legal intent on part of the Pakistani government, to ensure an effective command and control, and the safety and security of its nuclear assets. Some news reports however, appeared to give the impression that the Ordinance was meant to establish the National Command Authority, which obviously was not the case.[21]

It is evident, therefore, that Pakistan has since May 1998 covered a lot of ground in terms of establishing organizational, administrative and legislative structures to manage and oversee its nuclear assets. However, these efforts have to some extent failed to reassure the sceptics who continue to express concerns about Pakistan's ability to keep its nuclear weapons and materials safe and secure in the face of multiple security threats it is facing. Some critics also raise doubts about the effectiveness of Pakistan's command and control structures in the light of past security lapses epitomized by the A.Q. Khan episode. The detractors also cite the strong religious orientation of some Pakistani nuclear scientists and engineers and as a corollary assume that they would have a soft corner for the religious extremists of the Al Qaeda and Taliban types. A lot of this criticism is due to lack of information and first hand knowledge of the actual situation. This is borne out by the fact that those foreign academics and officials who have had the opportunity to interact with the Pakistani nuclear establishment are far more sanguine about these issues. One thing is clear, however, that Indian and Pakistani nuclear command and control structures are still at an early stage of evolution and would further mature and consolidate with the passage of time.

NOTES

1. Draft Report of National Security Advisory Board on Indian Nuclear Doctrine, Embassy of India Washington, DC, indianembassy.org and Jasjit Singh, 'Indian Draft Nuclear Doctrine: Some Reflections', Pugwash Online, also see 'India's Draft Nuclear Doctrine', Arms Control Association, Arms Control Today, July/August 1999.
2. Ashley J. Tellis, *India's Emerging Nuclear Posture: Between Recessed Deterrence and Ready Arsenal*, RAND, Santa Monica, 2001. For a review and summary of the book, see RAND Research Brief, RB-63 (2001).
3. Mattoo, op. cit., pp. 11–15.
4. Perkovich, op. cit., p. 441.
5. Bharat Karnad, 'A Thermonuclear Deterrent', in Amitabh Mattoo (ed.), *India's Nuclear Deterrent*, p. 111.
6. Ibid., pp. 113–26.
7. Ibid., p. 136.
8. Kanti P. Bajpai, 'The Fallacy of an Indian Deterrent', in Amitabh Mattoo (ed.), 'India's Nuclear Deterrent', pp. 151–2.
9. Ibid., pp. 153–4.
10. Ibid., p. 154.
11. Agha Shahi, Zulfiqar Khan & Abdul Sattar, 'Securing Nuclear Peace', *The News International*, 5 October 1999. P.R. Chari et al., pp. 190–92
12. Ibid.
13. Strategic Issues, Institute of Strategic Studies, Islamabad, March 2000, pp. 2–3.
14. Ibid., p. 55.
15. Abdul Sattar, address at the National Defence College, Islamabad, 24 May 2000.
16. Ibid.
17. Inamul Haq, Foreign Secretary of Pakistan, Statement in the Conference on Disarmament, Geneva, 25 January 2001.
18. Ibid.
19. Abdul Sattar, Keynote Address at the Carnegie International Non-Proliferation Conference: 'New Leaders, New Directions' on 18 June 2001, Washington DC.
20. President Promulgated National Command Authority Ordinance, Associated Press of Pakistan, 13 December 2007.
21. 'National Command Authority Established', *The Business Recorder*, Karachi, 14 December 2007.

7

Deterrence, Stability, Confidence Building Measures and Restraint Regime

The South Asian nuclear deterrence situation does not lend itself to an easy comparison with the Cold War model of deterrence between the two super powers, for reasons of both geography as well as history. The contiguity of India and Pakistan, disparity in their sizes, and a history of active hostilities including three major wars, some minor skirmishes and some near misses, distinguish the two South Asian antagonists from the US–USSR rivalry during the cold war. The China factor, which despite recent warming of Sino–Indian relations, weighs heavily in Indian security calculations and further complicates the situation. Since the mid-1980s a virtual deterrence situation was established in South Asia, variously described as the 'non-weaponized deterrence' or 'recessed deterrence'. Many analysts attribute the peaceful resolution of serious predicaments, such as the 1986–87 Brass Tacks crisis and the 1990 crisis over Kashmir, to the prevalence of this peculiar form of deterrence. The advantage of this kind of deterrence was greater crisis stability and low probability of an unauthorized or unintended nuclear strike, due to the inbuilt time/space buffers. In the period immediately following the nuclear tests in May 1998, the state of deterrence in South Asia remained tenuous at best, and a cause of concern for not only the two South Asian nuclear rivals but for the world at large. The Kargil conflict in the summer of 1999, and a year long military stand off in 2001–02 following the terrorist attack on Indian Parliament, seemed to confirm the worst fears of the proliferation pessimists. All kinds of doubts were expressed about the abilities of the two new entrants into the nuclear club, with regard to responsible nuclear stewardship. The 9/11 events and the ensuing 'war on terror' further complicated the situation, by raising concerns about terrorist attempts to acquire nuclear weapons or materials, and the possibility of terrorist attacks against nuclear installations. With the resumption of a composite dialogue between India and Pakistan in 2004 the situation has gradually improved, with agreements on a number of nuclear related CBMs and the general reduction in tensions in the region. It appears that the two South Asian neighbours are steadily moving up the nuclear learning curve and towards a stable nuclear deterrent situation. Meanwhile, both countries have set up command and control mechanisms, which are maturing as the time goes by. Pakistan announced the establishment of its National Command Authority and its various components in February 2000, while India announced the setting up of its Nuclear Command Authority in January 2003. Export controls have also been strengthened through the introduction of new and comprehensive export control laws, by Pakistan in 2004,[1] and by India in 2005.[2] With the gradual appreciation of the nuclear reality, the rhetoric has also given way to more responsible and sober statements by the leadership in both countries. However, serious disputes, including that over Kashmir, remain unresolved and unless there is a positive movement towards their resolution, the potential for another nuclear standoff between India and Pakistan will remain lingering in the background.

INDIAN THINKING ON LIMITED WAR AND COLD START STRATEGY

Indian thinking on limited war has been clearly influenced by their experience of the Kargil conflict in 1999. A few months after the termination of that episode a flurry of public statements by senior defence managers triggered an intense debate on the issue. Another reason for India's interest in a limited war doctrine can be found in the criticism by a segment of the Indian strategic community of the government's decision to go overtly nuclear in May 1998. Their criticism revolved around the argument, that it provided an opportunity to Pakistan to demonstrate its own nuclear capability and as a resultant India's conventional advantage vis-à-vis Pakistan was neutralized. A plausible justification, therefore, had to be found for maintaining a vast conventional military infrastructure. By propounding a limited war doctrine the Indian leadership was trying to achieve the twin objectives of justifying the need to maintain a large conventional force, and sending a message to Pakistan that the nuclearization of South Asia had not completely foreclosed India's options for the use of force. During this public discourse Indian defence minister, George Fernandez, and former army chief of staff, General V.P. Malik, emerged as the main proponents of the limited war doctrine.

In his inaugural address at a national seminar on 'The Challenges of Limited War', organized by Institute of Defence Studies and Analysis in New Delhi on 5 January 2000, Fernandez said; '...we kept all the wars limited in the past. No civilian targets were attacked, and the wars were terminated at the earliest opportunity'.[3] He went on to add that:

> We had understood the dynamics of limited war especially after India declared its nuclear weapons status nearly two years ago. Nuclear weapons did not make war obsolete; simply imposed another dimension on the way warfare could be conducted. The Kargil War, therefore, was handled within this perspective with obvious results.[4]

The Indian defence minister tried to reinforce his argument about the feasibility of a conventional war between two nuclear armed rivals by citing the example of the 1969 border clashes between China and the former Soviet Union, stating that, 'while war, in our context was kept limited in the past by choice, our interests would require that it should be kept limited in future as a matter of necessity'.[5]

Coinciding with the large-scale mobilization and deployment of forces along its borders with Pakistan in early 2002, Indian Army Chief General Padmanabhan said, 'The military situation with

Pakistan is serious and could spark a 'limited conventional war'. Adding that, 'To say that there is scope for a limited conventional war is a truism, yes it is there, but it all depends on the circumstances'.[6] However, at the same time other statements emanating from New Delhi indicated thinking reflecting anything but a limited war concept. For instance, Prime Minister Vajpayee in a statement on 2 January 2000 said, 'Whatever weapon is available we will use it to defend ourselves. And if because of that weapon the attacker is defeated......if he is killed, we should not be held responsible'.[7]

This muddled thinking and these conflicting statements drew criticism from many quarters within India. For instance, a prominent strategic analyst, Raja Mohan, pointed out that such statements reinforced the characterization of South Asia as a nuclear flash point and urged that, 'It is in India's interest to elaborate in greater detail its compulsions in adopting a strategy to fight a limited war, and commitment to maintain nuclear restraint.'[8] Another pre-eminent Indian strategist, General Raghavan, termed the statements made by George Fernandez and V.P. Malik as, 'ill informed references to limited war'.[9]

General V.R. Raghavan was very critical of the cavalier attitude with which the 'limited war' concept was being propounded in India, and expressed his apprehensions over India and Pakistan. Almost simultaneous statements made by Defence Minister George Fernandez and Army Chief of Staff General V.P. Malik, declaring that, 'India will not hesitate to fight a limited war with Pakistan, regardless of its nuclear weapons capability' is illustrative of the former while latter is amplified by General Raghavan's formulation that:

> The risks involved in fighting a limited war over the Kashmir issue and the potential for such a war to escalate into a nuclear exchange are at best inadequately understood and at worst brushed aside as an unlikely possibility......a close examination of Indian and Pakistani military and nuclear doctrines reveals elements that could contribute to the rapid escalation of a limited war to include nuclear weapons....the political objectives that a limited war might seek to achieve have also

not been articulated in official and public discourse in the two countries.[10]

He goes on to argue that the ongoing conflict in Kashmir, Pakistani belief that nuclear weapons have curtailed India's military options, and the Indian belief that despite Pakistan's nuclear weapons capability, a limited conventional war could be fought and won against Pakistan, create a situation fraught with dangers.[11]

The biggest paradox of limited war is that the escalation it is intended to avoid may become a necessary requirement for its termination. Professor John Garnett has summed up the views of many Western strategists who point out that:

> Military force is a blunt, crude instrument, better compared with the wood cutter's axe than the surgeon's scalpel. Inevitably, therefore, war is not usually a nicely calculated, precisely controlled business. More frequently it is a bloody, messy, painful and savage affair, which because it inflames the passions, provides an emotionally charged environment in which miscalculations and misperceptions flourish. The theory of controlled escalation ignores the crudity of the military instrument and seriously underplays the psychological pressure on each belligerent to misread his enemy's moves and to misjudge his own.[12]

While discussing the problems of limited war, Henry Kissinger highlighted the complexities of limited war and was of the view that it poses much greater psychological problems as compared to an all-out war. He went on to argue that, 'since limited wars offer no inherent guarantee against their expansion, they may gradually merge into an all-out war'.[13] Kissinger, while highlighting the intricacies of limited war said that, 'Limited war is not simply a question of appropriate military forces and doctrines. It also places heavy demands on the discipline and subtlety of the political leadership and on the confidence of the society in it'.[14]

IMPLICATIONS FOR SOUTH ASIAN SECURITY

It would appear that both India and Pakistan are in the process of assimilating the strategic implications of the nuclearization of South Asia. As these lessons gradually sink in, a degree of maturity, both in terms of actions as well as pronouncements, is likely to come about. Ten years is a rather short period of time, especially in view of the major distraction and distortion caused by the events of 9/11, to grasp the essentials of the nuclearization of the region. Profound changes have been brought about in the regional security environment as a consequence. Despite the advantage of hindsight, the two South Asian neighbours have tried to reinvent the wheel and have gone through their own versions of the 'Berlin Crises' and the 'Cuban Missile Crises' in the form of Kargil (1999) and a military stand-off in 2001–02. It appears that they could gradually settle down into a more stable and manageable relationship.

The sternest test faced by India's limited war doctrine was during the prolonged military stand off in 2002. Indian military planners must have realized the inadequacies of this concept. Their inability to apply it to an actual situation was obviously due to a rational cost–gain analysis by Indian military planners, keeping in mind its serious escalatory potential. The options were, therefore, confined to brinkmanship and the limited use of coercive diplomacy, rather than limited use of the military instrument. An alternative explanation could be that the Indians employed a 'strategy of compellence' which places more stringent demands on its practitioners, such as overwhelming superiority in the balance of forces. Pakistan adopted a 'strategy of deterrence', which is far less demanding. There was therefore an inherent dichotomy in Indian strategic thinking, keeping in view their advocacy of the limited war at the declaratory level, and their attempts at compelling Pakistan to do their bidding at the operational level. This mismatch in theory and practice resulted in their inability to achieve results commensurate with their effort. This experience might well have been the prime motivation behind the efforts to revert to the composite dialogue process in order to resolve the outstanding disputes between the two countries. The limited war doctrine however, continues to remain an integral part of Indian strategic jargon, though it is no longer so forcefully and publicly propounded. The current trend towards the resolution of disputes through a sustained process of dialogue will hopefully eliminate the incentives for recourse to the use of force—'limited' or 'unlimited'.

It is an irony of geography that the peculiar shape and size of Pakistan, which gives it with limited strategic depth is advantageous from the point of view of quicker mobilization of forces when compared to India. In 2001–02 the Indians found that, by the time they had completed the movement of their forces towards the international border, the Pakistanis were already there, waiting to receive them. Frustrated by this experience, the Indians came up with a new concept called the 'Cold Start Strategy'. This involves the reorganisation of their defensive formations stationed close to the international borders, and the augmentation of their offensive capability with greater mobility, and the emphasis on combined air–land operations. These formations would then be used to undertake offensive operations and make initial gains, exploiting the element of surprise, while the strike formations move up from the hinterland to consolidate and further exploit the gains. However, there are serious flaws in this concept because Pakistani forces would still be able to move up and counter these offensive actions well before the Indian offensive formations arrive on the scene. Irrespective of whether this is a sound strategic concept or not, this will be viewed as offensive and provocative by Pakistan and will make the risk of surprise attacks perennial, adding to the tensions and mutual suspicions. Pakistan has, therefore, been insisting, during the talks on conventional CBMs, that the two sides should abandon such offensive doctrines, that have the potential to destabilize the security environment.

HOW ROBUST IS SOUTH ASIAN NUCLEAR DETERRENCE?

The first serious crisis of the post nuclearization era in South Asia was the 1999 conflict in the Kargil region of the disputed state of Kashmir. Analysts are divided in their views about this conflict, with one group terming it as a failure of deterrence while the other citing it as another manifestation of the evolving nuclear equilibrium in South Asia. In his opening remarks before unveiling the Indian nuclear doctrine, India's national security advisor, Brajesh Mishra, acknowledged that the Kargil conflict remained confined to a limited sector and did not spill over to other parts of the Line of Control or the international border, due to the existence of nuclear deterrence. There is a general misconception regarding the prevailing conventional balance in South Asia. Although, the balance is clearly tilted in India's favour, what is generally overlooked is the fact that India's conventional advantage is by no means overwhelming, and Pakistan has so far been able to maintain a manageable ratio of forces. The doomsday scenarios projecting a contemplation of the use of nuclear weapons by Pakistan at a very early stage of the conflict is therefore, grossly misplaced. There is also a fairly widespread misperception that the Kargil conflict was likely to turn into a nuclear war between India and Pakistan, had a ceasefire not been brought about through the intervention by President Clinton. Some former American officials have also stated that they had evidence of imminent Pakistani preparations for a nuclear war and that Prime Minister Nawaz Sharif, during his one-to-one meeting with the US president, was presented with evidence of the Pakistani military's preparations for a nuclear war without his knowledge.[15] Senior officials in the Pakistani nuclear establishment have emphatically debunked this story, and insist that no such moves were made, and neither did the military situation warrant any such steps.[16] However, if India continues to acquire large amounts of 'state of the art' military hardware from Russia, Israel, France, Britain and even the United States, it will not be long before the disparity will become unmanageable. This will have the undesirable effect of lowering Pakistan's nuclear threshold. India has substantially increased its defence expenditure over the past few years. Pakistan, in accordance with its declared policy of avoiding the temptation of getting embroiled into a debilitating arms race with India, has kept its own defence budget frozen over the same period, catering only for the impact of inflation.

The military crisis in 2001–02 tested the limits of deterrence. Fortunately, the deterrence held, due to the fact that the existing conventional balance did not allow India the freedom of action or the confidence in its ability to make any meaningful gains. Against the backdrop of a mutual nuclear deterrence situation, any military adventure entails very high risks and costs. One thing however, has clearly emerged, that the last time around things did not spiral out of control, due to sustained high level diplomatic efforts by the US and to a lesser extent other friendly countries. In the absence of such high-level mediation, the possibility of an intended or unintended disaster cannot be ruled out. The propensities for sabre rattling and brinkmanship need to be curbed, and coercive use of military force must not be employed once too often. In the very early stages of the military standoff India tested a modified version of MRBM Agni, with a range of 700 km, and declared it as a Pakistan specific missile. Pakistan on its part conducted a series of missile tests at the height of the tensions in May 2002, to send a signal of its resolve. However, both sides were careful to give prior notification of the tests to each other to avoid any misunderstandings. General Sundararajan Padmanabhan, the Indian army chief at the time, in a statement devoid of any subtlety or finesse, hurled nuclear threats at Pakistan, warning it that launching any nuclear attack would unleash a backlash from India. Padmanabhan declared that: 'The perpetrator of that particular outrage shall be punished, shall be punished so severely that the continuation of any form of fray will be doubtful'.[17] In a statement in reply, the Pakistani President cautioned India that, 'unconventional' means would be used by Pakistan if India ventured across the LOC. Given the fact that India and Pakistan are nuclear weapon powers, this statement was interpreted as a threat to use nuclear weapons. Later on efforts were made to clarify that unconventional means in this case implied the use of guerrilla tactics. There were, however, not many takers for this explanation. Such actions and pronouncements do not inspire much confidence either within the region or outside. One can only hope that with the passage of time, and greater understanding of nuclear jargon, due care will be exercised in public pronouncements, especially during crises.

Nuclear Risk Reduction Measures

The concept of nuclear risk reduction measures is relatively new to the two South Asian nations. Such ideas could not be discussed bilaterally or at any multilateral forum due to the fact that both countries had covert nuclear programmes and were reluctant to acknowledge the existence of military nuclear capabilities. However, the May 1998 nuclear tests brought their respective programmes into the open, thereby removing the biggest barrier in the way of discussion of nuclear risk reduction measures. Prior to 1998, the only agreement in the nuclear realm was the 1988 Agreement on 'Non-attack on each other's nuclear facilities'.[18] This agreement required an exchange of lists of respective nuclear installations on 1 January every year. The agreement has held its ground so far, and even at the peak of tensions between the two countries at the beginning of January 2002, the lists were exchanged as had been the conventional practice.[19] This is not only a good omen, but also indicative of the importance both countries attach to this agreement and the seriousness with which it is followed.

Pakistan's Strategic Restraint Regime Proposal

In October 1998, during the expert level talks between India and Pakistan in Islamabad, nuclear risk reduction measures also came under discussion. During the course of the debate Pakistan made a comprehensive proposal for a 'Strategic Restraint Regime' in South Asia. This proposal contained not only nuclear and missile restraint measures, but also suggestions regarding conventional balance and restraint, in view of the close linkage between conventional and nuclear conflict. The restraint measures covered the complete spectrum from development to testing and deployment. However, the Indian side expressed its inability to discuss the suggestion until they had carefully evaluated and analysed the proposal.[20] Some of the ideas discussed during the Islamabad meeting were duly reflected in the Lahore MOU. Unfortunately, the dialogue process broke down after the Lahore

MOU, and there has been no further formal discussion of the Strategic Restraint Regime between the two countries.

THE LAHORE MOU

The Lahore MOU listed a total of eight measures for promoting a stable environment of peace and security between India and Pakistan. Out of these, five measures are directly related to nuclear risk reduction, while two others, i.e. 'periodic review of the implementation of existing CBMs and the setting up of appropriate consultative mechanisms to monitor and ensure their effective implementation' and the 'review of existing communication links between the two DGMOs with a view to upgrading and improving these links' are also complementary to the nuclear risk reduction measures. The last one pertains to agreement on 'prevention of incidents at sea'. The five specific measures related to Nuclear Risk Reduction are:

- The two sides shall engage in bilateral consultations on security concepts and nuclear doctrines, with a view to developing measures for confidence building in the nuclear and conventional fields, aimed at avoidance of conflict.
- The two sides undertake to provide each other with advance notification in respect of ballistic missile flight tests and shall conclude a bilateral agreement in this regard.
- The two sides are fully committed to undertaking national measures to reducing the risks of accidental or unauthorized use of nuclear weapons under their respective control. The two sides further undertake to notify each other immediately in the event of any accidental, unauthorized or unexplained incident that could create the risk of a fallout with adverse consequences for both sides, or an outbreak of a nuclear war between the two countries, as well as to adopt measures aimed at diminishing the possibility of such actions, or such incidents being misinterpreted by the other. The two sides shall identify/establish the appropriate communication mechanism for this purpose.

- The two sides shall continue to abide by their respective unilateral moratorium on conducting further nuclear test explosions unless either side, in exercise of its national sovereignty decides that extraordinary events have jeopardized its supreme interests.

- The two sides shall engage in bilateral consultations on security, disarmament and non-proliferation issues within the context of negotiations on these issues in multilateral fora.[21]

It also stipulated that where required, the technical details to implement the above measures would be worked out by experts of the two sides in meetings to be held on mutually agreed dates, before mid-1999, with a view to reaching bilateral agreements.[22] This anticipated meeting of experts could not take place due to the Kargil episode. As a result the agreed upon risk reduction measures could not be formalized into bilateral and binding agreements.

An interesting area however, is the ballistic missile flight-testing in which the two sides had established a norm with regard to pre-notification of these tests. In April 1999, when India conducted the test of an advanced version of its medium range ballistic missile Agni, a notification was given to Pakistan. Similarly, when Pakistan responded to this test by testing its own medium range missiles 'Ghauri' and 'Shaheen-I', India was duly notified. Pakistan has since then notified all its missile tests to India. India on the other hand, after the April 1999 test, discontinued notification of its missile tests, probably as a reaction to the Kargil conflict resulting in the next six tests not being pre-notified. However, in early January 2002 while India was in the midst of its largest troop mobilization since the 1971 War, and conducting the maiden test of its, shorter range version (700 km) of the Agni missile, it did provide a prior notification to Pakistan. Similarly, at the peak of tensions during the 2002 military standoff, when Pakistan conducted a series of missile tests in the last week of May that year, India was pre-notified. Since then both sides have continued to notify each other of their respective tests on a regular basis. Another positive aspect of this issue is that even in the absence of any formal agreement in this regard, both sides have been very careful in ensuring that they do not point the missiles in each other's direction during the test flights, to avoid any possibility of a misunderstanding or misperception.[23]

In addition to the establishment of the norm on notification, two other positive developments also took place. Firstly, in 1999 Pakistan took a conscious decision to break the action–reaction cycle with regard to missile testing and to conduct the tests only when dictated by the need to validate some technical parameters. Secondly, as a result of the norm on notification and the care taken by both sides to test the missiles at locations away from their common borders, the missile tests by both sides are now accepted as a routine activity of a technical nature. An interesting episode in this regard happened in March 2004, at the time of the first ever test firings by Pakistan of its Shaheen-II missile. This was the first time that Pakistan carried out an 'over the sea' missile test. On this occasion not only was prior notification given to India, it was also asked to issue a NOTAM to the international maritime and civil aviation traffic in the area, since the intended impact point of the missile fell in the jurisdiction of Mumbai air traffic control, and the request was complied with. This was by far the clearest indication that, when the two countries are convinced about the utility of a particular risk reduction or confidence building measure, they abide by it whether or not a formal agreement exists in this regard or not. The missile test pre-notification agreement was finalized during the expert level talks, held in New Delhi in August 2005,[24] and was signed into a formal agreement by the two foreign ministers in October 2005.[25]

The other significant agreement in the Lahore MOU related to the two sides abiding by their respective unilateral moratoria on nuclear testing, and the two sides have since refrained from nuclear testing. Pakistan has on several occasions proposed that these unilateral moratoria could be converted into a bilateral moratorium, which would not only enhance the credibility of the commitments by the two countries in this regard, but would also be reassuring for the international community. India is unlikely to be amenable to this proposal and would most probably prefer to maintain the status quo, particularly now that the CTBT is in abeyance and there is no international pressure on India and Pakistan to sign the CTBT.[26]

With regard to the reduction of risks of accidental or unauthorized use of nuclear weapons, the two countries have moved to establish requisite command and control structures. Pakistan announced the establishment of a three tiered nuclear command and control structure in February 2000,[27] with the National Command Authority (NCA) as the apex decision making body. India, for its part, announced the establishment of its Nuclear Command Authority in January 2003. This consists of a political committee, an executive committee and a tri-service strategic force command.[28]

On the issue of bilateral consultation on security, disarmament and non-proliferation within the context of negotiations on these issues in multilateral fora, no formal consultative mechanism has evolved, though there is a lot of scope for cooperation in this area since, on many issues, the two countries have identical concerns and more often than not their interests and positions coincide. However, formal cooperation and adoption of joint positions can only come about in the context of an overall improvement in the bilateral relations and discernible progress towards the resolution of long standing disputes.

THE WAY FORWARD

Some areas where mutuality of interest exists can easily be identified. For instance, the DGMOs hotline has served as the most reliable communication link between the two countries for years. It was decided to upgrade and improve this channel in the Lahore MOU as well. This was mainly an issue related to the sorting out of technical details and there were no political impediments or reservations in this regard. The original DGMOs hotline suffered from many technical deficiencies, since it was based on an antiquated overland telephone line maintained by the two sides within their respective territories. There were frequent breakdowns and the quality of speech was also not up to the standard required, due to high noise level.[29] A further problem with this line was that it was a voice communication channel, which is not the ideal media in which to communicate during crises and periods of high tension. With the availability of more reliable and secure fibre optic or satellite links, which also have greater capacity, it can be supplemented with Fax and computer based tele-type communication methods. Agreement to shift the DGMO hotline to the fibre optic link was formalized during the expert level meeting in New Delhi in August 2005[30] and has since been implemented. In addition to the DGMOs hotline, a hotline has also been established between the respective foreign secretaries, to facilitate the exchange of information on nuclear related matters, as had already been agreed to by the two sides during the first round of expert level talks held in New Delhi in June 2004.[31]

The second area that needed to be looked into is the inconsistent implementation of the existing CBMs. Recognizing this fact, it was decided at Lahore to periodically review the implementation of existing CBMs and to establish appropriate consultative mechanisms in this regard.[32] It is, therefore, imperative that a review and oversight mechanism should be established to meet biannually to review the progress on the implementation of existing CBMs. This forum could also be used to explore ideas on introducing improvements where possible or removing any technical impediments that may be hindering their smooth implementation. The review committee should hold any side not meeting its obligations to account. A case in point is the Indus Basin Treaty of 1962 which is by far the most successful CBM between India and Pakistan, principally because it is backed up by an institutionalized mechanism, in the form of the two Indus Water Authorities. The respective commissioners meet on a regular basis to review the implementation, and address complaints, by either side and have usually been able to resolve contentious issues at the technical level.

Another important confidence building measure between the two sides is the agreement to reduce the risk of accidents and unauthorized use of nuclear weapons. The agreement, which was formally signed in February 2007,[33] however, does not have any verification mechanism and appears to be based on good faith. A look at the text of the agreement reveals that no reciprocal or binding measures have been included, and the purpose has apparently been to reach an agreement without getting into contentious issues related to any kind of verification mechanism.

The most brilliant ideas and the most innovative schemes in the field of arms control, confidence building and risk reduction will not yield any positive dividends unless they are backed up by a matching political commitment, sincerity of purpose and determination and resolve on the part of both sides to make them succeed. In this regard it must also be kept in mind that only such measures would have any chance of success, in which both sides perceive a mutuality of interest. Any measure which is forced upon one party or the other, or which serves the interest of one side or the other and not both equally is doomed to failure.

NOTES

1. Gabrielle Kohlmeier, 'Pakistan Introduces Export Control Bill', *Arms Control Today,* Arms Control Association, September 2004 and Gabrielle Kohlmeier and Miles A. Pomper, 'Pakistan Advances Export Controls', *Arms Control Today,* Arms Control Association, October 2004.
2. Paul Kerr, 'India Passes Non-proliferation Legislation', *Arms Control Today,* Arms Control Association, June 2005.
3. Inaugural Address by George Fernandez at National Seminar Organised by IDSA on 'The Challenges of Limited War: Parameters and Options', New Delhi, 5 January 2000.
4. Ibid.
5. Ibid.
6. *Hindustan Times,* New Delhi, 11 January 2002.
7. Statement by Prime Minister Vajpayee on 2 January 2002, quoted in 'Disarmament Diplomacy', Issue No. 62, January–February 2002, Acronym Institute, UK.

8. Raja Mohan, quoted by General V.R. Raghavan in 'Limited War and Nuclear Escalation in South Asia', 'The non-Proliferation Review', Fall-Winter 2001, Vol. 8, No. 3, Centre for Non-proliferation Studies, Monterey Institute of International Studies, Monterey, CA, USA, p. 5.

9. Ibid., General V.R. Raghavan.

10. Ibid., p. 1.

11. Ibid., p. 3.

12. Garnett, p. 206.

13. Kissinger, pp. 167 and 143.

14. Ibid., p. 167.

15. Bruce Riedel, 'American Diplomacy and the 1999 Kargil Summit at Blair House', pp. 12–13. http://www.sas.upenn.edu/casi/publications/Riedel_2002.

16. In an interview with the author in 2002 after the publication of the Riedel story, Lt.-Gen. Kidwai, Director General of Pakistan's Strategic Plans Division termed the idea of any nuclear moves as ridiculous.

17. Ibid.

18. Kamal and Gupta, op. cit. Appendix-B-3.

19. 'Pakistan and India Exchange Annual Nuclear Lists', The News, Islamabad, 1 January 2002.

20. Based on the recollections of Brigadier Feroz Hassan Khan, former Director Arms Control & Disarmament Affairs, Strategic Plans Division, Joint Staff Headquarters, Pakistan.

21. Lahore MOU, op. cit. Also see Nazir Kamal and Amit Gupta, op. cit.

22. Ibid.

23. Based on the author's personal experience of the notification process.

24. Jawed Naqvi, 'Accord on nuke hotlines, missile tests with India', The Dawn, Karachi, 7 August 2005.

25. Qudssia Akhlaque, 'Pakistan-India sign two deals: missile testing, coastal information', The Dawn, Karachi, 4 October 2005.

26. As expected the two sides have reaffirmed their respective nuclear testing moratoriums as enunciated in the Lahore MOU. CNN, News Bulletin, 20 June 2004. Also see The Dawn, Karachi and The News, Islamabad, 20 June 2004.

27. Pakistan Ministry of Foreign Affairs, Organization of Pakistan's National Command Authority, http://www.forisb.org/NCA.html.

28. The Hindu, New Delhi, 4 January 2003.

29. Based on the personal inquiries and recent observations by the author.

30. Jawed Naqvi, op. cit.

31. Jawed Naqvi, 'Nuclear Hotline to be set-up, Pakistan–India to continue test ban', The Dawn, Karachi, 21 June 2004.

32. Lahore MOU, op. cit.

33. Jawed Naqvi, 'India opposes joint train blast probe: Pact signed to avert nuclear accidents risks', The Dawn, Karachi, 22 February 2007.

8

The A.Q. Khan Episode

Not many individuals evoke such starkly contrasting feelings and images as Dr Abdul Qadeer Khan, commonly known as A.Q. Khan. Despite the fact that his image has been tainted due to his indiscreet proliferation practices, he still remains a 'national hero', a saviour of the nation for a large number of Pakistanis. However, he is reviled as a villain in the West for his irresponsible, and at times reckless, nuclear proliferation activities. Consequently, he has become a controversial personality for the security and non-proliferation analysts and many books, articles, and news stories have been published on his role as a nuclear proliferator.

A British newspaper demonised him as far back as 1979 as, 'the most successful nuclear spy since Klaus Fuchs and Alan Nunn May took their secrets to the Kremlin'.[1] Former CIA Director George Tenet has described A.Q. Khan as 'a man who had, almost single-handedly, turned Pakistan into a nuclear power and was viewed as a national hero in his country'.[2] Many others call him the 'father of Pakistan's nuclear bomb'. However, a recent study by the International Institute for Strategic Studies (IISS), London disagrees. According to the authors of the study, 'A.Q. Khan can be accorded many epithets, including founder of Pakistan's uranium enrichment programme. However, it is not appropriate to call him, as many do, the father of Pakistan's bomb.'[3]

THE HISTORICAL PERSPECTIVE

A.Q. Khan, known to be a brilliant metallurgist, studied in Germany in the early 1960s and earned his Master's degree in metallurgy from Delft University in the Netherlands in 1967. In

1971 he went on to earn a scholarship in order to study for his PhD in the same subject from the Catholic University of Leuven in Belgium, under the supervision of Professor Martin Brabers.[4] He was severely traumatized by the tragic events of 1971 in which Pakistan's eastern half was dismembered through a combination of internal political revolt and Indian military action, and decided to return to his homeland. He was determined to make his country invincible so that it would never again have to face the kind of humiliation it had faced in 1971. However, his efforts to seek a job in Pakistan did not receive an encouraging response. While he was searching for a job to sustain himself and his family, he was told by one of his old Dutch classmates, Hank Slebos, about a job for a metallurgist in FDO, a Dutch company working on the development of centrifuges as a sub-contractor for the Dutch, British, German consortium Urenco. The job description matched Khan's area of specialization and, with a strong recommendation from his mentor Professor Brabers, he was appointed to the job.[5] This version of events clearly indicates that A.Q. Khan's finding a job at FDO was merely coincidental, and contradicts the stories which insinuate that he was probably planted by the Pakistani government by design, to steal secrets about centrifuge enrichment technology from Urenco. If the FDO management did not strictly follow the security regulations stipulated by the Urenco partners, and the Dutch bureaucracy did not carefully look into relevant details while processing his security clearance,[6] he should not be faulted at least on this account.

During the course of his work at the FDO, providence provided Khan with an opportunity to gain a deep insight into centrifuge technology. The Urenco plant at Almelo had received technical manuals on the improved German version of the centrifuge designs called the G-2. These manuals, however, were in German and needed to be translated into Dutch. This task required a person who not only knew both languages, but also had the technical know-how to be able to accurately translate the manuals, and Khan fitted the bill perfectly. This particular assignment not only provided A.Q. Khan with intimate technical details of centrifuge technology, but allowed him access to the highly classified parts of the plant. His translation work, spanning sixteen working days in the most sensitive parts of the enrichment plant, provided him with information which was to prove invaluable in years to come, when he would set about establishing a similar plant in Pakistan. His job at FDO also provided him with opportunities to interact with various contractors, vendors and suppliers. This information again was critical when he embarked upon the procurement of components for his plant at Kahuta, as he did not have to hunt around since he knew the exact locations of the suppliers.[7]

BEGINNINGS OF PAKISTAN'S URANIUM ENRICHMENT EFFORT

A.Q. Khan's desire to return to his homeland and contribute towards its nuclear programme turned into a firm resolve following India's nuclear test in May 1974. Having reservations about the likely response from the bureaucracy, including the PAEC establishment, he decided to write a letter to Prime Minister Zulfikar Ali Bhutto offering his services in the national cause. He was granted an audience by the prime minister during his annual holiday visit to Pakistan in December 1974, where he enthusiastically argued for the enrichment route to a Pakistani bomb, expressing his scepticism at the chances of success through PAEC's preferred plutonium route. While Bhutto was impressed by his confidence and enthusiasm, he was unsure of the viability of Khan's suggested plan of action. Bhutto decided to take his time and to obtain an evaluation of the young scientist's credentials, and Khan was asked to return to his job in Holland. He finally returned to Pakistan in December 1975 never to go back, sending his resignation to his Dutch employers in early 1976. There are contradictory accounts as to whether he was sent back at the end of 1974 to gather more information or to help in the procurement of key components for a Pakistani enrichment effort.[8]

Around this time some Pakistani procurement activities related to equipment and materials specifically related to centrifuge enrichment caught the attention of the Dutch authorities, and A.Q. Khan also came under suspicion. He was placed under active surveillance by the Dutch secret service. The lack of conclusive evidence of his involvement in surreptitious activities, however, created a split within the Dutch government authorities as to how to deal with him. The CIA was also brought on board. They counselled against arresting Khan and wanted to keep an eye on his activities in order to gain more information. While the Dutch foreign ministry was in favour of arresting Khan, the economic affairs ministry under Ruud Lubbers, who was to later become the Dutch Prime Minister, was against any such action which could kick up a scandal and work against the Dutch economic interests. The CIA advice tilted the balance decisively in favour of the latter. However, Khan was moved to a non-sensitive job in FDO.[9] After the public disclosure of the proliferation network in early 2004 a debate was renewed as to whether he could have been stopped in the mid-1970s had the CIA not decided to give him a long leash. Former CIA Director George Tenet has tried to justify the CIA approach arguing that:

> The natural instinct when you find some shred of intelligence about nuclear proliferation is to act immediately. But you must control that urge and be patient, to follow the links where they take you, so that when action is launched, you can hope to remove the network both root and branch and not just pull off the top, allowing it to regenerate and grow again.[10]

Khan was later tried on charges of nuclear espionage and convicted by a Dutch court in absentia. However, an appeal was mounted by lawyers hired by the Pakistani government to defend A.Q. Khan and the verdict was overturned. The court decision has also remained controversial to this day. A.Q. Khan and the Pakistanis argue that he was finally acquitted by the Dutch court of all charges of wrongdoing, and it is inappropriate to talk about his earlier conviction, while the sceptics would argue, as Tenet has done, that the 'verdict was overturned on a technicality'.[11]

A.Q. Khan returned to Pakistan equipped with the knowledge and insight he had gained about centrifuge technology during the course of his work with the FDO, as well as drawings of centrifuge designs. Based on the blueprints brought by Khan, and other requisite materials and technology acquired through 'an underground network based mainly in the developed countries of Europe',[12] Pakistan was able to lay the foundations of its own centrifuge uranium enrichment facility. Within a very few years Pakistan was able to master the complex technology and was even able to improve upon the Urenco designs with which it had started. Much has been made of Pakistan's clandestine procurement of materials and technology from Europe and elsewhere, but the greed and profit making by the European suppliers, who sold their wares not only to Pakistan but other countries including South Africa and India, is not taken into account.

PAKISTAN'S UNCONVENTIONAL APPROACH—CAUSES AND CONSEQUENCES

Pakistan was forced to adopt its unconventional approach to nuclear development as a result of the barriers erected by industrialized countries in the aftermath of the Indian nuclear test of May 1974. The London Suppliers Group (LSG) which was later named as the Nuclear Suppliers Group (NSG) developed control lists for nuclear and dual use items, which made it virtually impossible for countries like Pakistan to purchase any kind of nuclear plant from the industrialized countries. As described in Chapter 3, Pakistan's agreement with France for the purchase of an enrichment plant, covered by a stringent trilateral agreement between Pakistan, France and the IAEA, fell through due to intense US pressure on both Pakistan and France. Against this backdrop Pakistan opted for the purchase of individual components rather than complete plants, and assembled these in the country. Alongside this import effort, production facilities were constructed to replicate and mass produce some of these components. This also entailed the granting of financial and administrative autonomy to heads of various strategic entities, especially A.Q. Khan. His financial transactions were not subjected to any audit and the consignments of equipment imported by KRL could not be inspected by customs officials in the interest of maintaining secrecy. This lack of oversight and trust, reposed in individuals without effective verification, produced quick results but also provided loopholes and opportunities to individuals for malpractices and indiscretions, which later came back to haunt Pakistan and tarnish its international image.

Outside observers find it hard to believe that A.Q. Khan could indulge in his proliferation activities without the active connivance, or at least the knowledge of Pakistani government or Pakistan Army, which is believed to have been supervising and controlling the nuclear programme from the outset. The fact remains that while the Pakistan government can be faulted for inadequate oversight of its nuclear programme and the activities of some of its scientists, it cannot be accused of complicity. Commenting on this issue, Tenet appears to be ambivalent and does not give any definitive judgment, saying that, 'we had the goods on A.Q. Khan and his cohorts and we had reached a point where we had to act, but there were still some important matters to resolve. It remained unclear to what extent Khan's dealings were known and supported by his own government. It was our job to find out'.[13] To put the issue in perspective the following arguments may be of some help.

Firstly, assistance to the nuclear programmes of countries such as Iran, Libya and North Korea did not make any strategic sense. In fact, such cooperation with these countries ran counter to Pakistan's national security interests. Iran, for instance, shares land borders with Pakistan, is a political competitor within the comity of Islamic states and has had an uneasy relationship with Saudi Arabia, while enjoying very cordial relations with Pakistan's arch rival India. So would any Pakistani leader in his or her right mind allow nuclear cooperation with Iran, which would mean having another nuclear neighbour, a stronger and more influential competitor in the region and in the Islamic world in general, and putting its very close strategic relations with Saudi Arabia under severe strains? This line of argument has also been supplemented by Christopher Clary, an American analyst, who in a very comprehensive and systematic analysis of the issue says that, 'the nuclear assistance from Khan to Iran is remarkable because it dramatically complicated Pakistan's threat environment. Pakistan–Iran relations have been periodically turbulent and growing India–Iran entente is disconcerting to Islamabad'.[14]

Similarly, North Korea is situated in the backyard of Pakistan's closest strategic partner China, and Pakistan would never want to foment trouble in China's backyard. A nuclear-armed North Korea would have triggered a chain reaction in North East Asia whereby Japan, South Korea and possibly Taiwan would have decided to go down the nuclear route, thereby vitiating China's security environment. The whole thesis, of the missiles for nuclear technology deal is based on the assumption that Pakistan was forced to enter into this deal due to shortage of resources. However, the total value of the missile deal constitutes a small fraction of Pakistan's defence imports and annual defence outlay in the corresponding period. This has also been corroborated by the IISS study as in which it states that:

> Beginning with Benazir Bhutto, successive Pakistani governments have insisted that the ballistic missile cooperation with North Korea was based on a cash payment rather than a quid-pro-quo exchange for Pakistani nuclear technology. Pakistan claims it paid $210 million to North Korea for their missile package including transfer of technology…Given the enormous importance of the No-Dong missile to national defence, $210 million would have been within Pakistan's financial means. Despite its low foreign reserves, Pakistan's arms imports during 1995–6 time frame were valued at $819 million. The overall defence budget in the mid-1990s was around $3 billion annually.[15]

In the Libyan case, the total value of the deal by various accounts is purported to be $100 million, which is peanuts for a country of the size of Pakistan. Moreover, any cooperation with Libya did not afford Pakistan any politico-strategic advantage and ran the risk of putting Pakistan on the wrong side of the international community, given Libya's status as an international pariah.

Secondly, we would need to examine the prevailing international environment under which Pakistan was pursuing its nuclear ambitions, as well as the administrative arrangements which were put in place by successive Pakistani governments for the management of the nuclear programme. Pakistan began its nuclear weapons effort in earnest after the May 1974 Indian nuclear test, which as explained earlier, had resulted in the erection of all kinds of barriers in the way of nuclear commerce. When A.Q. Khan started his procurement activities he had to negotiate this obstacle course. According to Steve Weissman and Herbert Krosney, 'the clever Pakistanis were staying a step ahead of the game by buying individual parts and assembling more and more of the equipment themselves in Pakistan itself'.[16] Clary explains that:

> In many ways, the story of A.Q. Khan is reminiscent of an Indiana Jones movie. Our protagonist is racing down a long corridor, with non-proliferation barriers rising in front of him and he has to quickly navigate these obstacles lest he be crushed. After Khan overcomes each hurdle a new one emerges in front of him that he must circumvent to avoid failure...Khan stayed one step ahead of the competition for almost three decades.[17]

A.Q. Khan's procurement effort was also facilitated by the freewheeling and willing European middlemen and vendors. When a German journalist, Egmont Koch, termed Khan's activities as smuggling during the course of an interview, Khan retorted by saying that:

> ...Why do you paint a picture—smugglers, smuggling and sneaking... If you want to buy a thing, you place the order directly and you will get it. It is no problem...you are not willing to sell it to me, but you are willing to sell it to Tom. So Tom buys from you, he takes 10 per cent or 15 per cent and he sells it to me. This is purely a business deal.[18]

A.Q. Khan's former professor from the University of Leuven, Martin Brabers, attributes Khan's success in procuring equipment from European suppliers to his knowledge of the companies, his numerous acquaintances and friends that he had cultivated across Europe as a result of his language skills and his personal charm. Brabers believes that no other Pakistani would have succeeded in buying these items.[19] Khan himself pointed to the keenness of the European companies to enter into business deals with Pakistan, claiming that, 'they literally begged us to buy their equipment. We bought what we considered suitable for our plant and very often asked them to make changes and modifications according to our requirements'.[20]

In the process Khan had to deal with shadowy characters and had control over large sums of money that were not subjected to independent audit or book keeping. On their part Pakistani leaders dissatisfied with the slow progress of work by the PAEC, which they attributed to bureaucratic inertia, had given complete autonomy to A.Q. Khan to run his laboratory as he pleased. This obviously meant a lack of oversight and greater opportunities for corrupt practices. He was indeed treading on tricky terrain and according to Graham Allison, 'You don't find people of integrity who operate in that zone.'[21]

On the political front the US had adopted a hard line policy on nuclear proliferation, and Secretary of State Henry Kissinger had famously warned Prime Minister Zulfikar Ali Bhutto of dire consequences if he did not abandon his nuclear ambitions. Jimmy Carter, who took over the US presidency in early 1977, pursued a non-proliferation policy with much greater vigour, almost as an article of faith. Pressure was brought to bear on both France and Pakistan to abandon the reprocessing plant deal. Under these circumstances Pakistan was left with no choice but to pursue its nuclear programme in a covert mode, which also implied that a bare minimum of people would have any knowledge of the programme, in order to minimize the chances of any leakage of information. According to Clary, 'one imagines that there were hundreds of instances in the history of the Pakistani nuclear programme where the competing goals of secrecy and oversight were in conflict. It also seems likely that secrecy won more often than oversight'.[22] When the enrichment programme was initiated at the Engineering Research Laboratories (ERL) later renamed as the Khan Research Laboratories (KRL) Prime Minister Bhutto had appointed an independent board working directly under the prime minister, with the secretary of finance as its chairman and the secretary general of foreign affairs and secretary of general defence as its members. Their role however, was only limited to coordination and facilitating A.Q. Khan.[23]

When General Ziaul Haq assumed the presidency he constituted a Power Development Coordination Cell (PDCC) in 1978–79 through a presidential directive. The mandate given to this cell was to coordinate the weapons related programmes of both PAEC and KRL. A serving two star general, detached from the army, was appointed as Secretary of the PDCC and a brigadier was also assigned as Adviser Security PAEC. The primary responsibility of these officers was to keep President Zia informed of the progress of the various projects being undertaken by PAEC and KRL. Apparently the original members of the board appointed by Z.A. Bhutto were also included in the PDCC. After General Zia's death Ghulam Ishaq Khan, who found himself in charge of the nuclear programme, decided to bring the army chief into the loop.[24] However, contrary to the common perception of the military exercising total control over the programme, even the senior leadership except for the army chief, was not privy to the information related to the nuclear programme. It was only during General Waheed Kakar's tenure as army chief, in the early 1990s, that a two star general serving in the army headquarters as director general combat development was assigned by him to act as his liaison with A.Q. Khan and the PAEC chairman. The designated officer would receive periodic briefings from the heads of the strategic entities and keep the army chief posted about the developments.

Serving officers of the rank of brigadier/colonel were assigned to oversee the security of KRL. However, the overall responsibility for security rested with A.Q. Khan and these officers reported directly to him. The army made an error of judgment in the selection of these officers who were usually on the verge of retirement and were therefore tempted to associate themselves very closely to A.Q. Khan, with a view to gain his favours for their post retirement settlement. In the late 1970s, and especially in the early 1980s, the threat to the programme was perceived to be from external sources, and there were numerous press reports of Indian, Israeli, or joint Indo–Israeli plans to attack Pakistan's nuclear facilities. The focus of security was, therefore, oriented outwards and the insider threat was hardly taken into account. As later events were to prove, the oversight and security arrangements put in place to guard the highly sensitive areas of the programme were at best inadequate, and certainly not geared towards checking the indiscretions of some highly placed people.[25]

Analysts concede that, 'his security apparatus was not designed to monitor him, but rather to protect him and his organization from external spies and anything that might compromise his foreign procurement for Pakistan's nuclear programme'.[26]

THE REVERSE FLOW OF TECHNOLOGY

Throughout his procurement efforts, Khan used Dubai as the staging point, where he reportedly had a warehouse managed by his two associates, both Sri Lankan nationals, Farouq and his nephew Tahir. They also ran a computer import-export business in parallel under the name of SMB group. At some stage, starting in the late 1980s, A.Q. Khan realized that Pakistan's programme was reaching a plateau, and he could profitably use his technical expertise, knowledge of European suppliers and his personal rapport with them by reversing the flow of enrichment technology. In addition A.Q. Khan had developed a more efficient second generation centrifuge known as P-2. As the P-2s replaced the earlier P-1 centrifuges he had a surplus inventory of used P-1 machines.[27] It is hard to determine whether he and his Dubai based associates sought out potential buyers, or were approached by the interested buyers themselves. According to the IISS report in the context of his dealings with Iran and Libya, 'it may have been a case of interested customers first reaching out to the network, rather than the other way around'.[28] The methodology was simple. Khan would import more components than the quantity required by Pakistan and create a surplus inventory in Dubai, from where it could be shipped to countries like Iran, North Korea and Libya. According to the IISS study:

> Khan's nuclear acquisition activities were largely unsupervised by Pakistani government authorities and his orders of many more components than Pakistan's own enrichment programme required apparently went undetected. He had access to autonomous import and export privileges that no other organization in the country possessed.[29]

Another factor, which is either not commonly known or is generally ignored, is the fact that KRL had started utilizing its technical expertise and manufacturing capabilities to produce various types of conventional items of military equipment. These included weapon systems, such as the shoulder fired surface to air missile 'ANZA', the anti-tank guided missile 'Baktar Shikan', and items such as laser range finders and infra-red night vision devices. These pieces of equipment were also being exported to some Middle Eastern and North African countries such as Libya. Since all inbound and outbound cargo related to KRL was exempted from customs inspections, enrichment related components could easily be slipped into the cargo containers carrying these legitimate export items without anyone knowing about it.

There is a great controversy about who authorized nuclear co-operation with Iran and when. According to one segment of opinion President Ziaul Haq had authorized limited nuclear cooperation with Iran, which was later exploited by A.Q. Khan. It is however, hard to believe that a person like Zia, who had serious political as well as ideological differences with the Iranian leadership, could allow for cooperation in such a sensitive area.[30] It is a well-known fact that General Ziaul Haq, who was part of the

Organization of Islamic Conference (OIC) peace mission, with the remit of bringing the war between Iran and Iraq to an end, was not welcomed by the Iranians. This was chiefly because of his refusal to declare Iraq as the aggressor. If any nuclear cooperation with Iran had been authorized at all, it would have been confined to the area of peaceful nuclear technology.

It is alleged that the first contact with the Iranians took place in Switzerland. This was facilitated by a German engineer, Gotthard Lerch, a long time friend and supplier of Khan. The first substantive exchange is reported to have taken place in Dubai in 1987, in a meeting attended by Farouq, Tahir, and another German engineer, Heinz Mebus. The network is purported to have handed over a one-page hand written offer to the Iranians. This paper included different packages of technology from which the Iranians could choose, with prices ranging from millions to hundreds of millions of dollars.[31]

The Iranians reportedly struck a deal for $3 million, and were handed over a fifteen-page document which, among other things, included the procedure for the conversion of enriched uranium hexafluoride gas into uranium metal and its further casting into hemispheres. The documents shared by the Iranians with the IAEA inspectors in 2005 regarding the 1987 deal also included detailed drawings of P-1 components, a description of the manufacturing process, assembly, operating procedures and layout for a 168-machine cascade.[32]

The investigations conducted by the Pakistani officials and other sources have established that most of Khan's proliferation activities reportedly took place between 1988 and 1999. This coincided with the end of the Ziaul Haq era, a period in Pakistan's political history during which new power sharing arrangements were evolving. After A.Q. Khan had become a national icon, and was held in high esteem and blindly trusted by both civilian and military power elites. General Mirza Aslam Beg is often accused of complicity, particularly in Khan's dealings with Iran, but such accusations are conjectures based mainly on Beg's advocacy of the need for a strong Islamic block in West and Central Asia, and his theory of strategic defiance. If General Beg was the prime mover behind this cooperation, it is hard to explain the continuation of this relationship long after his retirement in 1991 as army chief.[33]

There are further allegations concerning the involvement of high-level Pakistani officials. For instance, the IISS report contends that 'Several sources have reported that an agreement was reached in 1991 between General Asif Nawaz, Beg's successor as chief of army staff, Rafsanjani and General Mohsen Rezai, head of the Revolutionary Guard, which involved Pakistani nuclear weapons technology in return for Iranian oil'.[34] However, this accusation is totally unfounded and is contrary to the reality on the ground. There is no evidence to suggest that Pakistan imported Iranian oil either in the early 1990s or later, and it continued to depend for its oil supplies on Saudi Arabia and Kuwait. This would indicate that the whole thesis of the 'oil for nuclear technology' swap is based on suppositions and conjectures similar to those suggesting the 'missiles for nuclear technology' barter deal with North Korea. The fact that interactions between the Khan network and the Iranians continued, despite the tensions and frictions in the relationship between Iran and Pakistan over growing sectarian problems inside Pakistan and the rise of Taliban in Afghanistan ostensibly with Pakistani support, is further proof that Khan's dealings with Iran did not have official sanction.[35]

According to Christopher Clary, 'the extent of state authorization of Khan's nuclear dealings is debatable. The available evidence seems to indicate that Khan was largely a rogue actor, acting without the approval of the state writ large....It is Khan's nuclear dealings with Libya that indicate the highest degree of nuclear freelancing. The benefits to the Pakistani state are unclear, while the benefits to Khan as an individual are obvious'.[36] Clary further argues that A.Q. Khan's proliferation network was a mutation of the procurement system devised by Pakistan in the 1970s and 1980s, and that 'Khan did not create the world market place for dual use and proscribed goods, but he was the most successful individual ever to tap into it'.[37]

When the National Command Authority was formally established in February 2000, Strategic Plans Division (SPD) started sending out its tentacles into the strategic organizations. It immediately met resistance from A.Q. Khan, who did not want anyone to pry into his domain. There were, however, indications that something was amiss, but without concrete evidence laying hands on a person of A.Q. Khan's stature would have been political suicide by the Pakistani government. Around the same time US diplomats were also expressing their concerns and suspicions about Khan's activities during meetings with their Pakistani counterparts, but whenever they were asked to provide some evidence to proceed against him, they expressed their inability to do so. Based on an intelligence tip off, an early morning raid was conducted by the ISI on a chartered aircraft destined for North Korea, but nothing was found except some bags of rice and crates of mangoes. It is difficult to make a definitive judgment on whether the intelligence information was inaccurate or A.Q. Khan had been cautioned about the raid. In any case, Khan was called up by senior military officials and cautioned.[38] The raid itself was a major departure from the norm and a serious effort to disrupt any illegal transfers of sensitive technology. Referring to the same raid, Clary argues that, 'The fact that there was an unannounced search would seem to indicate that Pakistani authorities did not regularly screen such cargo'.[39]

Against the backdrop of lingering suspicions of foul play, and Khan's resistance to any oversight of his operations by the newly created command and control set up, a decision was made to relieve him of his position as the chairman of KRL. He was consequently retired on the expiry of his term of office at the end of March 2001. This was a tough decision to take by the Pakistani government and was highly unpopular with the public. The political opposition also criticized the decision and accused the government of halting the development of Pakistan's nuclear weapons capability. However, to soften the blow and to keep a semblance of control over his movements, he was appointed advisor to the prime minister on science and technology.

In October 2002, when news about a secret North Korean uranium enrichment programme surfaced for the first time, A.Q. Khan was asked if he had anything to do with this, but he flatly denied any such accusations. Then in 2003, when IAEA inspectors found traces of enriched uranium at one of the Iranian facilities, the Iranians conceded that it came from contaminated centrifuge components imported from abroad. They did not directly name A.Q. Khan however. Suspecting fingers once again pointed in his direction. Towards the end of 2003 the Pakistan government ordered an investigation, and some of the closest associates of Khan were arrested. George Tenet claims to have shared evidence of A.Q. Khan's illegal trade in nuclear technology with President Musharraf in September 2003, while the latter was in New York in connection with the UN General Assembly meeting, and was assured by Musharraf that, 'I will take care of this'.[40] In October 2003 a German cargo ship, named BBC China, bound for Libya was intercepted in the Mediterranean. The ship was carrying centrifuge components manufactured in a factory in Malaysia. By then the Libyans had struck an agreement with the British and American officials to dismantle their WMD programmes. They promptly named Khan as the source of technology and also handed over documents including the blueprints for a nuclear weapon.

In the meantime, in November 2003, Pakistani authorities had started their full-scale investigations into the affair and had arrested some of the close Pakistani associates of A.Q. Khan. Khan tried to wriggle out of the situation by using his media contacts and, in one of his interviews with a private TV network, he went to the extent of claiming that he had single-handedly given Pakistan the nuclear and missile capability which had made its defence impregnable, and asked the viewers to look at the way he was being 'rewarded' for his efforts. After this incident he was confined to his house, and his telephone and other contacts were restricted. A.Q. Khan was not about to go down without a fight. He wrote a letter to his Iranian friends asking them not to mention his name to IAEA under any circumstances, and to give them the names of dead people, as he was doing in Pakistan. He had indeed named two such people, who had already passed away, as the ones who had directed him to get in touch with the Iranians. He also advised them to blame the contamination found in Iran as mischief making on part of the IAEA inspectors. The second letter was written to his daughter, in which he instructed her to go public with Pakistan's nuclear secrets, with the help of some British journalists. Unluckily for him the letters were intercepted by the Pakistani intelligence agencies.[41]

PAKISTANI VERSION OF THE EVENTS

The official Pakistani version of the above events has been articulated in some detail by President Pervez Musharraf in his book *In the Line of Fire*:

> Revelations began to flow. Our investigations revealed that A.Q. had started his activities as far back as 1987, primarily with Iran. In 1994–1995 A.Q. had ordered the manufacture of 200 P-1 centrifuges that had been discarded by Pakistan in the mid-1980s. These had been dispatched to Dubai for onward distribution...One branch of his network was in KRL. It included four to six scientists...Most of them proved to be unwitting participants, working on A.Q.'s orders without comprehending the real purpose or outcome.
>
> The other branch of the network was based in Dubai and dealt with procurement and distribution. It included several shady individuals and various European businesses.[42]

Initially, A.Q. Khan was in a defiant mood, but as he was confronted with more and more evidence gained from the interrogation of his close associates, as well as that received from foreign intelligence agencies, he finally broke down.[43] On 25 January 2004 Pakistani investigators publicly acknowledged that A.Q. Khan had indeed assisted the Iranian nuclear programme, without any government sanction, in return for millions of dollars. Consequently, he was removed from his last official position as scientific advisor to the prime minister. This was followed by another official pronouncement, in early February 2004, stating that Khan had signed a confession admitting to having provided blueprints, as well as material, for the Iranian, Libyan and North Korean programmes. On 4 February 2004, Khan appeared on national television and in a brief speech stated: 'I take full responsibility for my actions and seek your pardon.' Expressing his deepest 'sense of sorrow, anguish and regret', he maintained that his actions were taken 'in good faith but were errors in judgment. There was never ever any kind of authorization for these activities from the government'.[44]

This interview, which was ostensibly aimed at pacifying public sentiments and anxiety, attracted a lot of criticism and failed to satisfy Khan's admirers, who remained sceptical. To this day they view this as an act of public humiliation of a national hero. Some even credited him with making yet another sacrifice for the nation by personally taking full responsibility and saving the people responsible for these lapses. There was no dearth of sceptics in the international community as well, who continued to express doubts about the possibility of Khan undertaking his proliferation activities without the knowledge or active participation of the Pakistani government. They have been very critical of the pardon granted to him by former president Musharraf, who explained this particular event as follows:

I wanted to meet A.Q. myself and talk to him. When we met and I confronted him with the evidence, he broke down and admitted that he felt extremely guilty. He asked me for an official pardon. I told him that his apology should be to the people of Pakistan and he should seek his pardon from them directly. It was decided that the best course of action would be for him to appear on television and apologize personally to the nation for embarrassing and traumatizing it in front of the entire world. I then accepted his request for a pardon from trial but put him under protective custody for further investigation and also for his own sake.[45]

The findings of the investigation were shared with the IAEA as well as friendly intelligence agencies. However, it was declared in no uncertain terms by the Pakistan government that neither IAEA inspectors nor foreign intelligence agencies would be allowed any direct access to A.Q. Khan. Any further queries by the IAEA or friendly countries could be referred to the Pakistani authorities, who would obtain answers from Khan and honestly pass them on to them. According to George Tenet, '...Musharraf pardoned him but placed him under permanent house arrest. While we would have preferred to see Khan face trial and wanted to have US and IAEA investigators extensively question him about his dealings, the outcome was still a major victory'.[46] Despite this, demands for the granting of access to A.Q. Khan have been periodically made by various groups, including some in the US Congress. From a Pakistani perspective these demands appear to be entirely unreasonable and unjustified, as they are unlikely to lead to any further revelations in addition to what has already been extracted by the Pakistani investigators. The Pakistanis feel that, besides impinging on their sovereignty, it will amount to an admission that Pakistani investigators were incapable of interrogating Khan. There is also an acute awareness of the fact that any such move would have very serious domestic political consequences. In a hypothetical situation, if some foreign investigators were to be allowed to question Khan, and he refused to answer the questions, what other means do they have at their disposal to extract the desired information from him? Surely they cannot expect to be permitted to use any third degree interrogation techniques? Conversely, if Khan answered their questions, and the answers did not match their expectations, they could turn around and say that he was telling lies or not telling the whole truth. So the whole debate is unnecessary, meaningless and is extremely irksome to most Pakistanis, who feel that they have gone overboard in cooperating with the IAEA and sharing their findings with the international intelligence agencies.

TAKING STOCK

From a non-proliferation perspective, black markets are not a new phenomenon, nor were they invented by A.Q. Khan. In attempting to lay all the blame on his doorstep we may be in danger of missing the wood for a tree, with an adverse impact on the future efforts by the international community to prevent further proliferation. Tenet has pointed out that, 'In the new world of proliferation nation states have been replaced by shadowy networks like Khan's capable of selling turnkey nuclear weapons programmes to the highest bidders'.[47] Alluding to the possibility of the existence of other underground networks capable of proliferating nuclear technology, Tenet says that, 'what we don't know is how many networks similar to Khan's may still be out there—operating undetected and offering deadly advice and supplies to anyone with the cash to pay for them'. In an obvious reference to the Libyan deal, he maintains that, 'In the current marketplace, if you have a hundred million dollars, you can be your own nuclear power'.[48] This may, however, be an oversimplification, because the fact remains that despite receiving almost all the essential hardware, the Libyans were unable to put together a functional enrichment plant. The bulk of the equipment was not even unpacked and remained languishing in warehouses in the shipping crates. The Libyans did possess enough cash, but simply did not have the human and industrial resources to assemble and run these sophisticated and complicated machines successfully.

The volume and type of technology sold by the Khan network has been amplified by former president Musharraf. According to him:

> Doctor A.Q. Khan transferred nearly two dozen P-I and P-II centrifuges to North Korea. He also provided North Korea with a flow meter, some special oils for centrifuges, and coaching on centrifuge technology, including visits to top-secret centrifuge plants. To the Iranians and Libyans, through Dubai, he provided nearly eighteen tons of materials, including centrifuges, components, and drawings.[49]

The bulk of the equipment and components for Libya were manufactured in factories, facilities, and through suppliers in three continents, involving nationals from over twenty countries including Malaysia, Turkey, South Africa, Spain, Germany,

Switzerland, the UK and the Netherlands etc. In the North Korean case, the handful of machines supplied were meant to be templates for replication and mass production, and were too few to be of any use even in the setting up of a single cascade. To bulk produce the centrifuges, North Korea needed specialized materials, and its efforts to procure such materials from Europe faltered when a ship carrying specialized aluminium from Germany was intercepted.

It may be worth taking stock of the extent of supply operations of the A.Q. Khan network, and the damage it has caused to international security, since this issue has been generally overplayed. This is exemplified by Tenet's terming Khan 'the Merchant of Death'.[50] Many other writers have compared him with Osama bin Laden in terms of the harm he has caused. But that is certainly not a fair characterization. A.Q. Khan supplied enrichment technology to Iran, Libya and North Korea. Fortunately, for everyone, owing to a change of heart by Colonel Gaddafi, in large part due to the behind the scenes efforts by the British and American intelligence operatives, Libya's nuclear ambitions have been laid to rest. North Korea, as a consequence of the agreement put together in the six party talks, has begun a dismantling of its nuclear programme and this is well underway. Finally Iran, which is the only recipient of technology from the network to have installed a modest but functional uranium enrichment facility, has its options severely curtailed due to intrusive and persistent IAEA inspections, the tightening of export controls worldwide, a perpetual focus by international intelligence agencies on possible Iranian procurement activities and pressure brought to bear by the UNSC sanctions. This is not meant to defend A.Q. Khan's despicable actions, but to present a more realistic assessment of the situation. Given the outcome of the above three cases, one could feel reassured that in an environment of greater international cooperation and awareness, and increasingly effective and proactive counter-proliferation measures, the potential proliferators would think twice before embarking on this hazardous and expensive enterprise whose chances of success are diminishing by the day.

While castigating A.Q. Khan for his role in the network, and the Pakistani Government for not prosecuting him, not much is said about the fate of rest of his associates and how they have been dealt with by their respective governments. One of the most prominent cases among these has been that involving a Dutch national, Henk Slebos, a university classmate, and long time friend and associate of A.Q. Khan. Slebos was tried by a Dutch court on several counts of violation of the Dutch export control regulations. He was sentenced to twelve months imprisonment, of which eight months were a suspended sentence. He had to serve four months in jail and pay a 100,000 Euro fine. One of Slebos' employees, Zoran Filipovic, was also sentenced for violating export regulations. His punishment included 180 days of community service and a fine of 5,000 Euros. Peter Griffin, a British national who is also known to have been a long time supplier for the network, has not been indicted in any court. Griffin filed a lawsuit against the Guardian newspaper for defamation and received £50,000/$94,000 in damages. Three Swiss nationals, Friedrich Tinner and his two sons Urs and Marco, have been in the custody of the Swiss authorities since September 2005, but their trial has ground to a halt due to the refusal of the US government to provide relevant information. It is widely believed that the Tinners' are likely to be acquitted of all charges as a result of their cooperation with the CIA. Ernst Piffl, a German national, was tried and convicted in 1998 for the violation of export control laws and was sentenced to three years and nine months imprisonment and fined $240,000, while another German, Rainer Vollmerich, was convicted in 2005 on charges of filing false end-user certificates and licensing documents, and has been sentenced to seven years and three months in prison. However, another more prominent German associate of the network, engineer Gotthard Lerch, extradited to Germany in 2005 after being arrested by the Swiss authorities in 2004, was indicted in a court in April 2006, but the trial was suspended after four months due procedural glitches. Two German nationals living in South Africa are under trial in a South African court for several infringements of import and export laws.

B.S.A. Tahir, one of the closest associates and who was termed by President Bush as the chief financial officer of the network, was instrumental in the setting up of the centrifuge components' manufacturing facility in Malaysia. He was not found in violation of Malaysian laws. He remained under detention without trial under the Malaysian Internal Security Act for over two years, and is now reported to have returned to Dubai. Tahir has been reportedly released as a result of his cooperation with Malaysian and CIA investigations into the activities of the network. Meanwhile, in Pakistan A.Q. Khan remains in detention, four years after he was first confined to his house, while all the other individuals including both the members of security and Khan's personal staff, as well as some KRL engineers, have been released after being detained and questioned for varying periods of time ranging between a few weeks to two and a half years. Two of these, Brigadier (retd.) Sajawal Khan Malik and Major (retd.) Islamul Haq, remain under house arrest, while the activities of those released are being closely monitored.[51]

Another issue which needs to be addressed is that of the safety and security of Pakistan's nuclear assets. Whenever there is a mention of the A.Q. Khan episode it is presumed, by implication, that Pakistan's nuclear oversight is weak and unreliable, and that there is a serious danger of these assets falling into the wrong hands. As the history of the non-proliferation network indicates, most of the illicit proliferation activities predate the setting up of a formal system of command and control set up to oversee Pakistan's nuclear assets in February 2000. Some activities still took place up until Khan's retirement from his position as the chairman of KRL in April 2001. However, beyond that there is no evidence to suggest that there was any leakage of technology from Pakistan. Supplies to Iran and Libya from 2001 onwards were arranged for and delivered by Khan's Dubai based associates. The components designated for Libya were manufactured at many sites around the globe, brought to Dubai and shipped to that country. Pakistan has, over the past few years, taken legislative, administrative and organizational measures to strengthen its custodial controls.[52] It has tried to be as transparent as is consistent with the needs of security, in sharing the information about the measures put in place to prevent the recurrence of any such activity in future. This is evident from the number of briefings held recently for visiting foreign dignitaries, diplomats based in Islamabad and local as well as foreign media persons.

NOTES

1. *The Observer*, London, December 1979 quoted in Steve Weissman and Herbert Krosney (eds.), *The Islamic Bomb*, New York Times Books, 1981, Chapter 12.
2. George Tenet, *At the Center of the Storm—My Years at the CIA*, Harper Collins Publishers, NY, 2007, p. 285.
3. 'Nuclear Black Markets: Pakistan, A.Q. Khan and the rise of proliferation networks—A Net Assessment', IISS, London, 2007, p. 15.
4. Douglas Frantz and Catherine Collins, *The Nuclear Jihadist*, Hachette Book Group, New York, 2007, pp. 12–15.
5. Ibid., pp. 16–17.
6. Ibid., p. 17.
7. Frantz, op. cit., pp. 33–36.
8. Frantz, pp. 36-40.
9. Ibid., pp. 40–48. Also see 'Dutch let Khan go at CIA's request', *Dawn*, Karachi, 10 August 2005.
10. Tenet, op. cit., pp. 282–3.
11. Tenet, p. 282.
12. Pervez Musharraf, *In the Line of Fire*, Free Press, New York, 2006, p. 284.
13. Tenet, p. 284.
14. Christopher O Clary, 'The A.Q. Khan Network: Causes and Implications', Naval Postgraduate School, Monterey, California, p. 37.
15. IISS, op. cit.
16. Steve Weissman and Herbert Krosney, *The Islamic Bomb*, quoted in Clary, p. 28.
17. Clary, p. 29.
18. Steve Coll, 'The Atomic Emporium—Abdul Qadeer Khan Iran's race to build the bomb', *The New Yorker*, 7 & 14 August 2006, New York, p. 56.
19. Clary, p. 26.
20. Clary, op. cit., p. 27.
21. Ibid., p. 29.
22. Ibid., p. 34.

23. Based on interviews with senior officials of Strategic Plans Division—the secretariat of Pakistan's National Command Authority in January 2008 and earlier briefings on the subject attended by the author.

24. Interview with senior officials of the SPD op. cit.

25. Ibid.

26. IISS, p. 66.

27. Clary, pp. 38–39.

28. IISS, p. 66.

29. Ibid.

30. IISS, p. 67.

31. Ibid., p. 69.

32. Ibid.

33. Clary, p. 44.

34. IISS, p. 70.

35. IISS, p. 71.

36. Clary, p. 12.

37. Ibid., p. 21.

38. Musharraf, pp. 287-8.

39. Clary, p. 65.

40. Tenet, pp. 285–6.

41. Musharraf, p. 296.

42. Ibid., pp. 291–2.

43. Briefing to the newsmen by a senior Pakistani official.

44. Tenet, pp. 286–7.

45. Musharraf, pp. 292–3.

46. Tenet, p. 287.

47. Ibid.

48. Ibid.

49. Musharraf, p. 294.

50. Tenet, p. 281.

51. Kenley Butler, Sammy Salama & Leonard Spector, 'Where is the Justice?', *Bulletin of the Atomic Scientists,* November/December 2006. For a detailed expose of the Henk Slebos story see Frank Slijper, 'Project Butter Factory'— Henk Slebos and the A.Q. Khan network,' Transnational Institute, Amsterdam, September 2007.

52. For details of some of the measure instituted in this regard see Ken Luongo and Naeem Salik, 'Building Confidence in Pakistan's Nuclear Security', *Arms Control Today,* Arms Control Association, Washington, DC, November/December 2007.

9

Nuclear Safety and Security[1]

In pre-1998 days nuclear safety and security in South Asia was never a serious issue, mainly because both Indian and Pakistani nuclear assets were non-weaponized. However, following the nuclear tests in May 1998, and the moves towards operational capacity in their respective capabilities, this issue was brought to the fore. The events of 9/11 further heightened the concerns regarding the safety and security of nuclear weapons, fissile materials and nuclear storage sites, especially in view of the known desire of international terrorist organizations to gain access to nuclear weapons and/or materials. Though India has been facing active insurgencies in its north-east territory, as well as in Kashmir, for many years and its parliament was subjected to a terrorist attack in December 2001, concerns about Pakistan's nuclear safety and security have been much deeper and wider.

The reasons for the negative perceptions of nuclear safety and security in Pakistan have been varied. First, the surfacing of the A.Q. Khan network badly eroded international confidence in Pakistan's nuclear management. Second, the ongoing 'war on terror' in neighbouring Afghanistan, with its spill over into Pakistan's western borderlands, and third, the internal political turmoil and rising incidence of terrorist attacks, including a series of deadly suicide bombings especially during 2007, created fears that Pakistani nuclear assets could fall into the wrong hands. With national elections scheduled for early 2008, different scenarios were being conjured up, for instance that radical religious elements could take over the reins of power in Islamabad and with that the control of Pakistan's nuclear arsenal. While there are some genuine concerns about nuclear safety and security, there are many exaggerated and misplaced fears and misconceptions around the vulnerability of Pakistani nuclear weapons and materials.

After its overt nuclearization in May 1998, Pakistan moved very quickly to establish command and control over its nuclear establishment, which prior to that date was not under any central or institutional control. The heads of various nuclear establishments, especially the KRL, enjoyed a high degree of administrative and financial autonomy, and the perpetual rivalry between the PAEC and KRL also led to instances of the overstepping of their respective mandates. Although, Indian and Pakistani efforts to develop nuclear weapons capabilities were well known internationally, both countries continued to deny any such programmes, and both emphasized the peaceful nature of their respective programmes. In India there were a number of academic works on India's nuclear policy related issues. In Pakistan it largely remained a taboo subject. The result of this state of denial was the lack of public debate on issues such as nuclear doctrine, command and control, and safety and security. Even more surprising is the fact that there was no internal debate or systematic analysis of these issues within either the military or the civilian establishment.

ESTABLISHMENT OF THE NATIONAL COMMAND AUTHORITY

In the immediate aftermath of the May 1998 nuclear tests a team of officers was constituted within General Headquarters, and tasked with formulating recommendations for the setting up of an institutionalized command and control mechanism, and overall nuclear policy. The recommended structure for a National Command Authority (NCA) was tentatively approved by the army chief in early 1999, and a briefing in this regard was also given to the prime minister in April 1999. A core group, representing the Strategic Plans Division (SPD), which is the permanent secretariat of the NCA and Army Strategic Force Command (ASFC), had already started functioning from March 1999, pending formal government approval for the strategic command and control organization. The formal announcement regarding the establishment of the NCA and its various components was made in February 2000.[2] Since then it has matured into a professionally run and effective institutional mechanism. In addition to taking care of the operational and developmental aspects of the nuclear capability, the major role of SPD has been to establish oversight, financial and administrative controls over the activities of various strategic entities. This includes arrangements for the physical security of sensitive installations, which comprises multi-layered security perimeters, counter intelligence and personnel security. Additionally, a system of external audit, and procedures for material protection, control and accounting (MPC&A) has been established. The details regarding the organization, role and functions of the NCA have already been discussed in Chapter 6, on Nuclear Command and Control.

SECURITY AND SAFETY OF NUCLEAR WEAPONS AND MATERIALS

Over the years, and especially after 9/11, the Security Division of NCA, which is headed by a two star general, has grown exponentially and has 9000 to 10,000 personnel dedicated to the security of nuclear installations and materials. The Director General Security Division has his 'eyes' and 'ears' inside the strategic organizations. These are headed by a one star officer in each of the major organizations such as the PAEC, the KRL and NESCOM, who regularly report to him. The Security Division is also responsible for the implementation of the Personnel Reliability Programme (PRP), and coordinates the initial screening, background checks and clearance of personnel being inducted in any constituent part of the nuclear establishment.[3]

THE INSIDER THREAT

In recent times major concerns about nuclear security and safety in Pakistan revolve around not only the threat posed by various terrorist and extremist groups operating within and around Pakistan, but possible collusion between sympathetic insiders and these terrorist elements. The basis of this concern is the perception that there are religiously motivated elements within the Pakistani nuclear establishment, as well as the Pakistani military and security establishment. While it is not uncommon to find people with strong religious inclinations in the strategic organizations, it is not fair to equate a strong religious belief with fanaticism and extremism. The nuclear security establishment is sensitive to this issue, and makes a clear distinction between a good practicing Muslim and one who displays erratic behaviour and extremist tendencies. An interview by Peter Wonacott, the Islamabad based correspondent of the Wall Street Journal, with a senior official of the Pakistani nuclear security organization precisely highlights this fact. Wonacott writes that:

> Inside Pakistan's nuclear programme, scientists are allowed to grow long beards, pray five times a day and vote for this country's conservative Islamist politicians. Religious zeal doesn't bar them from working in top secret weapons facilities. But religious extremism does. It's up to the programme's internal watchdog, a security division authorized to snoop on its employees, to determine the difference— and drive out those who breach the boundaries.[4]

The personnel reliability programme instituted by Pakistan, besides looking into personal character, financial records and political affiliations, also takes into account religious motivation. During the interview the general pointed out that, while personal piety and religiosity is acceptable, people with an extremist bent of mind are not. He went on to cite an incident in which an employee was dismissed from his job for distributing leaflets of a religious party and trying to persuade his colleagues to join him in the mosque to attend the party's rallies. The employee concerned was cautioned and when he persisted in his practice, he was shown the door.[5] This particular case became known, and there may have been others which have not been publicized. It illustrates the fact that tolerance for such activities is very low. It also indicates that such activities do not go unnoticed, and invoke serious punitive actions. Linked with this aspect is the general perception of the radicalization of the Pakistani populace and its sympathetic outlook towards the Taliban and other religiously motivated militant elements. However, the national elections held in February 2008 have dispelled many of these myths and misperceptions, as a result of the overwhelming vote in favour of moderate and liberal political parties, and the near total rejection of religious political elements. The outcome of the elections should go a long way in alleviating many misgivings and concerns about extremist religious forces gaining control over Pakistan's nuclear assets.

In terms of the safety of nuclear weapons, various measures are in place. Pakistani officials have stated on numerous occasions that the warheads and delivery systems are stored separately, which precludes any possibility of the accidental or unauthorized launch of the weapons. The weapons are also equipped with electro-mechanical locks, commonly known as Permissive Action Links (PALs), and can only be activated when the requisite codes are fed into the systems. Finally, the 'two man' rule, a practice in vogue in all the established nuclear powers, is also followed.[6] This essentially means that orders and instructions at each level of command have to be authenticated by a second person before these can be executed. It is also generally believed that the weapons are stored at a number of different and dispersed sites, but it is difficult to speculate about the exact number and locations of these sites.

ESTABLISHMENT OF PAKISTAN NUCLEAR REGULATORY AUTHORITY

The Pakistan Nuclear Regulatory Authority (PNRA) was established in January 2001, partly as an obligation accruing out of Pakistan's accession to the Nuclear Safety Convention, and partly out of recognition of the need to have an autonomous oversight mechanism to ensure the safety of Pakistan's nuclear installations.[7] Before the coming into being of the PNRA, the safety of nuclear installations was being taken care of by the Directorate of Nuclear

Safety and Radiation Protection (DNSRP) within the PAEC. The PNRA is responsible for licensing the import and export of radiological sources and their 'cradle to grave' oversight, which essentially means that PNRA ensures the safety of radiological material from the moment it is imported into the country till its safe disposal after it has outlived its useful life. It also issues licenses for the running of nuclear power plants and for nuclear medical centres, private clinics and hospitals, which use radiological sources for diagnostic and treatment purposes. PNRA maintains an updated database of all radiological sources inside the country, and carries out periodic inspections to ensure that material is safely stored, does not pose any hazard to the public and is not vulnerable to theft or sabotage. It has already registered all the x-ray machines installed in various medical facilities.

PNRA has developed standards for the nuclear safety of nuclear power reactors being operated by the PAEC, and carries out regular safety checks. It strictly enforces its safety regulations, and on one occasion asked the Chashma Nuclear Power Plant to be shut down until the required safety checks were carried out. On another occasion it ordered the Karachi Nuclear Power Plant, which was due for relicensing on completion of its designed life of 30 years in 2002, to be shut down until all safety upgrades were completed. As a result, the plant remained out of use for almost one and a half years.

PNRA has also developed a five year National Nuclear Safety Action Plan, for which the government has provided the necessary funding. The implementation of the plan is already underway. Its aim is to protect the public from the hazards of radiation in case of an incident involving the release of radiation. The plan involves identifying and training the first responders, which would include the local administration officials as well as law enforcement agencies and the emergency support teams. It has already established its emergency response centre, which is on call around the clock, and has started training courses at its academy in Islamabad for the first responders, as well as border control agencies such as Pakistan Customs.

PNRA has benefited from IAEA sponsored workshops and seminars on issues such as Design Based Threat (DBT), and has closely collaborated with the IAEA. It invites IAEA experts for peer reviews of its activities and shares its inspection reports with the IAEA. The PNRA is basically responsible for the safeguarded peaceful segment of Pakistan's nuclear programme and does not have any sway over weapons related activities. However, it has also developed checklists and criteria for maintaining the highest standards of security for the weapons related facilities. These safety and security checks are carried out by the SPD under instruction by the PNRA.

NUCLEAR EXPORT CONTROLS

The history of Pakistan's export control laws goes as far back as 1950. These laws were supplemented from time to time by the Ministry of Commerce, through the issuance of Statutory Regulatory Orders (SROs). However, many of these laws were generic in nature. A need to augment these laws was identified after Pakistan's overt nuclearization in 1998. To begin with, in September 2000, the SPD issued internal export control guidelines for all strategic organizations.[8] Simultaneously, an inter-ministerial group was constituted under the overall supervision of the Ministry of Foreign Affairs with the remit to develop comprehensive export control legislation. This group included representatives from the ministries of Foreign Affairs, Commerce and Defence, as well as PAEC, SPD and PNRA.[9] After four years' strenuous efforts the law was finally promulgated in September 2004, and its related 'control lists' were also prepared and notified. The law stipulates severe penalties, including rigorous imprisonment of up to fourteen years as well as confiscation of property and hefty fines for any violations. The law has jurisdiction over all of Pakistan's territory and its citizens, whether inside or outside Pakistan. It covers exports and re-exports as well as transhipments. The control list conforms to the lists issued by the NSG, MTCR and Australia Group, and follows the pattern of notation used by the EU. In order to ensure the smooth implementation and effective enforcement of the export control law, a Strategic Export Controls Division (SECD-IV) has been established under the administrative control of the Ministry of Foreign Affairs. The SECD-IV includes officers from the Ministry of Commerce, Federal Board of Revenue, Customs, SPD, PNRA and Ministry of Foreign Affairs. A high-level oversight board has also been established under the chairmanship of the foreign secretary and includes senior officials from the concerned ministries. The Oversight Board will periodically review and oversee the implementation of the export control law.[10]

PAKISTAN–US COOPERATION

Like many other aspects of Pakistan's nuclear programme, Pakistan–US cooperation in the realm of nuclear security and safety has also been a subject of speculation and suspicion. The first problem arises from the fact that 'security' and 'safety' are usually mixed up and used alternately to mean the same thing, which is incorrect. While security pertains to physical security such as the perimeter security around nuclear sites, safety pertains to nuclear weapons and fissile materials, and this distinction has to be made clear. Much has been said, and speculated, about Pakistan–US cooperation in the media, and there have also been statements by former senior officials such as Richard Armitage, but many misconceptions still surround the issue.

In the immediate aftermath of 9/11, and on the eve of the US attack on Afghanistan, concerns were expressed in the US media about the security and safety of Pakistan's nuclear assets. Some reporters went to the extent of suggesting that US Special forces were training along with the Israelis, in order to go in and 'secure' Pakistan's nuclear weapons, and there were fanciful ideas suggesting the moving of Pakistani weapons to China for safe custody. Amidst all these noises Secretary of State Colin Powell, on a visit to Islamabad in October 2001, broached the subject with the Pakistani leaders and offered to share US expertise in securing its nuclear assets with Pakistan. There are obvious limitations to the scope of such cooperation, imposed by US obligations as an NPT member as well as domestic US laws. Pakistan for its part also has its own sensitivities and concerns. Pakistan laid down the limits beyond which it would not proceed. It was clearly spelt out that this cooperation would be strictly 'non-intrusive'. Pakistan was also wary of seeking any technology because of its possible security implications, and the cooperative activities were restricted to the exchange of 'best practices'. The significant areas of cooperation included PRP, training of security forces, and export control and border control related activities. Pakistan has obviously benefited from the far greater US experience in handling nuclear security related issues, but speculations about the US providing PALs or even the electronic security codes are far removed from the reality.[11]

Pakistan is a member of both the Nuclear Safety Convention as well as the Convention on Physical Protection of Nuclear Materials (CPPNM). In 2006 Pakistan signed an agreement with the US to become a member of the Container Security Initiative (CSI), and has also been negotiating participation in the Mega-ports Initiative with the US. Pakistan has also announced joining the US–Russian sponsored Global Initiative for Prevention of Nuclear Terrorism. However, despite all these measures, lingering fears concerning nuclear safety and security in Pakistan have not abated. The concerns emanate partly from the past failure of Pakistan to control the activities of A.Q. Khan and his associates, and are partly owing to the political instability and precarious law and order situation within the country. However, too much is made of political turmoil and the incidence of acts of terrorism in major cities. These incidents do send negative resonances, but have no direct impact on nuclear custodial controls. The nuclear assets are stored away in secure storage sites, which are more than adequately guarded through a multi-layered defence system. These are certainly not lying on the roadside, so that any passer-by can pick a few, put them in his sack and go away. Pakistan has its internal problems including extremism, poor governance and law and order, but state institutions are functioning and resilient. Loss of control of nuclear assets will only happen should the state institutions simply melt away and there is a total breakdown of order, which is certainly not on the horizon.

NOTES

1. For a detailed exposition of the subject see Kenneth Luongo and Naeem Salik, 'Building Confidence in Pakistan's Nuclear Security', Arms Control Today, Arms Control Association, December 2007.
2. 'Pakistan Announces Nuclear Command and Control Mechanism', Associated Press of Pakistan, 3 February 2000.
3. Luongo and Salik, op. cit., p. 13.
4. Peter Wonactt, 'Inside Pakistan's Drive to Guard Its A-Bombs', The Wall Street Journal, 29 November 2007.
5. Wonacott, op. cit., and author's discussion with the senior security official in January 2008.
6. Lt.-Gen Khalid Kidwai, 'Pakistan's Evolution as a Nuclear Weapon State', Center for Contemporary Conflict, Naval Post Graduate School, Monterey, California, October 2006. ccc@nps.edu.
7. Luongo and Salik, op. cit., p. 14.
8. Luongo and Salik, p. 15.
9. Author's personal recollection being a member of the group.
10. Luongo and Salik, p. 15.
11. Luongo and Salik, pp. 16–17.

Epilogue

Nuclear weapons are here to stay in South Asia, barring a historic international consensus on complete nuclear disarmament, which appears to be highly unlikely anytime in the foreseeable future. It is, therefore, imperative for India and Pakistan to redefine their bilateral relations in the light of new realities, in which the recourse to the use of force is no longer a feasible option. They should now move beyond confidence building measures and try to resolve their outstanding disputes through negotiation. At the same time, the international community also needs to reconcile itself to the reality of a nuclearized South Asia, and consider ways and means to accommodate the two nuclear-capable states into the mainstream of the nuclear non-proliferation regime. The recently concluded US–India civilian nuclear cooperation agreement, after its endorsement by the Nuclear Suppliers Group (NSG) and agreement on safeguards between India and the IAEA, would go a long way to recognize India's nuclear status. However, if Pakistan is kept out and discriminated against on the pretext of the past doings of the A.Q. Khan network, while there is a failure to acknowledge the measures it has taken to remedy the situation, this is likely to lead to consequences which would be undesirable both for regional stability as well as the cause of non-proliferation.

India's nuclear programme is unique among all nuclear weapon powers, in the sense that, unlike other nuclear programmes which were initiated with the purpose of developing nuclear weapons, its programme originated as a peaceful programme. That the development of a nuclear weapons option was always kept open by Homi Bhabha and his associates is another matter. India was, therefore, able to benefit from generous technological assistance until its programme had become largely autonomous. Incidentally, it was India's first nuclear test, in May 1974, which led to the formation of restrictive technology denial regimes such as the NSG and later

MTCR. Only time will tell whether or not India would again exploit the technological assistance being offered to it by the United States, within the framework of the civilian nuclear cooperation agreement, to further its nuclear weapons capabilities.[1]

The civilian nuclear cooperation agreement itself has some serious loopholes, as well as genuine opportunities, for India to substantially enhance its nuclear weapons capabilities. The biggest constraint India is facing at the moment is the scarcity of domestic uranium production and stocks. Once it is able to import nuclear fuel from abroad for its safeguarded nuclear plants, its domestic uranium would be freed up for use in the production of fissile materials for nuclear weapons. The very fact that India insisted on, and has succeeded in, keeping 8 of its nuclear power plants, which are without doubt purely civilian facilities, points to the fact that, after all, the nuclear agreement is not meant for promoting peaceful nuclear technology alone.[2] These power reactors are of 220 MW each and are based on CANDU design, which means that, technologically speaking, these are no different from the CIRUS (40 MW) and Dhruva (100 MW) research reactors. These had previously been the only reactors available to India for the production of fissile material. Some analysts argue that if India wanted to divert these reactors for fissile materials production it could have done so, even without this agreement. The problem with this argument is that for the utilization of these reactors for fissile material production, huge quantities of fuel would have been needed to meet the requirement to replace the fuel elements at low burn up, and India did not have that fuel. This would now be available under the terms of the agreement. In fact Australia has already entered into an agreement with India to supply uranium even before the agreement's endorsement by the NSG.[3] Currently the CIRUS and Dhruva reactors, assuming that they run at 60 per cent capacity, produce 36.5 kg of plutonium each year, whereas, each of these power reactors is capable of producing 48.2 kg of plutonium per year working at 60 per cent capacity. The cumulative annual plutonium production would, therefore, be 385.4 kg if all eight un-safeguarded power reactors are dedicated for fissile material production and would overtake within two years the total fissile material produced by India so far over the last forty-seven years since the inauguration of CIRUS in 1960. In all probability these reactors may not be used directly for the production of fissile material, but the burnt fuel generated by these reactors is likely to be used to feed the 500 MWe Fast Breeder Reactor (FBR) currently under construction. The breeder reactors have not been placed under safeguards under the terms of the US–India Nuclear Agreement. The new FBR will be able to produce 140 kg of plutonium per year, almost three times India's current plutonium production capability.[4]

Although, Pakistan has repeatedly stated that its nuclear policy is based on a 'minimum credible deterrence', given the dynamics of the India–Pakistan rivalry, Pakistan would be under great psychological and political pressures to respond to any major expansion in India's strategic capabilities. In the 1970s and 1980s, when faced with increasingly restrictive technology control regimes, Pakistan had adopted an unconventional approach towards nuclear development, taking grave risks, and had paid heavily in opportunity costs in the process. At the end of the day, however, it succeeded in acquiring nuclear capability, but the unprecedented administrative and financial autonomy granted to some entities and individuals became a cause of national embarrassment, most especially with the revelation of the irresponsible and unscrupulous activities of A.Q. Khan and his associates. This time around, however, Pakistan is in a position to harness its indigenous technological base and expand its own strategic capabilities. There are already some signals emanating from Islamabad pointing towards this likely outcome. Both the NCA[5] and the Ministry of Foreign Affairs[6] have made it clear that Pakistan is no mood to cede strategic dominance to India, and would take all possible measures to maintain the strategic balance in South Asia.[7] Some infrastructural work is already underway to turn these expressions of intent into practical reality.[8] This situation does not bode well for the advocates of nuclear restraint in South Asia. The proponents of the US–India deal were not prepared to give any serious thought to this eventuality, which will come back to haunt them in the not too distant a future. Such developments will be detrimental for both regional security and stability, and the international non-proliferation regime, and may also cast a dark shadow over the prospects for a Fissile Materials Cut Off Treaty.

Indian negotiators insisted, throughout the long and hard negotiations leading up to the finalization of the 123 agreement with the US, that they would not accept any restrictions on India's right to proceed with nuclear testing, despite the fact that India has announced a unilateral moratorium on nuclear testing since May 1998. The Indians finally succeeded in having their demands met in the final text of the agreement.[9] Chief US negotiator, Under Secretary of State Nicholas Burns, has stated that conducting nuclear tests is India's right as a sovereign state, conveniently forgetting that there are other sovereign states in the South Asian region and beyond, who can claim a similar right. These statements, and the agreement itself, are in contravention of the benchmarks set by the US Congress in the Hyde Act.[10] Resumption of nuclear testing by India would also be responded to by Pakistan, and would negate the prospects of a CTBT forever.[11]

Meanwhile, Pakistan is forging ahead with the testing of its varied missile delivery systems, including its latest air launched cruise missile 'RAAD', designated as Hatf-VIII.[12] This missile, with a range of 350 km and the announced capability to carry 'all types of warheads', gives Pakistan a strategic stand-off capability. It is also indicative of the fact that, after the development of medium and intermediate range ballistic missiles by India and Pakistan, competition in the development and induction of cruise missiles is now heating up. India has reportedly already inducted the 'Brahmos' cruise missile into its strategic forces. Brahmos can be fired from land as well as naval platforms, and its submarine launched version is expected to be ready for testing soon. Pakistan, after a series of successful test firings of its surface launched cruise missile 'Babur', has embarked upon diversification of its launch options by introducing an air-launched cruise missile, and one can assume that a submarine launched version of its cruise missiles would also be developed in due course.

India has by far the most advanced space programme in the developing world, and now has the capability to launch both Polar Satellite Launch Vehicles (PSLVs) as well as Geosynchronous Launch Vehicles (GSLVs). It already has surveillance satellites in orbit, and is likely to launch more capable satellites with better resolution, useful for military purposes. Pakistan's space programme is lagging behind due to lack of funding and official neglect in the past. However, its space programme is also picking up momentum. During former Prime Minister Shaukat Aziz' visit to China in March 2007, a space cooperation agreement was signed between the two countries.[13] Space could, therefore, become another area of competition and rivalry between India and Pakistan.

Although, only ten years into the overt nuclearization, India and Pakistan have rapidly moved up the nuclear learning curve, and a degree of maturity is clearly discernible in their thinking as they move towards the full operation mode of their respective nuclear capabilities. While one may not characterize it as a nuclear race, the fact remains that there is an ongoing competition between the two South Asian neighbours in the strategic field. The time has come for them to pause and think as to how far they can continue down this road. There is a need for the two countries to rein in their nuclear and missile development at levels commensurate with their declared policies of 'minimum credible deterrence'. They should think about some arms control measures, including the realm of conventional forces, and work out institutionalized risk reduction and crisis management structures. The basic foundations for these are already there, in the form of various confidence-building measures agreed upon by the two countries. There is, however, a need to arrange all these separate building blocks into a comprehensive restraint regime.

The two sides had agreed in a joint statement, following the First Round of Expert Level Talks in June 2004, to initiate a dialogue with the other nuclear powers, but no attempt has been made to realize this objective. They also agreed to coordinate their non-proliferation policies during negotiations at the international fora. Sadly, this has also not been followed up. It appears that the US-India civilian nuclear agreement has served as a disincentive for India to coordinate its policies with Pakistan, or to join hands with Pakistan to initiate a dialogue with other nuclear powers in the period since India has been granted a privileged status. But such policies are at best short sighted, both on the part of India as well as the US, because if past experience is any guide, Pakistan will do what it must to maintain its strategic autonomy, and would not let India get away with strategic dominance of the region.

India is not likely to have the capacity to catch up with China in the foreseeable future, but in attempting to do so it is likely to aggravate Pakistan's security concerns and upset the regional security balance. This will not be in India's best interest, and a more rational approach would be to remain sensitive to Pakistan's security concerns. The US may have pronounced that its relations with India and Pakistan are not a zero sum game any more, but it cannot remain oblivious to the ground realities, and the historical and psychological underpinnings of the Indo-Pakistan relations, in its attempts to build India as a possible strategic counterweight to China. The strategic dynamics in the Central Asian heartland are already undergoing a major transformation with Russia trying to reassert its military power, at the same time as a rising China. India and Pakistan are likely to play a significant role in these changing power equations, especially due to the fact that, unlike during the cold war, they are now nuclear powers. But the two countries can only play their due role if their nuclear status is accommodated in the international nuclear hierarchy, in the words of IAEA Director General Mohammad Al Baradei, 'through innovative and out of the box solutions.'[14] Such an arrangement, to be meaningful, has to accommodate all the three non-NPT nuclear states of India, Pakistan and Israel. Any attempt to make exceptions, and to keep one country or the other out of the mainstream, is likely to prove counter productive in the long run.

NOTES

1. For India's proliferation behaviour see, Adnan Gill, 'Seeds of Indian Proliferation—the illicit trade in nuclear technology', *Defence Journal*, Karachi, May 2006, Vol. 9, No. 10.; and Adil Sultan, 'The Myth of India's Impeccable Nuclear Non-proliferation Record', *Defence Journal*, May 2006, Vol. 9, No. 10.

2. 'India needs eight nuclear plants for self defence', *Daily Times*, Lahore, 8 April 2006.

3. 'Australia's uranium mines: The India Exception'—'The Deputy Sheriff does his bit for America's deal with India', *The Economist*, 23 August 2007. Also see Stephen de Tarczynski, 'Australia: Uranium Sales May Fuel Asian Arms Race', Inter Press Service (IPS) 27 August 2007.

4. International Panel on Fissile Materials, Global Fissile Material Report 2007.

5. 'Concern expressed at Indo-US deal: Deterrence satisfactory: NCA', *Dawn*, Karachi, 13 April 2006. www.Dawn.com. Also see 'Pakistan Nuclear Authority concerned at US-India deal', *People's Daily* online, 13 April 2006 and 'NCA warns of strategic implications of US-India nuke agreement', Associated Press of Pakistan, Rawalpindi, 2 August 2007.

6. 'Indo-US accord termed threat to security: Discrimination unacceptable': Foreign Office, *Dawn*, 18 March 2006. Also see 'Indian N-deal exceeds brief to Pakistan: Foreign Office', *Daily Times*, Lahore, 11 April 2006.

7. Iftikhar A. Khan, 'Pakistan warns against Indian nuclear tests', *Dawn*, 21 August 2007.

8. Joy Warrick, 'Pakistan Expanding Nuclear Programme', *Washington Post*, 24 July 2006. Also see ISIS report of 24 July 2006, by David Albright and Paul Brennan indicating the construction of second plutonium reactor at Khushab and David Albright and Paul Brennan, 'Pakistan appears to be building a Third Plutonium Reactor at Khushab Nuclear Site', ISIS, 21 June 2007.

9. Y.P. Rajesh, 'Terms seen met as US-India nuclear deal unveiled', Reuters, 3 August 2007.

10. See 'Congress Poised to Approve US-India Peaceful Atomic Energy Act', 7 December 2006. http://lugar.senate.gov/

11. Iftikhar A. Khan, 'Pakistan warns against Indian Nuclear tests', *Dawn*, 21 August 2007.

12. 'N-capable cruise missile test fired', *Dawn*, 26 August 2007.

13. Khaleeq Kiani, '27 Pacts signed with China: N-cooperation discussed: Aziz', *Dawn*, 18 April 2007.

14. Mohammed Al-Baradei, 'Rethinking Nuclear Safeguards', *Washington Post*, 14 June 2006.

Appendix 1
India's Fissile Material Stocks—An Estimate

India's fissile material production is based on two production reactors namely 'CIRUS' and 'Dhruva'. CIRUS, which started operation in 1960 is a 40 MW reactor, whereas Dhruva has a capacity of 100 MW and went critical in 1985. Dhruva was shut down soon after starting operation, but from December 1986 to mid-1987 it operated at 25MW capacity, while from mid-1987 to December 1987 it operated at 80 MW capacity.

A 40 MW reactor operating at 100 per cent capacity can produce 14.6 kg of plutonium per year, while the annual production of plutonium by a 100 MW reactor operating at the same capacity can yield 36.5 kg of Plutonium per year. Indian reactors normally operate at 60 per cent capacity and this figure is used as a benchmark by experts, such as David Albright, for calculating the size of Indian stockpiles. However, to be on the safer side for the purpose of this calculation a 70 per cent operating capacity has been assumed.

Working on this assumption CIRUS would produce 10.2 or 10 kg of plutonium annually, while Dhruva can produce 25.6 or 26 kg per year. The plutonium produced by CIRUS and Dhruva would therefore be as below:

Capacity	Operative Since	Annual output	Total output
CIRUS 40 MW	1960	10 kg	10 X 44 = 440 kg
DHRUVA 100 MW	1985-88	? kg	13 kg
	1988-2008	26 kg	20x26 = 520 kg
Total Output			973 kg

All of the plutonium produced so far is not available in ready stocks. There are inevitably some losses during reprocessing and some of it has also been used up in the nuclear explosions conducted by India in 1974 and 1998. Some plutonium has also been consumed for other purposes such as fuel for the Fast Breeder Test Reactor and for fuelling the initial core of the PURNIMA Reactor. The estimated consumption so far is as below:

Consumed for 1974 Test	10 kg
Estimated Consumption for 1998 Tests	25 kg
Processing losses	10 kg
Fuel for Fast Breeder Reactor	50 kg
Initial Core for PURNIMA Reactor	35 kg
Total Consumption	130 kg
Net Stock Available	973—130 = 843 kg

Assuming that the Indian warhead design requires approximately 5 kg per warhead, the total warhead production capacity would therefore, be 843/5= 168 warheads. However, this does not mean that all available plutonium has already been converted into warheads.

India also has 5 un-safeguarded CANDU Type Power Reactors, each with a capacity of 220 MW. Theoretically speaking these reactors are capable of yielding around 80 kg each of reactor grade plutonium per year, working at 60 per cent capacity, with a combined output of 400 kg per year. However, there is no evidence to suggest that all the fuel discharged from these reactors has been reprocessed. According to a RAND report, around 100 kg of plutonium has been recovered from power reactor fuel. It may also be pointed out that because of the low quality of reactor grade plutonium, due to a mixture of impurities in the form of Pu 240 and Pu 241, it is not ideally suited for weapons purposes and would require around 15 kg per warhead. The major problem with weapons based on reactor grade plutonium is the risk of pre-detonation, their yield is also unpredictable. Some reports in the Indian media, quoting a member of the team of Indian scientists who conducted the 1998 tests, suggested that one of the devices tested in May 98 was based on reactor grade or 'dirty plutonium'. However, it is difficult to verify the claim, or whether this experiment was a success or a failure. In the end India's ability to utilize its reactor fuel for weapons purposes will depend on its overall reprocessing capacity, which at present is not adequate to handle all the spent fuel being generated by its un-safeguarded reactors. In the event that India decides to use its power reactors for the production of fissile material, it will not only have to expand its existing reprocessing capacity, but will also have to enhance its uranium mining and fuel fabrication capability, since it will entail a greater turnover of fuel on low burn up.

Appendix 2
Pakistan's Fissile Material/Weapons Stocks—An Estimate

Unlike India, whose nuclear weapons programme is plutonium based, Pakistan's programme until recently was based on Highly Enriched Uranium (HEU) produced through the Gas Centrifuge Enrichment process. Plutonium is produced in what are known as plutonium production reactors, which burn natural uranium fuel and convert part of it into plutonium. This is then separated through a chemical process in a reprocessing plant. The amount of plutonium produced by such reactors can be calculated on the basis of the capacity and the operating history of a particular plant. For instance, a 40 MW plant running at 60 per cent capacity will yield approximately 9 kg of plutonium in a year. The same plant working at 100 per cent will produce about 15 kg of plutonium in a year. However, in case of HEU production it is difficult to estimate the production unless the number of centrifuges, the capacity of each centrifuge, its efficiency and the quality of feed material is known. This information is hard to obtain, and therefore all publicly available estimates of Pakistan's HEU stockpile are based on assumptions about the number of centrifuges, which has ranged from 3,000 to 10,000 machines in various studies, and their design features etc. The amount of plutonium required for each weapon is in the range of 5-6 kg while 15-25 kg of HEU is needed per weapon, depending on the sophistication level of the bomb design.

Of late Pakistan has also pursued the plutonium route and a 50 MW plutonium production reactor at Khushab has been operational since 1998. The International Panel on Fissile Materials (IPFM) has, in its Global Fissile Materials Report for 2007, estimated the annual production of plutonium by the Khushab reactor to be 13 kg. This calculation is based on the assumption that the plant works at 70 per cent capacity. However, if the reactor works at 60 per cent capacity its annual production would be around 11 kg/year. According to the same IPFM report, Pakistan's HEU inventory is estimated to be 1.3 metric tons or 1300 kg. Based on the above figure Pakistan should have between 110 to 130 kg of plutonium in addition to its HEU stocks. The median figure could be taken as 120 kg. Further, assuming that Pakistani weapons need 25 kg of HEU and 6 kg of plutonium, a rough estimate of Pakistan's nuclear weapons inventory could be as below:

| 1300 kg of Heu/25 | 52 weapons |
| 120 kg of Pu/6 | 20 weapons |

This would mean that Pakistan has an estimated capacity of around 70 nuclear weapons of nominal yield. However, this is just a rough estimate and does not in any way mean that all the fissile material has already been converted to into weapons.

Appendix 3
A Suggested Model for Minimum Nuclear Deterrence

How to work out the size of a minimum deterrence force

Having discussed various descriptions of minimum deterrence and differing views on its nature and scope, the question as to what is really meant by minimum deterrence and how one can arrive at some rough figure to determine its size, still lacks an answer. The reason for this is obvious, it is because there is lack of clarity of the concept itself and there are real difficulties in practicing the minimum deterrence strategy. For instance, it is politically correct for any country to adopt and declare a minimum nuclear deterrence policy, but when it comes to putting the concept into practice various complications arise. The military planners always base their calculations on the worst case scenario and would like to err on the side of safety, and therefore there is always a tendency to have something available just in case some unforeseen contingency arises.

Then there is the technological imperative. The scientific community relentlessly pursues Research and Development programmes, and once they achieve a breakthrough they will always press for the newly developed weapon systems to be inducted. The influence of the military/industrial complex is not yet very pronounced in the case of India and Pakistan, since most of the entities involved in the strategic programmes are currently state owned in both the countries. Then there is a clash of contradictory goals and ambitions, especially in case of India, which would like to project itself as a responsible and self-restrained country. At the same time, India harbours a strong desire to be reckoned as an important player in the global power hierarchy and a competitor to a rising China. In this kind of situation it becomes difficult to reconcile the declarations of good faith with raw ambition. This explains, to some extent the great diversity of views among Indian analysts regarding the envisaged size of their minimum deterrent.

Putting these difficulties to one side, I would suggest criteria, or a rough guide, by which one could work out the approximate size of a minimum deterrence force. This has nothing to do with the ground realities, especially in South Asia, where both sides have kept their options of upgrading and building up their arsenals open by declaring their respective minimum deterrents as 'dynamic', but an attempt at explaining what it ought to be.

The rationale for this model is based on the fact that nuclear weapons have tremendous destructive power, and even a single weapon can cause unacceptable damage. The second pillar of this concept is the fact that deterrence does not require the killing of every living being in a city or razing to the ground every standing structure in that city. Imagine a nuclear weapon of Hiroshima size, i.e. around 20 kiloton, exploding in a mega city of 10 million inhabitants. Based on various technical characteristics of the weapon, the target area and the prevailing weather conditions, it may kill say just 50,000 to 100,000 people, but imagine the fate of the remaining 9.9 million residents of that city. They would be without electricity, water, sewerage, medical facilities or even food, in addition to the danger of becoming victims of the immediate as well as residual radiation, which means that these people will have to be evacuated to a safer place. One can imagine the chaos and stampede it would cause in a panic-stricken populace. Then where do you find the means of transportation to move such large numbers, and enough space to accommodate them? Even if these problems are overcome there would be the additional problems of providing food, water and shelter to so many people, and after a week or so the hygiene and sanitation would become a nightmare. The conclusion one can draw from this discussion is that one does not really need a large number of very powerful megaton range nuclear weapons for deterrence, unless the objective is the total destruction or wiping off of a nation from the map of the world.

In view of the above, a simple method which can lead us to some realistic figure would be to determine, in general terms, the 'pain threshold' of the opponent. This would vary with the level of development and affluence in a country, and how much value it assigns to human lives. Some people argue that autocratic regimes are less concerned about the loss of lives as compared to countries ruled through democratic dispensations. This may not be entirely true in all cases.

The second step is to identify the most valuable assets, the loss of which would really hurt the adversary. This could be major population centres, industrial complexes, major military bases, communication hubs or a combination of all these. These can then be prioritised. Let us say that 'x' number of targets are selected as absolutely critical. Then there is the question of determining the number of warheads and the type of delivery systems that would be required to engage each of these targets. Given the uncertainty, especially in the fog of war, of system failures and the penetrability and reach of each system, and the overall value and size of the target, 2–3 warheads may be assigned to each, with a variety of delivery means to optimize the chances of the weapons reaching their intended targets. Obviously, one would not like to expend all one's assets in a single strike, so there would be a need to cater for some reserves. This should lead us to a rough figure. But then the extraneous factors described earlier, come into play. For instance, if there is a possibility of a surprise first strike by the enemy, which could take out 50 per cent of one's own assets, the number determined earlier would have to be doubled. Similarly, if the adversary has deployed Missile Defence

Systems and effective air defences, capable of intercepting 50 per cent of the incoming missiles/aircraft, the number would again have to be doubled. In mathematical terms it would appear to be something like the following:

No. of targets selected	X
No. of warheads with 2 warheads/target	X x 2
Add 50 per cent reserves	2X + X = 3 X
Add 50 per cent for system failures	3 X + 1.5 X = 4.5 X
Add 50 per cent for enemy missile defences	4.5 X + 2.25 X = 6.75 X

Now let us suppose that the value of 'X', i.e. the number of targets, is 10. The number of warheads would come to 10 x 6.75 X = 67.5. This can be rounded off to 68 or 70. The actual size of the arsenal would, however, depend on the number of targets actually identified as critical, the faith in the performance of one's weapons and delivery systems and whether the objective is just to deter and not to totally devastate the opposing country. The other important factors are, of course, the survivability of one's own weapons system in the face of a pre-emptive first strike, and whether or not the other side has deployed missile defence systems. This latter factor is important because it significantly increases the size of the arsenal, even if 50 per cent interception capability is assigned to the defences. As is evident from the hypothetical example the numbers jumped from 45 to 68 with a 50 per cent interception. If the defences have greater interception capability, say in the 90 per cent range or above, the size of the arsenal would be doubled to 90 or so weapons. The figures would of course vary with a lesser or greater number of targets.

Bibliography

Books

Ali, Chaudhry M., *The Emergence of Pakistan*, Columbia University Press, New York & London, 1967.

Karnad, Bharat (ed.), *Future Imperilled*, Viking, New Delhi, 1994.

Bhargava, G.S., *South Asian Security after Afghanistan*, Lexington Books, Massachusetts, 1983.

Bhutto, Z.A., *The Myth of Independence*, Oxford University Press, London, 1969.

Bhutto, Z.A., *If I am Assassinated*, Vikas Publishers, New Delhi, 1979.

Blackwill, R.D. and Allan Carnesale (eds.), *New Nuclear Nations-Consequences for US Policy*, Council on Foreign Relations, New York, 1993.

Cirincione, Joseph, Jon B. Wolfsthal, Miriam Rajkumar, *Deadly Arsenals: Nuclear, Biological and Chemical Threats*, Carnegie Endowment for International Peace, Washington, D.C., 2005.

Cohen, S.P., and R. L. Park, *India: Emergent Power*, Crane, Russak & Company, Inc., New York, 1978.

Dittmer, Lowell (ed.), *South Asia's Nuclear Security Dilemma: India, Pakistan and China,* New Delhi, Pentagon Press, 2005.

Ebinger, C.K., *Pakistan: Energy Planning in a Strategic Vortex*, Indiana University Press, Bloomington, 1981.

Frantz, Douglas and Catherine Collins, *The Nuclear Jihadist*, Hachette Book Group, New York, 2007.

George, T., Robert Littwak, and Shahram Chubin, *Security in Southern Asia India and the Great Powers*, IISS, Gower Publishing Company Limited, Hampshire, 1984.

Goldblat, J. (ed.), *Non-proliferation: The Why and the Wherefore*, SIPRI, Taylor & Francis, London, 1985.

Gupta, B.S., *Nuclear Weapons? Policy Options for India?*, Sage Publications, New Delhi, 1983.

Jackson, R., *South Asian Crisis: India Pakistan Bangladesh*, IISS, Chatto & Windus, London, 1975.

Jones, Owen Bennett, *Pakistan—Eye of the Storm*, Yale University Press, New Haven & London, 2002.

Jones, Rodney (ed.), *Small Nuclear Forces and U.S. Security Policy: Threats and Potential Conflicts in the Middle East and South Asia*, Lexington Books, Lexington, MA, 1984.

Kapur, A., *India's Nuclear Option Atomic Diplomacy and Decision Making*, Praeger Publishers, New York, 1976.

Kapur, A., *International Nuclear Proliferation Multilateral Diplomacy and Regional Aspects*, Praeger Publishers, New York, 1979.

Kapur, A., *Pakistan's Nuclear Development*, Croom Helm, New York, 1987.

Kaushik, M., and D.N. Mehrotra, *Pakistan's Nuclear Bomb*, IDSA, New Delhi, 1980.

Kolodziez, E.A., and R.E. Harkavy (eds.), *Security Policies of Developing Countries*, Lexington Books, Lexington, Mass., 1982.

Kux, Dennis, *The United States and Pakistan, 1947–2000: Disenchanted Allies*, Woodrow Wilson Center Press, Washington, D.C., 2001.

Lefever, E.W., *Nuclear Arms in the Third World*, The Brookings Institution, Washington, 1979.

Malik, H., *Dilemmas of National Security and Cooperation*, Macmillan, London, 1993.

Malik, Z., *A.Q. Khan and the Islamic Bomb*, Hurmat Publications, Islamabad, 1999.

Marwah, O., and J.D. Pollack (eds.), *Military Power and Policy in Asian States: China, India, Japan*, Westview Press, Boulder, Colorado, 1980.

Schulz, A., and Onkar Marwah (eds.), *Nuclear Proliferation and the Near Nuclear Countries*, Ballinger Publishing Company, Cambridge, Mass., 1975.

Matinuddin, K., *The Nuclearization of South Asia*, Oxford University Press, Karchi, 2002.

Mattoo, A. (ed.), *India's Nuclear Deterrent—Pokhran-II and Beyond*, New Delhi, Har Anand Publications, 1999.

Mian, Z. and Ashish Nandy, *The Nuclear Debate: Ironies and Immoralities*, Colombo: Regional Center for Strategic Studies, July 1998.

Musharraf, Pervez, *In the Line of Fire*, Free Press, New York, 2006.

Nolan, J.E., *Trappings of Power—Ballistic Missiles in the Third World*, The Brookings Institution, Washington, D.C.

Palit, N.K., and P.K.S. Namboodiri, *Pakistan's Islamic Bomb*, Vikas Publishers, New Delhi, 1979.

Perkovich, G., *India's Nuclear Bomb: The Impact on Global Proliferation*, University of California Press, 1999.

Quandt, W.B., *Saudi Arabia in the 1980s*, Brookings Institution, Washington, D.C. 1981.

Quester, G.H. (ed.), *Nuclear Proliferation: Breaking the Chain*, The University of Wisconsin Press, London, 1981.

Simpson, J., eds., *Nuclear Non-Proliferation: An Agenda for the 1990s*, Cambridge University Press, Cambridge, 1987.

Rehman, S., *The Long Road to Chaghi*, Print Wise Publications, Islamabad, 1999.

Simpson, J. (ed.), *Nuclear Non-proliferation an agenda for the 1990s*, Cambridge University Press, Cambridge, 1987.

Singh, J. (ed.), *Nuclear India*, New Delhi, Knowledge World, 1998.

Sinha, P.B., and R.R. Subramaniam, *Nuclear Pakistan: Atomic Threat to South Asia*, Vision Books, New Delhi, 1980.

SIPRI Yearbook 1975, The MIT Press, Cambridge Massachusetts and London,

Johnson S.E. and William H. Lewis (eds.), *Weapons of Mass Destruction: New Perspectives on Counter Proliferation*, National Defense University Press, Washington D.C., 1995.

Subrahmanyam, K. (ed.), *Nuclear Myths and Realities*, ABC Publishing House, New Delhi, 1981.

Tellis, Ashley J., *India's Emerging Nuclear Posture: Between Recessed Deterrence and Ready Arsenal*, Rand Corporation, Santa Monica, 2001.

Tenet, G., *At the Center of the Storm: My Years at the CIA*, Harper Collins Publishers, NY, 2007.

Thomas, R.G.C., *The Great Power Triangle and Asian Security*, Lexington Books, Mass., 1983.

Weissman, S., and Herbert Krosney, *The Islamic Bomb. The Nuclear Threat to Israel and the Middle East,* Times Books, New York, 1981.

Williams, S.L., *The US, India and The Bomb*, The John Hopkins Press, Baltimore, Maryland, 1969.

Wolpert, Stanley, *Roots of Confrontation in South Asia*, Oxford University Press, Oxford, 1982.

Dissertation

Christopher Clary, *'The A.Q. Khan Network: Causes and Implications'*, Master's thesis submitted to Naval Postgraduate School, Monterey, California, December 2005.

Journals/Periodicals

Ebinger, C.K., 'US Nuclear Non-proliferation Policy: The Pakistan Controversy', *The Fletcher Forum*, Vol. 3, No. 2, 1979.

Cheema, P.I., 'Pakistan's Quest for Nuclear Technology', *Australian Outlook,* Canberra, August 1980.

Interview with Dr Abdul Qadeer Khan on Pakistan's Nuclear Program, *The Arms Control Reporter*, IDDS, Massachusetts Avenue, Cambridge, Massachusetts, March 1984.

Jones, R.W., 'Nuclear Proliferation: Islam, The Bomb, and South Asia', *Washington Paper No. 82*, Sage Publications, Beverly Hills, CA, 1981.

Jones, R.W., 'Nuclear Supply Policy and South Asia', prepared for the Nuclear Suppliers and Nuclear Non-proliferation Seminar, *CSIS*, Washington, D.C., 28–29 June 1984.

Khan, M.A., 'Nuclear Energy and International Cooperation', *The Rockefeller Foundation/RIIA working paper*, September 1979.

Maddox, J., 'Prospects for Nuclear Proliferation', *Adelphi Paper*, No. 113, IISS, London, 1975.

Mehdi, S.S., 'India's Nuclear Program, how much peaceful?', *Pakistan Horizon*, Pakistan Institute of International Affairs, Karachi, Part I in Vol. 26, No. 4, 1983.

Marwah, O., 'India's Nuclear and Space Programs Intent and Policy', *International Security*, Vol. 2, fall 1977.

Siddiqi, A.R., 'Pakistan Seeks Atoms for Peace', *Defence Journal*, Karachi, Vol. 2, No. 3, 1976.

Proceedings of the International Conference on Nuclear Non-proliferation in South Asia, Organized by the Institute of Strategic Studies, Islamabad, on 12 September 1987, *Strategic Studies*, Vol. XI, No. 1, Summer & Autumn 1987.

Tahir Kheli, S., 'Pakistan's Nuclear Option and US Policy', *Orbis*, Vol. 22, No. 2, Summer 1978.

Tomar, R., 'The Indian Nuclear Program: Myths and Mirages', *Asian Survey*, Vol. 20, No. 5, May 1980.

Indian Defence Review Digest, Vol. IV, Lancer Publications, New Delhi, 1992.

Disarmament Diplomacy, Acronym Institute, Issue No. 23, February 1998.

Miller, M. and Lawrence Schienman, 'Israel, India and Pakistan: Engaging the Non-NPT States in the Non-proliferation Regime', *Arms Control Today*, December 2003.

Strategic Studies, Vol. X, No. 4, Summer & Autumn 1987, Institute of Strategic Studies, Islamabad.

Salik, Brig. Naeem Ahmad, 'Strategic Dynamics and Deterrence: South Asia', *Contemporary Security Policy*, Vol. 25, No. 1., April 2004.

Seymour Hersh, 'On the Nuclear Edge', *The New Yorker*, 29 March 1993.

Rizvi, Hasan A., 'Pakistan's Nuclear Testing', *Asian Survey*, 41, 6, 2001, pp. 943–955.

Arms Control Association, *Arms Control Today*, January/February 2004.

'Curbing Nuclear Proliferation', an Interview with Mohammad El Baradei, *Arms Control Today*, November 2003.

Jones, R.W., 'Pakistan's Nuclear Posture: Quest for Assured Nuclear Deterrence- A Conjecture', *Regional Studies*, Vol. XVIII, No. 2, Spring 2000, Institute of Regional Studies, Islamabad.

Rasgotra, M., Non-Proliferation Issues: The South Asian Context, *Strategic Studies*, Summer & Autumn 1987, ISS, Islamabad,

Simpson, J., 'The Nuclear non-proliferation regime, back to the future?', *Disarmament Forum- One 2004*, UNIDIR, Geneva.

Arms Control Association, *Arms Control Today*, News Briefs, August/September 1998. [http://www.armscontrol.org/act/1998_08-09/bras98.asp?print]

'No Harm in Signing the CTBT: Qadeer,' *Pakistan Link*, 25 September 1998, http://www.pakistanlink.com, quoted in Gaurav Kampani, 'CTBT Endgame in South Asia?', *Center for Non-proliferation Studies*, January 2000.

Cohen, A. and Thomas Graham Jr., 'An NPT for non-members', *'Bulletin of the Atomic Scientists'*, May/June 2004, Volume 60, No. 3, pp. 40-44.

Indian Defense Review Digest, Vol. IV, New Delhi, Lancer Publications, 1992.

Milhollin, G., 'India's Missiles—With a Little Help from Our Friends', *Bulletin of the Atomic Scientists,* November 1989.

Banerjie, I., 'Indian Defence Review Digest', Lancer Publications, Pvt. Ltd., New Delhi, 1992,

Koblenz, G., 'Theatre Missile Defence and South Asia: A Volatile Mix', *The Non-proliferation Review*, Vol. 4, No.3, Spring/Summer 1997, p. 54.

Strategic Issues, Institute of Strategic Studies, Islamabad, March 2000.

Kohlmeier, G., 'Pakistan Introduces Export Control Bill', *Arms Control Today*, Arms Control Association, September 2004 and Gabrielle Kohlmeier and Miles A. Pomper, 'Pakistan Advances Export Controls', *Arms Control Today*, Arms Control Association, October 2004.

Paul Kerr, 'India Passes Non-proliferation Legislation', *Arms Control Today*, Arms Control Association, June 2005.

General V.R. Raghavan in 'Limited War and Nuclear Escalation In South Asia', '*The non-Proliferation Review*', Fall-Winter 2001, Vol. 8, No. 3, Centre for Non-proliferation Studies, Monterey Institute of International Studies, Monterey, CA.

Coll, S., 'The Atomic Emporium—Abdul Qadeer Khan and Iran's race to build the bomb', *The New Yorker*, 7 & 14 August 2006, New York.

Kenley Butler, Sammy Salama & Leonard Spector, 'Where is the Justice?' *Bulletin of the Atomic Scientists*, November/December 2006.

Ken Luongo and Naeem Salik, 'Building Confidence in Pakistan's Nuclear Security', *Arms Control Today*, Arms Control Association, Washington, DC, November/December 2007.

Defence Journal, Karachi, May 2006, Vol. 9, No. 10. and Adil Sultan, 'The Myth of India's Impeccable Nuclear Non-proliferation Record', *Defence Journal*, May 2006, Vol. 9, No. 10.

Documents/Reports

CIA *World Fact Book*, ttp://www.odci.gov/cia/publications/factbook/index.html.

CIA, Scientific Intelligence Report, '*Indian Nuclear Energy Program*', 26 March 1958.

CIA, *Central Intelligence Bulletin*, 20 May 1974.

CIA, National Foreign Assessment Center, '*Indian Nuclear Policies in the 1980s—An Intelligence Assessment*', 10 September 1981.

CIA, Directorate of Intelligence, *India's Nuclear Program-Energy and Weapons—An Intelligence Assessment*', July 1982.

CIA, Directorate of Intelligence, *India's Potential to Build a Nuclear Weapon'—An Intelligence Assessment*, July 1988.

Classified Report to Congress on the Non-proliferation Policies and Practices of the People's Republic of China, September 1997.

Dept of State, Intelligence Note, dated 13 June 1974.

Draft Report of National Security Advisory Board on Indian Nuclear Doctrine, Embassy of India Washington, DC, http://www.indianembassy. org. and Jasjit Singh, 'Indian Draft Nuclear Doctrine: Some Reflections', *Pugwash Online*, also see 'India's Draft Nuclear Doctrine', Arms Control Association, *Arms Control Today*, July/August 1999.

Durrani, M.A., Major General (retd), 'Pakistan's Strategic Thinking and the Role of Nuclear Weapons', *CMC Occasional Paper/37*, Cooperative Monitoring Center, Sandia National Laboratories, Albuquerque, New Mexico, USA, July 2004.

Slijper, Frank, 'Project Butter Factory'—Henk Slebos and the A.Q. Khan Network, *Transnational Institute*, Amsterdam, September 2007.

Galluci, R., *Background Paper—'Pakistan and the Non-proliferation Issue'*, Department of State, Washington, D.C., 22 January 1975.

Government of India, *Department of Atomic Energy*, Annual Report 2005–2006.

Intelligence Report, Office of Near Eastern, South Asian and African Analysis, CIA, 29 May 1998.

Jones, R.W., Mark G. Mcdonough, et al. (eds.), 'Tracking Nuclear Proliferation—A Guide in Maps and Charts', *Carnegie Endowment for International Peace*, Washington, D.C., 1998.

Krepon, M., and Mishi Faruqee, Occasional Paper No. 17, *'Conflict Prevention and Confidence Building Measures in South Asia-The 1990 Crisis'*, The Henry L. Stimson Center, Washington, D.C., April 1994.

National Security Archive, *Electronic Briefing Book No. 187*, Washington, D.C.

Nuclear Black Markets: Pakistan, A.Q. Khan and the rise of proliferation networks—A net assessment, *IISS*, London, 2007, p. 15.

Pakistan's Nuclear Programme, published by Directorate of Films and Publications, Ministry of Information and Broad casting, Government of Pakistan, Islamabad, March 1987.

Pakistan Television Corporation Limited, National News Bureau, English News Headlines, 1800 hrs dated 11 September 1998. file://H:\ The%20Government%20of %20PakistanENGLISH19ENG26-1998. htm

Post Mortem Report—An Examination of the Intelligence Community's Performance Before the Indian Nuclear Test of May 1974, for the Director Central Intelligence, July 1974.

Reiss, M. and Harald Muller (eds.), *Working Paper No. 99*, Woodrow Wilson Center for Scholars, Washington D.C., January 1995.

Special National Intelligence Estimate Number 31-1-65, 'India's Nuclear Weapons Policy', *Directorate of Central Intelligence*, 21 October 1965.

United States Atomic Energy Commission, Washington, D.C., 2 October 1974, 'Prospects for Further Proliferation of Nuclear Weapons'.

Electronic Sources

'US Intelligence and the Indian Bomb', National Security Archive, Electronic Briefing Book No. 187, April 2006. nsarchiv@gwu.edu.

'China, Pakistan and the Bomb', National Security Archive, Electronic Briefing Book No. 114, March 2004. nsarchiv@gwu.edu.

Index